T0320129

Competition in the Railway Industry

TRANSPORT ECONOMICS, MANAGEMENT AND POLICY

Series Editor: Kenneth Button, *Professor of Public Policy, School of Public Policy, George Mason University, USA*

Transport is a critical input for economic development and for optimizing social and political interaction. Recent years have seen significant new developments in the way that transport is perceived by private industry and governments, and in the way academics look at it.

The aim of this series is to provide original material and up-to-date synthesis of the state of modern transport analysis. The coverage embraces all conventional modes of transport but also includes contributions from important related fields such as urban and regional planning and telecommunications where they interface with transport. The books draw from many disciplines and some cross disciplinary boundaries. They are concerned with economics, planning, sociology, geography, management science, psychology and public policy. They are intended to help improve the understanding of transport, the policy needs of the most economically advanced countries and the problems of resource-poor developing economies. The authors come from around the world and represent some of the outstanding young scholars as well as established names.

Titles in the series include:

European Union Port Policy
The Movement Towards a Long-Term Strategy
Constantinos I. Chlomoudis and Athanasios A. Pallis

Structural Change in Transportation and Communications in the Knowledge Society
Edited by Kiyoshi Kobayashi, T.R. Lakshmanan and William P. Anderson

Globalisation, Policy and Shipping
Fordism, Post-Fordism and the European Union Maritime Sector
Evangelia Selkou and Michael Roe

Cost–Benefit Analysis and Evolutionary Computing
Optimal Scheduling of Interactive Road Projects
John H.E. Taplin, Min Qiu, Vivian K. Salim and Renlong Han

The Future of Automated Freight Transport
Concepts, Design and Implementation
Edited by Rob Konings, Hugo Priemus and Peter Nijkamp

Telecommunications, Transportation and Location
Kenneth Button and Roger Stough with Michelle Bragg and Samantha Taylor

Competition in the Railway Industry
An International Comparative Analysis
Edited by José A. Gómez-Ibáñez and Ginés de Rus

Competition in the Railway Industry

An International Comparative Analysis

Edited by

José A. Gómez-Ibáñez

Professor of Urban Planning and Public Policy, Harvard University, USA

Ginés de Rus

Professor of Economics, Universidad de Las Palmas de G.C., Spain

TRANSPORT ECONOMICS, MANAGEMENT AND POLICY

Edward Elgar

Cheltenham, UK • Northampton, MA, USA

Published by
Edward Elgar Publishing Limited
The Lypiatts
15 Lansdown Road
Cheltenham
Glos GL50 2JA
UK

Edward Elgar Publishing, Inc.
William Pratt House
9 Dewey Court
Northampton
Massachusetts 01060
USA

Reprinted 2015

A catalogue record for this book
is available from the British Library

Library of Congress Cataloguing in Publication Data

Competition in the railway industry : an international comparative analysis
/ edited by José A. Gómez-Ibáñez, Ginés de Rus.
    p. cm. – (Transport economics, management and policy series)
    Includes bibliographical references and index.
    1. Railroads–Deregulation. 2. Railroads–Management. I. Gómez-Ibáñez
José A., 1948- II. Rus, Ginés de. III. Transport economics, management
and policy.
    HE1051.C56 2006
    385'.1–dc22
        2006005900

ISBN 978 1 84542 903 4

Printed and bound in Great Britain by the CPI Group (UK) Ltd

Contents

Figures

Tables

Contributors

Javier Campos
Associate Professor of Economics
Economics of Infrastructure and Transport (EIT)
University of Las Palmas, Spain

Ginés de Rus
Professor of Economics
Economics of Infrastructure and Transport (EIT)
University of Las Palmas, Spain

Stephen Glaister
Professor of Transport and Infrastructure
Department of Civil and Environmental Engineering
Imperial College London, UK

José A. Gómez-Ibáñez
Professor of Urban Planning and Public Policy
Graduate School of Design and Kennedy School of Government
Harvard University, USA

Jorge Kogan
Senior railway adviser
Corporación Andina de Fomento

Chris Nash
Professor of Transport Economics
Institute for Transport Studies
University of Leeds, UK

Emile Quinet
Emeritus Professor
Centre d´Enseignement et Recherche en Analyse Socio-économique
École Nationale des Ponts et Chaussées, Paris, France

Clifford Winston
Senior Fellow
Brookings Institution

Introduction

José A. Gómez-Ibáñez and Ginés de Rus

At the end of the 20th century, many countries adopted radical reforms in an attempt to strengthen their railways. The railways' share of passenger and freight traffic had been declining at an alarming rate in part because of increasing competition from autos, buses, airplanes, trucks, waterways and pipelines. In countries with private railways, such as the US and Canada, bankruptcies were threatening to eliminate many services. In countries with government-owned railways, such as in Europe or the developing world, the subsidies required to maintain service were becoming a serious burden on the state.

Most countries tried to improve railway performance by introducing added competition, although they differed in the forms of competition employed. One method was to separate or 'unbundle' train operations from infrastructure so that independent train operating companies could compete with one another over common tracks. The idea was inspired in part by telephones and electricity where potentially competitive activities (such as long distance or mobile telephony) were being separated from less competitive ones (local hard-wire service); it was also inspired by highway and air transportation where trucking and airline companies have long competed while using highways and airports provided by separate entities. The second approach was to privatize the railways in the hope that competition among investors for ownership or control of the company would put pressure on managers to be more efficient. Finally, some countries also loosened government controls on railway tariffs and services that dated from the late 19th and early 20th centuries, when the railways enjoyed a near monopoly on transport. The idea was that these outdated regulations were preventing the railways from responding effectively to the intense competition they now faced from other modes.

In practice the countries divided into two camps depending upon whether they chose to rely primarily on unbundling or on privatization. Europe and Australia decided to unbundle train operations from infrastructure, in some cases while also privatizing ownership but in other cases not. North America, Japan and the developing countries relied on privatization instead of unbundling, in some cases while also deregulating railway tariffs and services but in other cases not.

This book examines the experiences with these reforms, focusing particularly on the debate between unbundling and privatization. The contributors, all prominent railway scholars from Europe, North America and Latin America, disagree and each side offers reasonable arguments. The proponents of privatization argue that the train-on-train competition has been slow to emerge in Europe or Australia and is unnecessary given the intense competition from other modes. Moreover, they contend that unbundling greatly complicates the coordination of train operations and infrastructure maintenance. They blame this complexity for contributing to the accidents and cost overruns that led to the spectacular bankruptcy in 2001 of Railtrack, Britain's private railway infrastructure company. Proponents of unbundling respond that the policy has performed reasonably well outside of Britain, and attribute the British disaster to the half-hearted implementation of the policy by the Labour Government. They also point out that privatization has sometimes proven difficult as well, particularly in developing countries where private railway operators and governments have become embroiled in disputes over tariffs and conditions of services.

The book opens with a chapter that introduces the reform options, the experience and the debate. The main body of the book is then divided into two parts: the first dealing with countries that have unbundled and the second with those that have not. The section on unbundling consists of four chapters and begins with a chapter that describes the European Commission's efforts to require the unbundling of European railways and the main alternative models that have emerged, including those of Britain, Sweden and Germany. The next chapter (Chapter 3) examines the British model in more detail, since Britain pursued the most ambitious and controversial reforms in Europe by comprehensively unbundling and privatizing its railways. Chapters 4 and 5 consider the policies in France and Spain – both less enthusiastic reformers. Some French government officials hope that the establishment of a separate infrastructure company will help them control the powerful French railway company. But most French officials are skeptical about the merits and practicality of train-on-train competition, although some competition seems inevitable particularly for contracts from regional governments to provide subsidized regional passenger services. In Spain the prospects for train-on-train competition are probably limited to some freight and regional services but are unlikely in the new high-speed intercity passenger system that Spain has been building.

The second part, consisting of three chapters, examines efforts to introduce competition through privatization rather than unbundling. Chapter 6 recounts the US experience with deregulating its private freight railroads. After decades of mergers the US industry has consolidated into four giant freight railways: two west of the Mississippi and two east of the Mississippi.

Deregulation has proven remarkably beneficial for both shippers and the railways despite the fact that many shippers have little choice of which railway to use, particularly in the short run. Chapter 7 describes Latin America's efforts to privatize its railways as integrated concessions. Privatization has stimulated a remarkable improvement in railway performance in most cases, although conflicts between the railways and the government have been a problem particularly where the governments did not feel they could loosen regulation while they privatized. The book concludes with a final chapter that attempts to draw together the lessons about the prospects for introducing competition in railways.

The contributions to this volume emerged from a conference on railway competition held at the Rafael del Pino Foundation (Madrid, Spain) in September 2004. The editors are indebted to Amadeo Petitboo for his comments, patience and encouragement and to Matt Pitman and David Vince for their editorial advice. Both the conference and this book were made possible though the generous financial support of the Rafael del Pino Foundation.

1. An overview of the options

José A. Gómez-Ibáñez

THREE OPTIONS FOR COMPETITION

Many countries have attempted to improve the performance of their railways since 1980 by introducing or strengthening competitive or market forces. Three distinct methods have been used: vertical unbundling, privatization and deregulation. All three represent radical departures from past practice, but they are not necessarily consistent with one another and their relative merits are the subject of intense debate.

One option is to encourage railroads to compete with one another by mandating that they provide competing railroads or train companies access to their tracks. In the past, virtually all the railroads in the world combined infrastructure and train operations in a single company, with no or few rights to access the tracks of other railroads. Different railroads usually served different countries or regions within a country, so that some shipments might originate in the territory of one railroad and terminate in the territory of another. The railroads usually had agreements to exchange cars so that interchange traffic did not have to be unloaded and reloaded in transit. But each railroad owned all or most of the locomotives, tracks, yards and stations needed for the region it served. In the parlance of economists, the railroads were horizontally separated in that they served different territories but vertically integrated in that they provided all the key functions needed to serve their territories.

Beginning in the 1980s, a number of countries, particularly in Europe, began to vertically 'unbundle' their railways by requiring that existing railways grant other railways or independent train operating companies access to their tracks. In some cases the incumbent railways were also broken into separate train operating and infrastructure companies to facilitate the introduction of competition. The idea of vertically unbundling was inspired in part by the experiences of the telephone and electricity industries where reformers had begun to separate activities with the potential to be competitive, such as long-distance calling or wholesale power generation, from activities that seemed inherently monopolistic, such as local hard-wire telephony or high-voltage electricity transmission. There were

1

also obvious parallels with road transportation, where competing trucking and bus companies had long shared access to highways that were built and maintained by independent highway agencies. If vertical unbundling and open access seemed successful in telephones, electricity and highways, why not in railroads?

A second option is to introduce competition for corporate control by turning to the private sector to provide railway services. From roughly World War II until the 1990s, railway services in most countries were provided by government-owned corporations. The primary exceptions were in North America, where all the major freight railways in the United States and one of the two in Canada were privately owned. Beginning in the late 1980s, over a dozen countries transferred their government-owned railways to the private sector either by selling the railway outright or by granting a private company a concession to operate the railway for 10 to 50 years. The idea is to harness competition in the market for corporate control to encourage railways to cut costs and offer attractive services. Investors or managers who ignore opportunities to cut costs or offer non-profitable services will lose the competition to purchase the railway company or concession or, once in place, will lose control through bankruptcy or a takeover challenge from more competent investors.

The final option is to enhance competition by relaxing government controls over the prices railways can charge and the types of services they can offer. Although private railways had long been the norm in North America, they were tightly regulated by government agencies that enjoyed the power to dictate tariffs and prohibit the abandonment of services or the merger of companies. The powers of government regulators to intervene in the private railroads' affairs were sharply restricted in Canada beginning in 1967 and in the United States in 1980. And some of the Latin American countries that privatized their railways in the late 1980s and 1990s did so without strong controls on prices and services. The idea is that government controls on tariffs are an anachronism since modern railways face intense competition not just from other modes of transportation but also from other locations and products. A railroad cannot raise its tariffs too high or the businesses on its lines will be disadvantaged in competing with businesses at other locations. Deregulation is more common for freight and intercity passenger services than for commuter services in major metropolitan areas, where the forces of intermodal and locational competition are thought to be weaker.

Although these three options are used in various combinations, in practice the most controversial decision is whether to introduce competition through vertical unbundling. Vertical unbundling conflicts fundamentally with deregulation and to a lesser extent with privatization in that unbundling requires fairly intimate government involvement in the industry while deregulation and privatization imply a reduction in government involvement. Unbundling does reduce involvement in as much as government regulation or ownership can be confined to the infrastructure companies, where the fear of monopoly is greatest, while train operating companies can be governed by market forces, with minimal government interference. But as long as some segments of the industry are thought to be monopolistic, the government must remain involved as regulator or owner. And mandating access arguably makes the government's task more complicated since it is now responsible for supervising the coordination of track and train operations provided by separate companies. Privatization can be pursued with or without unbundling. But deregulation is impossible with unbundling, if only because regulation is necessary to prevent the natural tendencies of the companies to consolidate into vertically integrated companies again.

This book examines the experiences with railway reform, focusing primarily on Europe, North America and Latin America. This introductory chapter provides an overview of the reform experiences around the world and advances the argument, not shared by all the other authors, that introducing competition thorough vertical unbundling has proven more problematic than introducing competition with vertical integration. The basic reasoning is that inducing train operators to compete with one another by unbundling is of limited value since most railways already face such substantial competition from other modes and locations. Moreover, the quality of railroad service depends heavily on the close coordination of infrastructure and train operations, and this coordination seems much harder to achieve when the two activities are provided by separate companies.

The main body of the book is then divided into two parts. The first part, consisting of four chapters, examines efforts to introduce competition through vertical unbundling, both with and without privatization. Chapter 2 describes the European Commission's efforts to require unbundling in its member states and the main alternative models that have emerged, including those of Britain, Sweden and Germany. Chapter 3 then examines the British model in more detail, since Britain pursued the most ambitious and controversial reforms in Europe by comprehensively unbundling and privatizing its railways. Chapters 4 and 5 consider the policies in France and Spain, both less enthusiastic reformers. The second part, consisting of three chapters, examines efforts to introduce competition with vertical integration. Chapter 6 recounts the US experience with deregulating its private freight railroads, while Chapter 7 describes Latin America's efforts to privatize its railways as vertically integrated concessions. The book concludes with a final chapter that attempts to draw together the lessons about reform.

THE IMPETUS FOR REFORM

Railroad policy has been shaped by the decline in railroad market share and profitability during much of the 20th century, a trend rooted in increasing competition from autos, buses, trucks, pipelines and airlines. Before the development of the highway and air modes, the railroads enjoyed a near monopoly in transporting intercity freight and passengers, the principal exceptions being on routes where inland waterway or coastal shipping was a realistic option. By the 1920s these new modes had begun to encroach noticeably on the railroads, and after World War II the competition intensified significantly. The appeal of alternative modes was reinforced by rising per capita incomes, which made passengers more willing to pay for the speed and convenience of highway and air service, and by the declining share of agriculture and raw materials in the economy.

The railroads' decline provoked a round of reform immediately before and after World War II, when many countries in Europe and the developing world bought out or expropriated their private railways. The hope was that consolidation and reorganization under government ownership, perhaps accompanied by a one-time infusion of new capital, would help arrest the industry's decline. An additional motive among developing countries was economic nationalism, since their railroads were usually owned by foreign investors.

Within a few decades, many industry observers came to believe that governments' close involvement in the railroads, either as owner or regulator, was counterproductive because that involvement made it harder for the industry to adapt to its new environment. Public ownership was usually accompanied by public subsidies, which were helpful. But it also was accompanied by requirements to attend to employment, regional development and other social goals that competed with the railroads' basic transportation function. Railroads were typically pressed to employ more staff than they needed, for example, or to maintain branch lines and services that were lightly used and no longer profitable, and the costs of these obligations often exceeded the subsidies they received. In North America, government regulators usually required the privately owned railroads to attend to many of the same social goals. These privately owned railroads were typically not subsidized, however, in part because public subsidy was less politically acceptable unless accompanied by public ownership.

Efforts to reduce government involvement in railroad management began in the 1960s and 1970s when some countries experimented with converting their railroads from government agencies into publicly owned corporations. The hope was that the corporate form would strengthen the accountability of managers for key performance objectives while freeing them from interference in day-to-day affairs. Corporatization was a disappointment, however, largely because it proved ineffective in shielding the managers from pressures to pursue conflicting or unrealistic goals. By the 1980s, a number of countries were ready to experiment with vertical unbundling, privatization or deregulation as a means of more clearly defining and limiting the role of government in the industry and redirecting the efforts of railway managers.

In the end, vertical unbundling was adopted primarily in Europe and Australia, in some cases with privatization and in many cases without. The rest of the reformers maintained vertically integrated railways, although sometimes with requirements to provide competing railways access to limited segments of track where there were important concentrations of customers. Canada and the United States deregulated their already private freight railways, while New Zealand took the radical step of privatizing and deregulating at the same time. Japan and many developing countries in Latin America and Africa privatized their railways but left some provisions for regulation, although these were often fairly nominal in the case of freight services.

VERTICAL UNBUNDLING: EUROPE AND AUSTRALIA

Motives

All the countries that vertically unbundled did so in the hope of inducing competition among train operators, but some had other objectives as well. In Australia competition was the primary motive: railway unbundling came about after an independent inquiry to review Australia's competition policies recommended requiring open access in all network industries, including railways. For the European Commission (EC) improving international through services was equally important. The EC had long been concerned that delays and inefficiencies of transferring rail cars between national railroads reduced the quality and inhibited the growth of international long-distance services on the continent. It hoped that through service operated by a single train operator would be significantly better. Finally, some countries, particularly in Scandinavia, were interested in vertical unbundling as a means to put rail and road transportation on an equal footing. The intention was to develop access charges for railways and highways that reflected their full social costs, including accidents and air pollution, so that shippers and passengers would make socially responsible choices between the two modes.

The Extent of Required Access and Separation

Differences in objectives and circumstances have led to differences in the extent to which access and separation is required. Australia requires open access over virtually all of the track network, for example, but there is no requirement to separate infrastructure and train operations into different companies.[1] The national interstate track network and the intrastate track of New South Wales are maintained by infrastructure-only companies. The intrastate track in the other states is provided by vertically integrated companies, although some of these companies have 'ring fenced' the management of infrastructure from that of train operations to provide more assurance that independent train operators will be treated fairly. There is no requirement or consistent policy concerning privatization. The two infrastructure-only companies are both publicly owned but most of the vertically integrated companies have been privatized.

In Europe, the EC issued a series of directives beginning in 1991 specifying deadlines for the railroads to provide access for certain types of services. These directives, described in more detail in Chapter 2, also mandate that vertically integrated railways separate accounts for infrastructure and train operations and take other steps to make their infrastructure costs and access charges more transparent. While the EC directives eventually envision access for a wide variety of services, the EC's priority, in keeping with its concerns, is to require access for international services first.

The countries of continental Europe have embraced the idea of open access and vertical separation with varying degrees of enthusiasm. Sweden reorganized its national railway into separate infrastructure and train companies in 1988, for example, three years before the first EC directive. Sweden also forced the incumbent train company to compete with independent operators for contracts to provide subsidized passenger services. At the other extreme, Spain and France have been relatively slow to reform, as explained in Chapters 4 and 5. Privatization has been even less of a priority in continental Europe than in Australia; none of the large publicly owned railways has been privatized as of 2005.

Britain is unique in that it has pursued both vertical separation and privatization more aggressively than the rest of Europe or Australia, although with some important restrictions on access. As explained in more detail in Chapter 3, Britain divided its national railway into more than 70 different companies, the most important being Railtrack, which was responsible for track, stations and other infrastructure, and 25 passenger train operating companies, each specializing in a particular type of service and route. Beginning in 1996, the government sold Railtrack through a public stock offering and tendered the train operating companies as franchises ranging in duration from seven to 15 years. A separate regulator was established to set the charges the train operating companies paid Railtrack for using its tracks and stations. The regulator allowed open access for freight operators, capacity permitting, but severely restricted the access that other passenger train companies could have to a franchisee's routes. Most of the passenger train franchises were unprofitable and were to be awarded to the bidder requesting the least subsidy, and the regulator and the Department of Transport were concerned that allowing open access would increase the franchise risk and the amount of subsidy the bidders would request.

Railtrack went bankrupt in 2001 because of unexpected costs caused by a series of fatal train accidents and by difficulties encountered in a major upgrade of the West Coast Main Line. By that time the Labour Party was in control of government and, being less sympathetic to private companies, it took the opportunity to reorganize Railtrack as a not-for-profit company called Network Rail.

Entry

The early experience with vertical unbundling suggests that encouraging entry by independent train operators is harder than expected. Where an integrated railroad was broken into separate infrastructure and train operating companies, the incumbent train operator has typically faced few successful challengers, and where an integrated company was left intact but with a mandate to open access, there have been few access seekers. Only a handful of new international freight services have emerged in continental Europe, for example, despite over a decade of EC directives to encourage them. In Australia, relatively few competing freight services developed between 1995 and 2002, and the most important were operated by existing freight forwarders who took the not-very-risky step of shifting their own freight to their own trains (BTRE, 2003, pp. 101–102). Similarly, incumbent train operators have lost only a small fraction of the passenger train service contracts that have been tendered in Sweden and Germany, although the challengers are gradually becoming more successful.

Entry may be discouraged because existing operators and services are already fairly efficient. Railroads have always had incentives to interchange cars or trains smoothly if they fear that otherwise they will lose through traffic, for example, so that the advantages of through service provided by a single operator may be less than the EC presumes, and if incumbent operators are not efficient at first, the threat of entry may be as effective as actual entry in stimulating improvements. Some Australian shippers report, for example, that the presence of an open access regime alone has been enough to stimulate incumbent railroads to offer lower freight rates particularly for coal (BTRE, 2003, p. 101).

Many observers suspect, however, that entry is discouraged less by the incumbents' efficiency than by the difficulties challengers face in assembling the necessary inputs and complying with conflicting technical standards and regulations. Finding suitable locomotives, rolling stock and train crews can be difficult, especially since the equipment and skills are fairly specialized and the markets for experienced workers or used equipment are likely to be thin or non-existent. The British managed to attract reasonable numbers of bidders for their train operating companies only because they essentially auctioned their existing train companies intact, complete with a trained labor force and leases for the necessary locomotives and rolling stock. The problems of new entrants are compounded for train services that cross international boundaries since the countries may have incompatible technical standards and regulations. The EC is now considering the creation of a European railway agency with a mandate to harmonize standards so as to reduce barriers to entry.

Coordination

A more troubling lesson of the recent experience is that vertical unbundling seems to cause coordination problems that are far more serious and difficult than proponents expected. Vertical unbundling involves a tradeoff between the benefit of introducing competition to more activities and the cost of reduced coordination between the newly separated segments of the industry (Gómez-Ibáñez, 2003, pp. 247–263). A train operating company cannot offer reliable, high-speed passenger service, for example, unless the infrastructure company maintains the tracks to a high standard and makes them available when scheduled. Before unbundling, the coordination of infrastructure and train operations took place within a single company. The two activities may have been in separate divisions of the company, but at least they reported to a common boss. After unbundling, by contrast, coordination must be arranged through contractual agreements between separate firms that have some common but many conflicting interests. If the infrastructure provider is thought to have elements of monopoly power, those agreements may have to be supervised by a government regulator. The fact that virtually all the world's railways were vertically integrated before the current round of reforms strongly suggests that integration once offered important opportunities for coordination that were difficult to achieve with separate firms.

The key to resolving the coordination problems is to establish charges and other terms of access that provide the appropriate incentives for both the infrastructure and the train operating company. One oft-cited complication is that infrastructure is characterized by substantial sunk costs and economies of scale, so that the marginal cost of carrying an additional train is typically less than the average cost, especially if the network has excess capacity. Charges set at marginal costs will encourage the efficient use of existing capacity, but they will not generate enough revenue to make the infrastructure company financially self-supporting. One solution, adopted primarily in Scandinavia, is for the government to subsidize the infrastructure company to make up the losses from marginal cost pricing. A more popular alternative is to allow the infrastructure company to discriminate among its customers by charging the least price-sensitive customers more than their marginal costs. Price discrimination avoids the drain on the public treasury and the potential incentive problems of public subsidies, but it makes charge setting more subjective and controversial.

An even more troubling difficulty is that the appropriate access charges and conditions can vary greatly among trains because the infrastructure requirements of train operations are so varied. For high-speed passenger trains, for example, it is very important that the track is relatively straight and super-elevated on curves and that there are few or no grade crossings. For slow-speed freight trains, by contrast, straight track and few grade crossings are less important while super-elevation increases maintenance problems by shifting heavy axle weights onto the inside wheel and rail. The variety of train and infrastructure types makes synchronizing the design of the infrastructure and the train operating plan important to a railroad's financial success. This problem of tailoring and optimization is less critical if there is excess capacity in the infrastructure, so that different services can share the facilities with minimal extra cost and conflict. But when the infrastructure reaches capacity and new investment is needed, the level of required access charges is likely to increase and the very specific and often conflicting needs of operators become more apparent and serious.

The complexity of the coordination problem has led to a debate as to whether infrastructure companies should be required to post a standard schedule of access charges and conditions or whether charges and conditions should be negotiated on a case-by-case basis. Standard posted charges and conditions are more transparent and avoid the potentially considerable delays and other costs of negotiation. Unless the posted schedules are very complex, however, they may not provide sufficient opportunities for price discrimination or for tailoring infrastructure services and charges to train operations. The EC favors standard charges because of the difficulties it has faced in encouraging international services, for example, while Australia relies somewhat more on negotiated access charges.

The problems of coordination have been most apparent in Britain, perhaps because Britain is the first country where infrastructure demands have greatly exceeded capacity after vertical unbundling. Britain's railroad reforms were a major success initially because they cut the amount of public subsidy the railway system required while maintaining or improving the quality of service. But problems with the access charges soon caused congestion and a host of related problems to develop. The access charges for train operators were posted as long as there were paths available in the network. If the train operators wanted Railtrack to increase the capacity of the tracks they used, however, they had to negotiate with Railtrack over additional fees, with the government regulator to intervene in the event of an impasse. The posted access charges were set on the assumption that the network had excess capacity, so that they consisted of a large fixed annual fee plus a very small variable charge per train operated. But the small variable charge encouraged the train operators to ask for so many more train paths that the network quickly became congested. Meanwhile, the capacity improvements that were to provide relief proved very difficult to negotiate because the train operators, Railtrack, and the regulator often disagreed about the design of the improvements needed, how much they should cost and how those costs should be shared. The congestion on the system made track maintenance more difficult, probably contributing to the accidents that helped bankrupt Railtrack, and the difficulties of negotiating capacity improvements seem to have played a role in the poor design of the West Coast Main Line enhancement project – the other main cause of Railtrack's failure. The collapse of Railtrack forced the government to substantially increase its financial support of the rail system and contributed to the widespread impression that the reforms were a failure.

Both of the British contributors to this volume argue that Britain's problems do not demonstrate that vertical unbundling is inherently difficult in railways. Chris Nash (in Chapter 2) blames hasty implementation, while Stephen Glaister (in Chapter 3) argues that the strategy was inherently sound but was undermined by a combination of haste and political compromises. In particular, Glaister contends that the incentives of competition were undermined by the initial reluctance of government to allow the train operating companies or Railtrack to go bankrupt when they got into trouble. Moreover, the mounting financial problems of Railtrack finally gave the Labour Government, which had come to power after the railway reforms and never liked them, the excuse to essentially renationalize the company.

The fact that vertical unbundling has not caused serious problems in the rest of Europe or Australia seems, at first glance, to support Nash and Glaister's arguments. Perhaps the more gradual or piecemeal introduction of vertical unbundling has, or will, allow these other countries to fix coordination problems before they become too serious. One might also argue that the rest of Europe and Australia have been spared because the few infrastructure-only companies they have created are still in public rather than private hands, and thus possibly less dogged in pursuing their self-interest at the expense of the train companies. But it is also striking that the rest of Europe and Australia have seen relatively little entry and competition for infrastructure capacity compared with Britain. The lesson seems to be that vertical unbundling works best when there is excess infrastructure capacity, and that encouraging coordination when capacity is constrained is very challenging.

DEREGULATION: NORTH AMERICA AND NEW ZEALAND

North America

The United States and Canada deregulated their freight railways after it became apparent that regulation was hastening the industry's decline. In the United States, federal railway regulation began in 1887, when Congress established the Interstate Commerce Commission (ICC) to prevent railroads from exercising 'undue prejudice' by, for example, charging higher tariffs to small shippers or shippers served by only one railway. In the following decades Congress expanded the agency's powers to allow the ICC to specify the tariffs a railway could charge and to make ICC permission necessary before a railroad could abandon track or merge with another.

In 1980, the US Congress responded to the rapidly deteriorating financial condition of the American railroads by sharply limiting the ICC's powers to regulate freight tariffs, mergers or abandonment. The ICC could set tariffs only if it made two findings: first, that the shipper in question was 'captive' to the railroad in the sense that he had few practical alternatives and, second, that the tariffs were in excess of 180 percent of the railroad's variable costs. Even then, the ICC had to determine whether the railroad involved was earning a reasonable return on its investments as a whole and, if not, had to take the railroad's revenue shortfall into account in its decision. These restrictions have limited the number of tariff cases in which the ICC intervenes to a handful per year. Most tariffs are now set by private negotiations between railroads and shippers with the ICC, which was later renamed the Surface Transportation Board (STB), involved in only the most egregious suspected cases of monopoly abuse.

Mandatory track access plays only a relatively minor role in the new US deregulated system. American railroads have long exchanged track rights on a voluntary basis, where one railroad has a more direct or level route, for example. But these arrangements are uncommon and usually do not include the right to pick up or drop off traffic on the host's track. Government-mandated track access was extremely rare before 1980, if only because ICC tariff regulation made it unnecessary, but the practice expanded somewhat as the industry consolidated after deregulation. By 1997, several waves of mergers had left the United States with only four major freight railroads: two to the east and two to the west of the Mississippi River. The STB conditioned its approval for the last few mergers on specific exchanges of track rights so that shippers who had a choice of two railroads before the merger would still have the same choice after. However, the percentage of track involved is relatively small.[2]

As Clifford Winston explains in Chapter 6, deregulation brought about a remarkable revival of the US freight railroad industry. The average tariff per ton-mile dropped by roughly half in real terms, stimulating an increase in railroad traffic of all types, and the railroads were able to cut costs faster than they cut tariffs, so that the industry's profitability was restored. The railroads complain that they still earn less on their investments than other comparable private industries, and some shippers argue that they have not enjoyed much tariff relief because they are still captive to a particular railroad. But the industry is once again able to attract capital, and even the so-called captive shippers are paying less than they did before deregulation.

Canada took a similar path to deregulation. In 1967, concerned that regulation was hindering the railroads' ability to compete with other modes, the government gave the railroads more pricing freedom by restricting the circumstances under which the Canadian Transport Commission[3] could set maximum rates and by allowing the railroads to set rates collectively. By 1987, however, the government had become convinced of the need to promote competition among railroads as well, and to that end eliminated collective ratemaking, introduced confidential contracts with shippers, and made best-and-final offer arbitration available in case of an impasse in negotiations between a shipper and a railroad.

Competition was also aided by an 'inter-switching' requirement that dated from the early 1900s and had been originally designed to prevent railroad overbuilding in urban areas. The inter-switching provision allows a shipper with access to only one railroad to ask that the shipment be transferred to a second railroad at standard regulated rates as long as the distance from the origin or destination to the interchange point is no more than 30 kilometers. In 1995 the government took the further step of selling off the Canadian National Railway, so that both of Canada's transcontinental railways are now privately owned. Freight rates declined by approximately one-quarter in real terms in the decade immediately following the 1987 reforms, although there are signs that large shippers have enjoyed the biggest rate reductions while small shippers may have been left out (Canada Transportation Act Review Panel, 2001, pp. 39–41).

New Zealand

In 1993, New Zealand leased its railroad to a private company for 80 years and the company operated reasonably successfully with minimal regulation for over a decade. New Zealand adopted its so-called 'light-handed' approach to regulation because it is a small country and wanted to avoid establishing a large regulatory bureaucracy (Bollard and Pickford, 1997). When New Zealand began to privatize its telecommunications and other utilities in the 1980s it established a single Competition Commission with the responsibility over all sectors. Utilities were enjoined by law from abusing their 'dominant position' and competitors or customers could sue in the courts for relief. As a last resort, the government could ask the Commerce Commission to set prices.

The Competition Commission's price setting powers were never invoked for the railroad, perhaps because it faced so much competition from trucks and coastal shipping. The private operator significantly increased efficiency and market share and reported profits through the 1990s. But the profits had been inflated by capitalizing maintenance and deferring renewals, and in the end the efficiencies were not enough to make rail freight truly profitable in the face of only modest traffic densities, short lengths of haul, and a modern highway and trucking system. The government bought back the rail infrastructure from the company in 2004 after the railroad, near bankruptcy, announced its intention to abandon passenger service and some freight lines. A private operator continues to operate the trains, but the government controls and subsidizes the infrastructure.

Competition and Long-term Contracts

Deregulation was successful in North America and New Zealand because the rail freight market proved far more competitive than traditionally believed. North America's railroads specialize in carrying bulk commodities that are of too little value and high weight to warrant transport by truck and inter-modal containers moving over long distances. In the short run, some railroad shippers have effective transportation alternatives. Shippers of containers from east or west coast ports to the center of the country usually can choose between two railroads or more, for example, while shippers located on or near a waterway may have barges as an option. But the vast majority of rail shippers – such as mines, electricity generating stations, refineries and manufacturing plants – are served by only one railroad and not located on a waterway. In the long run, however, these apparently captive shippers often can avoid high railroad tariffs by shifting to other locations and products. For example, an electric utility with a coal-fired generating station can relocate the station to the tracks of another railroad or to a waterway, buy power wholesale over the grid from other utilities, or convert the station to burn natural gas or oil. The threat to relocate or shift products may not be credible in the short run because the shipper's plant is valuable, durable and expensive to move or modify. But these threats become real once the shipper's investment reaches the end of its economic life and has to be renewed.

One of the keys to making locational and product competition more effective has been to allow shippers and railroads to sign long-term contracts. A shipper can protect itself from future exploitation by making any investment on the railroad's network conditional on a long-term service contract; the contract locks in the leverage the shipper enjoys when a new investment is made or an old one is renewed. Long-term contracts have also proved useful in helping the railroads to reduce costs by allowing the railroads and shippers shape services in mutually advantageous ways. The contracts often include volume guarantees, for example, which allow the railroads to invest in specialized cost-saving equipment or to commit to frequent or regular schedules without sacrificing train or crew productivity. Indeed, the cost-saving advantages of contracts are so great that even non-captive traffic often moves under long-term contracts.

Long-term contracts are commonly used in other industries to protect parties that are making relationship-specific investments. A parts supplier would not invest in specialized machinery useful for only one customer, for example, without the protection of a long-term contract from that customer. Before deregulation the ICC prohibited railroads from signing private contracts with shippers for fear that contracts would be a device for favoring large shippers unduly. By permitting contracts, deregulation restored to the industry an important tool for protecting shippers and railroads from opportunistic behavior so that they could make mutually advantageous investments.

Deregulation has had its problems and limitations, perhaps the most important being that it works better for large shippers than small. Large shippers with multiple plants may not even need the protection of long-term contracts since they can more easily and rapidly retaliate against high railroad tariffs by shifting production and investment among their plants. Moreover, the time and costs spent negotiating a contract usually do not increase proportionately with the contract's size, which makes long-term contracting more worthwhile or practical for a large shipper than a small shipper. Freight forwarders and other intermediaries that consolidate small shipments may serve as effective negotiators on the small shipper's behalf. Deregulation was possible by the late 20th century in part because most of the small shippers who were so dependent on the railroads in the late 19th century had long since shifted to trucks. Even so, it is politically helpful to provide shippers with the option of appealing to a regulatory agency such as the STB, even if the agency is allowed to intervene only in extreme cases.

PRIVATIZATION WITH SELECTIVE ACCESS: LATIN AMERICA AND JAPAN

Horizontal vs. Vertical Separation

Latin America and Japan followed a third strategy of reform, relying primarily on privatization rather than vertical unbundling or deregulation. Unlike Europe and Australia, they typically broke their national company up horizontally into several regional, vertically integrated railways rather than vertically into separate infrastructure and train companies, and unlike North America and New Zealand, they retained some forms of tariff regulation rather than deregulate. But Latin America and, to a lesser extent Japan, incorporated elements of two other strategies. In particular, the territories of the regional railroads were often designed to create some direct or indirect forms of competition, and regulation was fairly light-handed particularly for freight but also for intercity passenger services.

In Japan, the territories of the new railways did not overlap so the emphasis was on indirect forms of competition. Passengers are the key concern in Japan since the relatively short overland distances and the availability of coastal shipping severely limit rail's share of the freight market. The Japanese national railway was broken into six regional passenger railways, three for the eastern, central and western parts of the main island of Honshu and one each for three smaller islands. A seventh company was created to operate freight trains over the tracks of the passenger railways. The hope of reformers was that the six passenger railroads would ease the task of government regulation by allowing regulators to benchmark the performance of each railroad against those of its peers.

In some Latin America countries, the territories of the new railroads were designed to overlap enough to encourage more direct competition between them. As explained in Chapter 7, Mexico was arguably the most successful in this regard, in part because it was one of the last to privatize and restructure its railroads and benefited from the experience of others. Freight is the main concern in Mexico, as there is very little passenger service. Mexico divided its national railway into three main freight railways, two to the north of Mexico City and one to the south. The three railroad networks were carefully designed so that all three railroads serve Mexico City, each railroad serves a major port on the Pacific and the Caribbean, two railroads each serve the major industrial cities of Monterrey and Guadalajara, while each northern railroad connects with a different US railroad at the border. The three railways together own a small railway that serves the valley of Mexico City, which provides all of them direct access to customers in the capital area. In addition, there are some exchanges of track rights in Monterrey and Guadalajara to allow the two railways that serve those cities access to all of the customers in the metropolitan area. The resulting system gives shippers in Mexico's three main markets a choice between at least two railroads, each with access to a Pacific and a Caribbean port and each connecting to a different US railroad. The required access rights are strictly limited to a few locations, however, and railroads are expected to negotiate access charges and terms, with the Secretary of Transport empowered to break impasses.

Other countries, such as Brazil and Argentina, were less successful in encouraging competition among railroads both because their networks were less suitable and because competition was an afterthought in restructuring (Campos, 2001). Brazil's freight network did not lend itself to an obvious competitive design since most of the main routes connect a separate port to its hinterland. The Brazilians made matters worse, however, by awarding the inner and outer portions of some routes as separate concessions, forcing the inner railroad to negotiate joint rates or access rights to get to a port. Argentina's intercity network consists mainly of lines that radiate out from Buenos Aires and is used almost exclusively for freight. The lines were awarded as five separate freight concessions, with the condition that provincial governments be allowed to access the tracks if they chose to inaugurate an intercity passenger service.[4] The five concessions do not overlap in the hinterland, but are close enough to one another that some shippers may have an effective choice of railroads. Nevertheless, the Argentine and Brazilian freight railroads have more to fear from trucks than from each other, especially since distances are short enough that trucking direct to the ports is often competitive with rail.

In short, Japan and the countries of Latin America all mandate track access but only in a very limited way. Where one use of the network predominates – passengers in the case of Japan or freight in the case of Argentina's intercity lines – access is usually required for the rare train of the minority use. Rights to use specific and relatively short segments of track are sometimes mandated to enhance competition (as in Mexico) or to correct flaws in concession design (as in Brazil). However, widespread access on the scale permitted in Europe and Australia is not required.

Regulation by Concession Contract

Latin America and Japan felt it necessary to regulate their private railroads but Latin America deliberately adopted a form of regulation designed to be less intrusive than the approach used previously in North America. Regulatory systems can be classified into two broad types: discretionary and contractual (Gómez-Ibáñez, 2003). Under the discretionary approach, a regulatory agency has broad latitude to set the tariffs charged by the companies it regulates. The agency is usually limited by its authorizing statute, which sets out the factors it must consider in reaching its decisions. Moreover, the company or its customers usually can appeal the agency's rulings to some independent body, often the courts, if they feel the agency has violated its statute. But the statutory guidance is fairly broad, so that the agency has substantial discretion in its interpretation. Under the contractual approach, by contrast, the government awards the company a contract that specifies in detail the tariffs the company can charge and other conditions of service. The contract is usually for a fixed term and awarded through competitive bidding. A regulatory agency monitors the company's compliance with the contract and, if warranted, imposes any fines or penalties for poor performance provided for in the contract. But the regulatory agency does not have the discretion to unilaterally change the terms of the contract.

The discretionary approach has long been the norm for regulating private railroads and other utilities in the United States, but the contractual approach is more popular among developing countries. Many developing countries privatized not just their railroads but electricity, telecommunications and other types of infrastructure during the 1980s and 1990s. Potential investors were concerned about the governments' commitment to private infrastructure, however, especially since many of the newly privatized companies had been nationalized only a few decades earlier. Investors were being asked to buy or build infrastructure that was durable and immobile, and once they did the government might be tempted to take advantage of the situation by reneging on promises to maintain reasonable tariffs. In this context, the contractual approach was more appealing than an approach that granted the government substantial discretion. The key limitation of the contractual approach is that one must draft a contract that is 'complete' in that it foresees all major developments that might affect the contract and provides appropriate contingencies. The more uncertain the industry or the government's needs, the harder it is to draft a complete contract. As a result, developing countries often used discretionary regulation for infrastructure such as telecommunications, where the technological or other uncertainties seemed great, but they relied more on contractual regulation for other forms of infrastructure, including railroads.

Freight and passenger concessions generally take different forms because governments typically expect freight service to be financially self-supporting while they are often willing to subsidize passenger service, particularly on urban commuter lines that serve congested metropolitan areas. Freight concessions are typically awarded to the firm offering the highest payment to the government or promising to make the largest investment while freight tariffs are often only loosely controlled. Passenger concessions, in contrast, are usually awarded to the firm requesting the minimum subsidy with both the minimum level of service and the maximum fare carefully specified. Freight concessions are often for 30 or more years (with comparable extensions allowed), a term dictated by the expected lifetimes of investments in rolling stock and track. Passenger concessions are much shorter, often ten or so years, because the government wishes to exercise greater control over its financial obligations and the level of service.

Performance

The privatized railway concessions were generally successful in improving service for shippers and passengers while significantly reducing the level of public subsidy the railroads absorb. A survey of 17 freight concessions in five Latin American and one African country found, for example, that traffic had increased in all 17 concessions and that tariffs had declined in 15 concessions for a total savings to shippers of US$900 million in 1999 (Thompson et al., 2003). Urban commuter railway and subway concessions in Buenos Aires and Rio de Janeiro have substantially reduced the amount of public subsidy required while also increasing ridership (Rebello, 1999).

While mandatory access is not a central element of the Japanese or Latin American reforms, it seems to have worked relatively smoothly. Complaints about the difficulties of negotiating the charges and other conditions for that access are common, but seldom reach the level where government regulators are asked to intervene. It probably helps that the access rights are relatively limited and that in some cases, such as Mexico, they are reciprocal. A railroad may be more sympathetic to a competitor requesting terms for accessing its track if that railroad is at times dependent on gaining access to the competitor's track.

The principal problem with these railroad concessions is that drafting a complete contract has proved to be much more difficult than expected. Virtually every railroad concession has had to be renegotiated at one time or another because economic crises, faulty traffic forecasts, or other unexpected developments have made it difficult for the concessionaires, the government, or both to comply with their obligations under the contract. The renegotiations have undermined both the security that the investors had hoped for and the support of railroad users and the general public for the concession system. If the concession is awarded through competitive bidding both the investors and the public are likely to accept the initial terms as fair. But there is no similar, transparently fair way to renegotiate a concession once it is awarded, which often raises investor and popular concerns about corruption or incompetence.

COMPETITION AND VERTICAL UNBUNDLING

It is hard to argue that railroads enjoy much monopoly or market power anymore, particularly in intercity freight and passenger service. In freight, trucks long ago stole the small and high value shipments, and even compete effectively for bulk commodities in countries, like Japan or Argentina, where the lengths of haul are relatively short. Barges and pipelines are an option for some longer hauls, but even where those modes are absent the railroads usually face intense competition from other locations and other products. In intercity passenger service, the automobile and the airline now dominate, particularly in North America where railroads account for less than 1 percent of the market. Even in Europe, which has been investing heavily in high-speed trains, rail's share of the passenger market has fallen to 6 percent while air's share is rising steadily and, with the spread of low-fare airlines, should soon exceed that of rail (Table 1.1). Only in urban passenger service might railroads enjoy some market power, and even then only for commuting in the most congested metropolitan areas, where there are no parallel metro lines, and where buses are not given priority in traffic.

The intensity of competition makes vertical unbundling less attractive in railroads than in telephones, electricity and highways. As noted earlier, vertical unbundling involves a tradeoff between the benefits of introducing competition to new activities and the costs from lost coordination when activities are provided by separate firms. There are reasons to believe that the coordination problems are more severe in railroads than in other industries (Gómez-Ibáñez, 2003, pp. 331–337). Train operations are more varied in their technical characteristics than telephone calls, electrons, or motor vehicles, for example, and thus the basic infrastructure required for railroads is less standardized than it is in other industries. Moreover, infrastructure accounts for a relatively large portion of railroad costs, particularly for passenger service, which makes the strategy of reducing coordination problems by building excess infrastructure capacity more expensive. We may have underestimated the coordination difficulties in other vertically unbundled industries – witness the growing concern in the electricity industry about the need for incentives to build additional

*Table 1.1   Passenger kilometres by mode in the 15 countries of the
             European Union*

	Passenger cars	Buses and coaches	Tram and metro	Railway	Air	Total
Passenger kilometers traveled (billions)						
1970	1582	269	39	219	33	2142
1980	2295	348	41	248	74	3006
1990	3199	369	48	268	157	4041
1995	3506	382	47	274	202	4410
2000	3789	413	53	303	281	4839
Share of passenger kilometers (%)						
1970	73.9	12.6	1.8	10.2	1.5	100.0
1980	76.3	11.6	1.4	8.3	2.5	100.0
1990	79.2	9.1	1.2	6.6	3.9	100.0
1995	79.5	8.7	1.1	6.2	4.6	100.0
2000	78.3	8.5	1.1	6.3	5.8	100.0

Source: European Commission, *Panorama of Transport: Statistical Overview of Transport in
the European Union, Data 1970–2000*, Part 2 (Luxembourg: European Communities, 2003).

high-voltage transmission lines. But coordination problems seem at least as
hard, if not harder, in railroads than in any other industry where a policy
of forced separation has been attempted.

If the extra competition introduced by unbundling is of little value,
however, then there seems little point in risking the loss of coordination.
Indeed it is striking that Britain, which completely separated its infrastructure and train operations, decided that it was unwise to encourage train-on-
train competition in passenger service. Most of the British passenger
services were going to require public subsidy, in large part because they
already faced such stiff competition from other modes, and the competition
among bidders for the train operating franchises promised to be intense
enough to significantly reduce the government's subsidy bill. In this
context, the government thought it risky and unnecessary to introduce still
more competition by allowing train operators to compete with one another
over the same tracks. If train-on-train competition was to be prohibited,
however, what was the point of unbundling? The government might have
been better served by auctioning off vertically integrated franchises and
avoiding the types of coordination problems that brought down Railtrack.

The case for vertical unbundling seems plausible only if it is very limited and
selective. Voluntary exchanges of track rights among railroads should be
allowed and even encouraged. But mandatory access also may make sense if,

as in Mexico, the United States or Canada, it is limited to a few key portions of the network where access provides a significant increase in competition. Even in such cases, however, it may be important to be sure that there is some symmetry in access requirements so that the railroads have incentives to behave reasonably when negotiating with one another over access terms and charges.

If the intense competition that the railways face makes vertical unbundling less attractive, it also increases the appeal of privatization and deregulation. Indeed, the developing countries that privatized but imposed concession regulation probably were too timid, especially for intercity freight and passenger services. Competition from trucks and buses is typically intense and private long-term contracts probably could ameliorate any remaining competitive problems. If so, those countries might have avoided concession regulation, and the attendant problems of drafting complete concession contracts. They might have maintained a regulatory agency with powers to intervene only in the most troubling cases, so that, as in Canada and the United States, the railroads were largely deregulated but regulation was available as a safety valve to solve serious problems that may arise.

NOTES

1. If a rail infrastructure provider refuses access on reasonable terms, then the access seeker can appeal to the National Competition Council (NCC) to determine that the track involved is a bottleneck with natural monopoly characteristics. With an affirmative NCC finding, the access seeker can ask the Australian Competition and Consumer Commission to arbitrate any dispute over access terms (BTRE, 2003, pp. 58–64).
2. The American Association of Railroads (2002) estimates that 14 percent of the route mileage in the United States, Canada and Mexico is under voluntary or mandatory track access agreements.
3. Since renamed the Canadian Transportation Agency.
4. A sixth freight concession attracted no bidders, and was eventually given to the employees. In addition, the commuter rail lines and the subway serving Buenos Aires were awarded as seven concessions. Finally, the most important intercity passenger rail line (connecting Buenos Aires with Mar del Plata) was given to the Province of Buenos Aires to operate.

REFERENCES

American Association of Railroads (2002), *North American Freight Railroad Statistics*, Washington, DC.
Bollard, Alan and Michael Pickford (1997), 'Utility Regulation in New Zealand', in Michael E. Beesley (ed), *Regulating Utilities: Broadening the Debate*, London: Institute of Economic Affairs, pp. 75–131.
Bureau of Transport and Regional Economics (2003), *Rail Infrastructure Pricing: Principles and Practice*, Department of Transport and Regional Services, Bureau of Transport and Regional Economics, Report 109, Canberra, Australia.

Campos, Javier (2001), 'Lessons from Railway Reforms in Brazil and Mexico', *Transport Policy*, **8**, 85–95.

Canada Transportation Act Review Panel (2001), *Vision and Balance: Canada Transportation Act Review*, Minister of Public Works: Toronto, Canada.

Gómez-Ibáñez, José A. (2003), *Regulating Infrastructure: Monopoly, Contracts, and Discretion*, Harvard University Press: Cambridge, MA.

Rebello, Jorge (1999), 'Rail and Subway Concessions in Rio de Janiero', World Bank Private Sector Note no. 183.

Thompson, Louis S., Karim-Jaques Budin, and Antonio Estache (2003), 'Private Investment in Railways: Experience from South and North America, Africa, and New Zealand', Paper prepared for the Public–Private Infrastructure Advisory Facility, project C060200/S/RWS/ST/1W.

PART I

Competition through vertical restructuring

2. Europe: Alternative models for restructuring

Chris Nash

INTRODUCTION

The pace of reform in the rail industry accelerated rapidly in the last decade under the pressure of successive European legislation. By 2005, many countries in Europe were in the process of completely separating infrastructure from operations and of introducing competitive tendering for at least some passenger services, while all were required to implement open access for freight services and to provide an opportunity to appeal on access issues to a regulator who is independent of the infrastructure manager. This chapter first reviews the legislation to distinguish the changes required by law from those implemented voluntarily by some member governments. It then examines the extent to which vertical separation and competition by means of open access or tendering have actually been introduced. The following two sections examine econometric evidence and case studies of the impacts of reform, focusing particularly on two different models: complete separation of infrastructure and operations as in Britain and Sweden, and continued vertical integration in the main operator as in Germany. The evidence suggests that the overall reforms are leading to improvement in the competitive situation of European railways but there is still a great deal of doubt about the precise combination of reforms that works best in any given situation.

THE DEVELOPMENT OF EUROPEAN RAILWAY POLICY

The recent round of rail reforms in Europe began in the late 1980s, with the separation of infrastructure and operations and introduction of competitive tendering in Sweden. Whereas in North America competition between separate vertically integrated operators had been preserved, at least on the most important routes, in Europe for many years rail services had been provided by government owned vertically integrated monopolies. Until 1989, European rail policy had concentrated on trying to turn these organisations into arm's-length commercial bodies, compensated by government for social obligations but otherwise operating independently without other financial aid. This approach was promoted in a set of regulations passed in 1969/70.

However, railways continued to be seen as a problem in most of Europe. They steadily lost market share (Figures 2.1 and 2.2), falling from 10 per

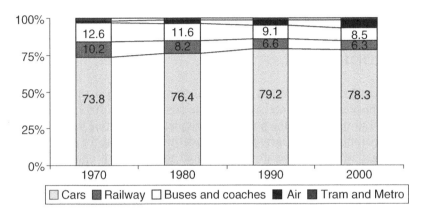

Source: Nash and Rivera-Trujillo, 2004.

Figure 2.1   Passenger modal share in the European Union (passenger/km %)

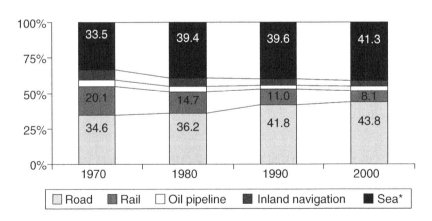

Source: Nash and Rivera-Trujillo, 2004.
*Intra-EU traffic including domestic traffic.

Figure 2.2   Freight modal share in the European Union (tonne/km %)

cent to 6 per cent of passenger kilometres and 20 per cent to 8 per cent of freight ton kilometres over 30 years. They also required high and increasing levels of subsidy; Table 2.1 shows that less than half of the total costs of rail transport in Europe were borne directly by passenger and freight customers. While data taken from company accounts give (sometimes very) different results, the figures in Table 2.1 are drawn from a major European Commission funded study, UNITE, which sought to measure all elements of capital and operating costs and revenues on a comparable basis. The UNITE study used the perpetual inventory method to value capital costs, so its results are comparable to those of a replacement cost depreciation approach.

A particular concern of the European Commission was that the railways were not performing well even in the rapidly growing international rail freight sector, where the long distances should have given rail a competitive advantage and where the growth of road haulage was seen as particularly problematic in terms of congestion and environmental pollution.

Table 2.1   Total rail transport costs and revenues 1998 (€ million)

Country	Revenue over total cost
Austria	0.31
Belgium	0.24
Denmark	0.54
Finland	0.66
France	0.41
Germany	0.43
Greece	0.18
Hungary	0.09
Ireland[1]	0.46
Italy	0.28
Luxembourg[2]	0.26
Netherlands	0.35
Portugal	0.22
Spain	0.27
Sweden	0.62
Switzerland	0.45
UK	0.57
Total	0.39

Notes:
[1] Operating, signalling and depreciation costs only.
[2] Rail owned buses included.

Source: Nash et al. (2002).

It was clear that rail was failing to provide a competitive combination of cost and quality of service, and an important reason for this was thought to be the existing structure of the industry. Whereas liberalisation in the road sector led to a position where any licensed operator could take freight from anywhere to anywhere within the European community, international rail freight was still handled by agreement between neighbouring railways, who passed the traffic from one to another at each border. This meant that there was no single operator who could be held accountable for the entire service, speed of reaction to market developments was slow and the entire operation was only as good as the weakest link in the chain. Other problems were the fact that each railway had its own technical standards, types of signalling and electrification, etc. Thus most often trains had to change drivers and locomotives at borders. Moreover the quality and capacity of infrastructure for international freight was also a problem, with investment tending to be concentrated on domestic passenger services.

The Commission's policy concentrated heavily on open access for international freight operators since international freight traffic was of particular concern. However, to achieve this it was necessary to probe much more deeply into the organisation of the railways. The first measure (91/440) introduced open access for operators of international inter-modal freight, and required non-discriminatory pricing and allocation of paths to allow them to operate. However, its impact was small and it rapidly became apparent that a range of barriers to entry still existed. First, to enter the market an operator had to obtain an operator's licence and safety certificate for every country through which it wished to operate. In addition, it had to obtain rolling stock and drivers authorised to run in every country through which it wished to operate, or arrange to change locomotives and drivers at borders. It also had to negotiate an access agreement and charges with each infrastructure manager. Even where infrastructure managers were cooperative, this was bound to be a time consuming business. But it was alleged that some infrastructure managers were far from cooperative, since they were either part of the main competing train operating company, or had the same owner, namely the government.

Thus a succession of further measures followed, culminating in the so-called first railway package of 2001, which extended the right of entry to all international rail freight operators, initially (in 2003) on an extensive Trans European rail freight network and ultimately on all lines. The same set of measures required that if passenger and freight train operators and infrastructure managers were part of the same organisation, they should at least be separate divisions, with separate accounts. They also required non-discriminatory allocation of paths, and that allocation of paths and the setting of track access charges should be carried out by an organisation independent of any train operating company. There was also to be a regulator, independent of train operating companies and infrastructure managers, to whom appeals could be made, and rules were laid down on which infrastructure charges were to be based.

In January 2002, the Commission adopted a further set of measures (known as the second railway package) that included: (i) a new directive on the regulation of safety and investigation of accidents and incidents on the community's railways; (ii) further measures to promote interoperability of railway rolling stock between countries; (iii) a regulation to establish a new European safety and interoperability agency; and (iv), and most fundamentally, an amendment to 91/440 so as to open up access to the infrastructure for domestic as well as international rail freight services by 2007.

Although the priority has been freight services, a proposal to open international rail passenger markets to competition was under discussion in 2005 as part of a third rail package. An earlier proposal to amend regulation 1191/69 to introduce compulsory competitive tendering for all subsidised services, passenger as well as freight, met with too much opposition in both the European Parliament and the Council of Ministers. A revised version permits competitive tendering or in-house operation of urban railways but excludes regional and long distance services from its scope.

The issue of open access cannot be separated from pricing policy. To have the right of access, but at whatever price the infrastructure manager chooses, is valueless. It has long been the declared aim of the Commission that pricing policies should promote economic efficiency, which requires prices that relate to marginal social cost. Originally, this was seen mainly in terms of charging for the marginal operating and maintenance costs of the infrastructure, but more recently the concern with environmental problems has led to an emphasis on the external costs of transport as well – congestion, accidents and environmental costs.

In 1998 the Commission published its proposals for the introduction of a common transport infrastructure charging framework, which placed a further emphasis on the marginal social cost pricing approach, while allowing mark-ups to be levied where this is not adequate for full cost recovery (CEC, 1998). The proposals on railway infrastructure charging emerging from the first railway package were enshrined in Directive 2001/14, on allocation of railway infrastructure capacity and levying of charges. In summary, the Directive determines that charges must be based on 'costs directly incurred as a result of operating the train service'. These may include:

- Scarcity, although where a section of track is defined as having a scarcity problem, the infrastructure manager must examine proposals to relieve that scarcity, and undertake them unless they are shown, on the basis of cost–benefit analysis, not to be worthwhile.
- Environmental costs, but only where these are levied on other modes.
- Recovery of the costs of specific investments where these are worthwhile and could not otherwise be funded.
- Discounts, but only where justified by costs; large operators may not use their market power to get discounts.
- Reservation charges for scarce capacity, which must be paid whether the capacity is used or not.
- Compensation for unpaid costs on other modes.
- Mark-ups where necessary for financial reasons, but these must not discriminate between different operators competing for the same traffic and they must not exclude segments of traffic which could cover direct cost. Exactly what this means is not clear; it appears that Ramsey pricing is permitted, but it is doubtful whether two part tariffs could be regarded as acceptable under this Directive for any traffic for which there is on-track competition.

This Directive reflects some quite sophisticated economic arguments. The list of elements that may be included in the charges suggests that 'the direct cost of operating the service' is to be interpreted as short-run marginal social cost. However, the fear that short-run pricing may lead infrastructure managers to artificially restrict capacity or to be unable to fund investments is addressed by special provisions. Moreover, there is an allowance for second-best pricing in the face of distorted prices on other modes, where little progress has been made on moving towards marginal social cost pricing. Nevertheless, the effect of these provisions, all sensible in themselves, is to considerably water down the likely effect of the Directive by giving infrastructure managers various loopholes under which they can argue for the maintenance of previous forms of infrastructure charging. In particular, the degree to which competitive charges for paths involving several countries, based on comparable pricing regimes, have been achieved is inevitably limited.

Although the subsequent White Paper (CEC, 2001) proposed a framework directive and methodology paper extending marginal social cost pricing to all modes of transport, there has been little progress on this. In the case of road haulage, an existing directive (the so-called Eurovignette

Directive of 1999) allows member states to require road haulers to buy an additional licence (the Eurovignette) to use their motorway system. The background to this was the wish of countries with high taxes on road haulage to even out the terms of competition with haulers based in low tax countries; the Eurovignette Directive permitted such a charge but required it to be levied on all operators regardless of nationality, and not to exceed the infrastructure costs of providing the motorway system (i.e. excluding externalities). A proposal to review the Eurovignette Directive on heavy goods vehicle charges put forward in 2003 would still tie the average level of charges to average infrastructure and uncovered accident costs, excluding other externalities, although these could be used to differentiate charges by vehicle type, time and location. It would also permit charges to be levied on all roads, rather than solely motorways. The proposal, which would still not fully internalise externalities in charges, was agreed late in 2005. Proposals for air and water transport have yet to be brought forward.

In summary, then, current European legislation leaves room for a great variety of approaches to railway reform. It does not (and under European law cannot) require privatisation of any part of the rail industry. Nor does it at present require separation of rail infrastructure and operations into totally separate organisations, although the requirement that – in the absence of this – key functions such as path allocation and the setting of charges be undertaken by a separate body – has led many countries to conclude that complete vertical separation is the simplest way to comply. It requires neither open access nor competitive tendering for the operation of passenger services, although a number of countries have implemented one or both of these measures. What it does require is open access for international rail freight operators, and by 2007 for domestic rail freight services as well.

ALTERNATIVE MODELS OF RAIL RESTRUCTURING

As commented above, the existing European legislation leaves the way open for a variety of models of rail restructuring. In practice, the main two approaches have followed either the Swedish model, with completely separate organisations still within the public sector responsible for rail infrastructure and for many rail services, or the German model, with a single vertically integrated public sector organisation still owning separate subsidiaries or divisions responsible for infrastructure and passenger and freight operations. The essential difference between these models is whether infrastructure and operations are still vertically integrated. However, within both models there are widely differing degrees of liberalisation in terms of the degree to which new entry is permitted. The position of the main countries is shown diagrammatically in terms of the two key dimensions of vertical separation and degree of competition in Table 2.2.

Britain has followed the vertical separation path but, unlike any other country in Europe, has completely privatised both infrastructure and operations with open access for freight operations and competitive franchising of virtually all passenger operations. The example of Great Britain is considered further in Chapter 3. At the other extreme France (discussed in Chapter 4) has separated infrastructure and operations but maintained both to date as public sector monopolies (Finland has also followed this model). Sweden has progressively opened up its rail freight market to competition and its subsidised passenger services to competitive tendering, and the same model is being followed – more slowly – by Denmark and the Netherlands. Germany has complete open access for commercial freight and passenger services and progressive spread of competitive tendering for regional passenger services, and is being followed more slowly by Austria, Italy, Poland and Belgium. At the time of writing, Spain, Greece and Ireland have yet to start the process of reform, although the separation

Table 2.2   Alternative models of rail restructuring

	Degree of competition		
Degree of separation	None	Open Access freight competition	Plus at least some competitive tendering for passenger
Vertically integrated (with separate accounting)	Greece Ireland	Belgium	Germany Austria
Separate public sector infrastructure manager	France Finland Spain		Sweden Netherlands Denmark Italy Portugal
Separate private sector infrastructure manager			Great Britain

of infrastructure and operations into separate public sector bodies is planned for 2005 in Spain. The situation as of early 2005 is listed country by country in Table 2.3.

The primary advantage of Germany's vertically integrated model is that it maintains the possibility of integrated planning of infrastructure and the main passenger and freight services, both in terms of short-term time-tabling and longer-term investment. Both of these areas have been problems particularly in the highly fragmented British rail network, although the degree of difficulty has been reduced by the introduction of tight control over timetables and investment by the government (initially through the Strategic Rail Authority, although that is now to be abolished – see Chapter 3).

These benefits of vertical integration would be largely lost, however, if open access for freight and competitive tendering for passenger services led to the majority of services being transferred to the private sector, as then there would in any case be a need to coordinate timetables and investment plans between a number of different organisations. Moreover there are some substantial disadvantages to continued vertical integration. First, under European legislation there must be a separate body responsible for path allocation and the setting of infrastructure charges, so complete vertical integration is not allowed. Second, the continued operation of both infrastructure and train services by a single large public sector company means that a private entrant must negotiate for access with its main competitor, who will gain knowledge of the traffic for which it plans to compete and will have much greater market strength (and possibly government subsidies or cross-subsidy) with which to compete for it.

Perhaps adequate rules, including 'Chinese walls' between the infrastructure and operating divisions and an independent regulator with adequate power and resources to investigate and remedy abuses might solve these problems of vertical integration. But under European legislation, while the regulator must be independent of the infrastructure manager, it may still be part of the Ministry of Transport. In some cases, indeed, the regulator is a single person, without resources or powers, located within the same ministry as is responsible for the finances of the infrastructure manager and state owned operating companies. In this case, whether infrastructure is separated from operations or not, there is a risk that decisions favour the incumbent, and the chances of rectifying abuses of power by a vertically integrated public sector operator appear uncertain.

Table 2.3 Rail organisation in Western European Railways (selected cases)

No.	Country	Degree of separation of infrastructure from operations	Degree of competition	Main operator	Infrastructure
1	Austria	Accounting separation	Limited to Regional passenger and freight services	OBB Integrated railway state owned	Mainly owned by the state (OBB Netz), 10% are privately owned
2	Belgium	Accounting separation	One freight operating company entrant	SNCB Integrated railway state owned	State owned (SNCB)
3	Denmark	Institutional separation	Freight and regional passenger services	DSB state owned	Public corporation (Banestyrelsen)
4	Finland	Institutional separation	None	VR state owned	State owned organisation (RHK)
5	France	Institutional separation	None	SNCF state owned	State owned organisation (RFK)
6	Germany	Organisational separation	All markets	DB AG Vertically integrated railway divided into groups and divisions	DB Netz AG state owned company; some private railways
7	Great Britain	Institutional separation	All markets	Private companies	Owned by Network Rail: 'not for profit' company
8	Greece	Accounting separation	None	OSE Integrated railway state owned	Owned by the state (OSE)
9	Ireland	Accounting separation	None	IE Integrated railway state owned	Owned by the state (IE)

10	Italy	Organisational separation	Freight and regional passenger services	FS state owned	State owned subsidiary (RFI)
11	The Netherlands	Institutional separation	Freight and regional passenger services	NS state owned	State owned organisation (PRORAIL)
12	Portugal	Institutional separation	Only one private passenger operator	CP state owned	State owned organisation (REFER)
13	Spain	Institutional separation	None	RENFE state owned	State owned organisation (ADIF)
14	Sweden	Institutional separation	Regional passenger and freight services	State owned passenger and freight companies	State owned organisation (Banverket)

Note: The term institutional separation is used to denote totally separate institutions; Organisational separation is used where infrastructure and operations are separate subsidiaries of the same holding company.

Source: Nash and Rivera-Trujillo (2004).

ECONOMETRIC STUDIES OF THE IMPACT OF RAIL RESTRUCTURING

Studies of the impact of rail restructuring fall into two broad groups: formal econometric studies and more qualitative case studies. The case studies tend to dominate the recent literature because of problems with obtaining comparable data and the short period of experience of most of the reforms.

A number of econometric studies of the period before the recent major reforms have established that railways with greater autonomy from government and lower subsidies were the most productive and had the lowest costs (Oum and Yu, 1994; Cantos, Pastor and Serrano, 1999; Gathon and Pestieau, 1995; Cantos and Maudos, 2000). However, a word of caution is in order since the direction of causation may be different from that usually assumed. While subsidies are often thought to encourage inefficiency, for example, it is also possible that already inefficient railways required high subsidies to survive. Similarly, high costs and low productivity might be the result of public service obligations to provide services such as peak commuter services which are costly but socially desirable.

On the issue of whether it was advisable to break up existing railway companies into smaller ones, Preston (1996) found that the optimal size for a vertically integrated railway was that of a medium-sized European company, such as the Norwegian or Belgian railway. If so, there might be advantages to splitting the larger European national companies into several separate companies. By contrast, the British approach of splitting passenger train operations between 25 train operating companies would lead to much smaller companies than appeared optimal. Preston's study was based on vertically integrated companies, however, so its implications for the optimal sizes of separate infrastructure and operating companies are unclear. But a later study by Cowie (2002) examined the British train operating companies, and concluded that they had unrealised economies of scale, so that a smaller number of larger companies would be preferable purely in terms of costs.

On the issue of vertical separation, Cantos, Pastor and Serrano (1999), using data envelopment analysis on data for a sample of 17 European railways from 1970 to 1995, found that the rate of technical change increased in the period 1985–1995 and attribute this partly to the rail reforms. The only countries to undertake vertical separation in the 1985–1995 period were Sweden in 1988 and Great Britain in 1994, however, so this evidence on the impacts of vertical separation is not very strong. Certainly, Sweden is singled out as having improved its already-good performance significantly post-1988, and, while there may be other causes including competitive tendering of passenger services and open access for freight, Sweden's success indicates that a package of measures including vertical separation may be a success. Sweden is discussed further later in this chapter.

Cantos (2001) studied the relationships between the marginal cost of passenger and freight services and the value of infrastructure capital. Rather curiously, he found that an increase in infrastructure capital reduced the marginal cost of freight services but increased the marginal costs of passenger services. This finding alone does not shed any light on whether these train and infrastructure services are best performed by the same or separate companies, although it certainly shows that if separation is the approach adopted then contractual relationships must be in place which give each party appropriate incentives in the light of these interrelationships.

Two recent studies have attempted to measure the effects on railway efficiency of the separation of infrastructure from operations and of open access. The first, by Friebel et al. (2003), uses a production function approach to examine the effects of three different reforms: (i) the separation of infrastructure from operations; (ii) independent regulation; and (iii) the introduction of competition. Friebel and his colleagues found that introducing any of the reforms individually or sequentially improved efficiency, while introducing them as a package was neutral in terms of efficiency. This result is somewhat puzzling, but may indicate the importance of at least undertaking some reform while suggesting that trying to do too much simultaneously is not beneficial.

However, the authors recognise a number of shortcomings. In the first place, the estimated production function is Cobb Douglas and the only inputs considered are staff and route kilometres; the outputs are passenger and freight tonne kilometres. Moreover, the study uses the date when legislative changes formally occurred to indicate reforms; thus for instance Spain and France are supposed to have introduced third party access in 1995 and 1997 respectively, although in practice entry remained blocked. Portugal is shown as having independent regulation, although the only competition is for a single franchise. Data for Britain is available only up to 1995, and the estimated immediate effect of the package was to worsen efficiency. Competition for the passenger market through franchising was much more significant than open access in Britain (which only occurred in the freight market) and came after 1995. Other studies (Pollitt and Smith, 2002) conclude that the British reforms did accelerate productivity growth until the dramatic changes triggered by the Hatfield accident in 2000. But when Britain is excluded, as it is from most of the analysis, institutional separation of infrastructure from operations (as opposed to organisational separation) is found to have a positive effect on efficiency.

The second study of the effects of infrastructure separation is by Rivera-Trujillo (2004). He uses a more sophisticated translog production function with staff, rolling stock and track as inputs and includes Britain throughout. A major limitation, however, is that he includes data on traffic staff only, and thus excludes infrastructure workers. Moreover, the distinction between traffic and infrastructure staff may not be consistent across the countries he studied and may have changed at the time of restructuring. (In fairness, these doubts probably apply to the measures of total staff used by Friebel as well, due to varying degrees of subcontracting.)

Rivera-Trujillo finds a significant positive effect on efficiency from the introduction of competition and a significant negative effect for separation of infrastructure from operations. The size of the two effects appears similar and the two variables are quite highly correlated. Excluding either one leaves the sign of the other unchanged but substantially changes the magnitude of the parameter. Taken at face value, this result suggests that separating infrastructure from operations makes train operations less efficient, unless it is necessary for the introduction of competition, and even then it is doubtful whether the overall effect is beneficial. However, in the period in question, open access competition was generally on a very small scale. Moreover, for passenger services franchising was probably the more effective way of introducing competition, and franchising was very limited in most countries over the period in question. Thus the ultimate benefits of allowing access to the infrastructure to new operators may be substantially understated, and the benefits of achieving this may be worth the costs of vertical separation unless those benefits can be achieved simply by requiring access to the network without vertical separation. Whether it is possible, through independent regulation, to ensure competitive access to infrastructure controlled by the incumbent operator seems doubtful.

In sum, the econometric evidence to date has been inconclusive on the important question of whether to separate infrastructure from operations. While some observers believe that the separation brings advantages in efficiency, transparency, neutrality and competition (Evans, 2003), others remain convinced that separation has been a fundamental mistake (Pfund, 2003).

CASE STUDIES OF ALTERNATIVE MODELS

Given the very different nature of the reforms introduced in different countries, a case study approach may provide insights that econometric studies miss. A group of researchers at IBM (2004) have compiled an index of rail liberalisation based on indicators of both the legal status of reform and actual implementation. In measuring implementation the authors put themselves in the position of a new entrant and examined the difficulties and costs of obtaining an operator's licence, safety certificate and paths on the infrastructure. The three countries found to have most liberalised their rail sectors were Britain, Sweden and Germany. It therefore seems appropriate to consider these countries in more detail, especially since – as discussed above – they represent very different models of liberalisation.

By way of introduction, Table 2.4 presents some overall indicators of the performance of the three railways pre and post reform, although relating only to the productivity of train operators' staff. These figures are certainly affected by the state of the economy, particularly in the case of Britain where the 1990s began with a recession and ended with a boom. Nevertheless, in every case there was much better performance after reform than before and the biggest improvement was achieved in Sweden.

Britain

The reforms in Great Britain are considered only briefly here, since they are discussed in detail by Glaister in Chapter 3. In Britain, infrastructure was separated from operations, competitive tendering was introduced for all passenger services and open access competition for freight. All parts of the industry were privatised. Infrastructure charges for passenger services were

Table 2.4   Analysis of reforms in three European countries (annual average rate of growth in %)

Country	Pre reform	Post reform
Train km/train operating staff		
Germany	3.98	5.73
Great Britain	−0.55	3.96
Sweden	0.45	10.15
Traffic units/train operating staff		
Germany	3.69	5.71
Great Britain	−3.48	6.18
Sweden	2.58	10.63

Notes:
For Germany the pre-reform period refers only to DB over 1977–93; the post-reform period to 1995–99. The period 1993–95 is distorted by the merger of DB and DR (the former East Germany operator).
For Britain, the periods are 1990–94 and 1994–99.
For Sweden, the periods are 1977–87; and 1988–99.

Source: Rivera-Trujillo (2004).

based on a two-part tariff with the variable part simply reflecting short run marginal social cost; initially freight charges were subject to negotiation, but subsequently were also simply based on short run marginal cost. These reforms were reasonably successful, until the cost explosion that followed the accident at Hatfield in October 2000, which eventually led to Railtrack's bankruptcy.

This author agrees with Glaister that Railtrack's failure was not a reflection of inherent problems with vertical restructuring (Nash, Matthews and Smith, forthcoming). Rather it was the consequence of a badly implemented and rushed reform, in which maintenance work was contracted out to separate infrastructure maintenance companies without competitive tendering and without adequate contractual safeguards, plus bad management on the part of Railtrack. These issues were being addressed by the Regulator and by Railtrack management when the Hatfield accident, and the unnecessary reaction to it of stringent speed restrictions across the network, precipitated Railtrack's downfall.

This is not to say that separation of infrastructure from operations was totally without problems. The difficulties in allocating paths, achieving an effective timetable and planning and implementing investment foreseen by opponents of such separation did indeed all emerge (Nash, 2002). Possibly an infrastructure charging regime that fully reflected scarcity of capacity and gave the infrastructure manager more incentive to expand capacity would have alleviated these problems, although the design of such a pricing system is certainly not without problems itself.

The poor performance of Railtrack may be partly the consequence of the badly set-up maintenance contracts which it inherited, but it does appear that the organisation was too concerned with short run share price movements relative to long term stewardship of its assets, while the initial regulatory regime – set up when Railtrack was still a public sector company and with no expectation of imminent privatisation – was not sufficiently firm to deal with the situation.

In practice, the solution to these problems pursued by the incoming government in 1997 was two-fold. First, it appointed a new regulator whom it knew would take a firmer line with Railtrack; he did indeed introduce new requirements, for instance to ensure greater investment. Second, it established a public sector planning body known as the Strategic Rail Authority (SRA). While the SRA took over the task of franchising, it also provided much clearer public sector direction as to the future strategy and finance of the industry as well as examining in detail issues such as the allocation of scarce capacity.

The SRA has come in for much criticism, particularly in respect of its over-optimistic strategic plan and its inconsistent policy on franchising.

However, given the dramatic change in the environment in which it was working, it is not clear how far it is to be blamed for these problems. Its initial policy was to seek a smaller number of longer franchises – of the order of 20 years – in return for participation in special purpose vehicles with banks and construction companies to undertake major enhancement of the rail network. This strategy fell apart after the Hatfield accident and the major increase in rail infrastructure costs. It was no longer affordable, and it was also doubtful whether the situation in which the infrastructure company was delivering a very poor standard of service and the whole future strategy of the industry was unclear was the right time to be letting long franchises. Instead, under instructions from the Secretary of State, a series of small extensions to existing franchises was negotiated. Moreover for a variety of reasons, including a desire to realign franchise boundaries and to avoid disputes over the liability for the failure of Railtrack to deliver contractually committed network improvements, some loss-making existing franchises were renegotiated with increased subsidies. All these reasons may well have led to a temporary reduction in competitive pressures on the train operating companies, but resumed competitive franchising was well underway, with many new franchises let, by the time that the government took the decision to disband the Strategic Rail Authority and take responsibility for franchising itself through the Department for Transport.

In summary then, the main problems of the British approach may have been problems of the detail of implementation, but there is clear evidence that both the separation of infrastructure from operations and the privatisation of the infrastructure manager are not without their problems. It may be that the tightening of regulation and the greater degree of planning provided by the Strategic Rail Authority would have resolved these problems had the Hatfield accident and the resulting bankruptcy of Railtrack not intervened. But the most important lesson of the British experience is to approach reform cautiously, ensuring that separation of infrastructure from operations is accompanied by adequate planning mechanisms to resolve the problems of developing efficient short run timetabling and operations strategies and long run investment and capacity plans, and that the infrastructure manager is only privatised if the government is sure that it has in place adequate regulatory arrangements.

Sweden

Sweden also has complete separation of infrastructure and operations, but with a publicly owned infrastructure company, Banverket. There remain publicly owned (but now completely separate) passenger and freight train operating companies, but all services requiring subsidy are subject to competitive tender and there is open access for freight. The result is an increasing number of private companies sharing the track with the publicly owned companies. Rail operators are simply charged short run marginal cost for use of the infrastructure, with the rest of the cost being borne by the taxpayer.

The introduction of competitive tendering in Sweden has not been without its problems. Alexandersson and Hultén (2003) conclude that competitive tendering has generally achieved cost savings of the order of 20 per cent but where higher savings or rapid revenue growth have been assumed by bidders, problems have typically followed. Sometimes the motives may be purely predatory. When the state owned operator won back a contract from the private operator BK Tag in 1993, it was found guilty of using its dominant position to put in a loss-making bid as a way of eliminating competition. This of course is always a fear when competition for contracts is between one major state owned operator and small private operators. More recently a new entrant which is part of a major international group, Connex, was accused of using the same tactics when it put in a bid implying a 41 per cent reduction in subsidies on a long distance service, as a way of breaking into the market.

In other cases it seems that the winning bidder simply was mistaken – the 'winner's curse'. An operator which won the contract for the West Coast Line on an assumption of greatly increased revenue went swiftly bankrupt, while the winner of the contract for the Stockholm suburban services assumed productivity increases which were not achieved, leading both to a shortage of drivers and consequent service unreliability and to losses for the operator.

Nevertheless, when Nilsson (2002) reviews the overall experience of Sweden he seems to regard it as a moderate success. We have already seen in Table 2.4 the impressive productivity gains of the train operating companies in Sweden. Nilsson reports that the infrastructure manager did not achieve similar economies in the use of labour, but did undertake a massive increase in investment. While passenger traffic grew freight traffic remained steady. He concludes that the combination of marginal-cost based infrastructure charges, open access for freight and competitive tendering for subsidised passenger services has probably worked well, and that the efficiency of Swedish railways is high. However, he believes that infrastructure charges are probably too low (since they do not include the cost of accelerated renewals or any element for congestion or scarcity), and he suspects that government spending on services and investment was too high. Even though infrastructure investment is subject to routine cost–benefit analysis, the fact that infrastructure investment decisions remain in the public sector leaves them open to manipulation for short-term political advantage. He believes open access should be extended to inter-regional passenger services, not in the expectation that on-track competition would be the permanent outcome, but rather to achieve a contestable market in which new entrants could totally supplant incumbents. He also argues that costs should be disaggregated to the level of individual routes, in order to promote greater transparency and make the assessment of value for money easier.

Germany

In Germany, infrastructure and the majority of operations are in the public sector. DBAG, a public limited company with share capital owned wholly by the Federal Government, was formed in 1994 by the merger of Deutsche Bundesbahn (the former Federal Republic of Germany operator) and Deutsche Reichsbahn (the operator of the German Democratic Republic). DBAG was essentially a holding company for five other companies: two responsible for the infrastructure and three train operators – one responsible for long-distance passenger services, another for regional passenger services and a third for freight services (the two passenger operating companies have since been merged).

In 1996, responsibility for regional passenger services was transferred entirely to the states. The states may use competitive tendering, but are also allowed to sign 6–15 year contracts with DB for the provision of services over their entire network provided that the contract provides for a 'sufficient' proportion of services to be subject to competitive tendering. Link (2004) argues that states are encouraged to sign such contracts by the argument that DB will not invest in rolling stock and other facilities unless they do and that the services the states subject to competitive tendering are usually the least attractive. By 2002 DB's competitors had won 8 per cent of train kilometres in regional services, having secured some 60 per cent of the contracts put out to competitive tender.

There is also open access for freight and commercial passenger services. Germany has always had a number of small private railways and these are increasingly operating over DBAG tracks, while there has been new entry in both freight and (in a very small number of cases) commercial passenger services. Nevertheless, DBAG remains very dominant, and there has been criticism that the organisational arrangements favour the incumbent (Link, 2004). Link argues that even though the access charges do not discriminate between operators for particular categories of traffic, they still deter entry, for instance by the presence of a surcharge on regional services, which is the sector of the market open to competitive tendering. Moreover, she criticises a lack of transparency as to how the charges are calculated, whether the regional surcharge is used to hold down prices in sectors where DB is the sole operator and whether DBAG can practice other forms of cross subsidisation. She also cites claims of discrimination in terms of access to facilities, including provision of information and access to depots.

Firms with complaints may (and do) appeal either to the Federal Railway Office (EBA) or the antitrust authorities, and it appears that the powers of the EBA are being strengthened in respect of issues relating to infrastructure charges and access. Whether these offer adequate protection, however, is something Link doubts; she advocates complete separation of infrastructure from operations and compulsory competitive tendering for all subsidised services. But despite these alleged problems with the competitive process, an improvement in the performance of DBAG following these reforms is also apparent from Table 2.4.

The history of rail infrastructure charges in Germany is complicated. Originally Germany had a system of charges per train kilometre differentiated by type of train and location and designed to recover total cost, except for those capital costs borne by government. In other words it was essentially an average cost pricing system. Modifications led to the introduction of a two-part tariff, in order to meet complaints from regions about the high marginal costs of high-frequency services. However, following complaints that the two-part tariff favoured large operators, and especially DBAG itself, it has reverted to a single-part tariff with a differentiated charge per kilometre.

Thus it may be seen that there are large differences in infrastructure charging systems between countries (Crozet, 2004). Partly these are philosophical; Sweden, for instance, subscribes to marginal cost pricing principles, while Germany appears to believe that average cost pricing is the basis of efficient allocation. Britain lies between the two, in that – at least at privatisation – it was believed important for efficiency that Railtrack covered its total costs from charges, while offering a variable charge related to marginal cost. But there are other reasons for the differences; for instance, the emphasis on open access in Germany makes non-discrimination a key issue, while the constraints on open access in Britain mean that two-part tariffs are more acceptable.

Overall then it seems that there have been benefits from the introduction of competition into rail markets, through competitive tendering for passenger and through open access for freight, whatever the overall structure of the industry, but that separation of infrastructure from operations has been more problematic. On the one hand there is some evidence that it has raised costs, and in Great Britain the private infrastructure manager became bankrupt, while under its successor costs have risen enormously (Chapter 4). On the other hand there are obvious problems in increasing competition in a situation in which the major operator still controls the infrastructure, as in Germany. However effective the 'Chinese walls' between the infrastructure and operating arms of the incumbent, small operators are bound to fear that the incumbent will use its position to disadvantage them. Perhaps, on the evidence here, the Swedish model with a publicly owned infrastructure company completely separate from all operators and charging short run marginal social cost is the one that has worked best to date.

CONCLUSIONS

The main elements of rail reform in Europe have been separation of infrastructure from operations, open access for freight services, competitive franchising for passenger services and independent regulation. We will seek to draw conclusions on each of these elements in turn.

Separation of Infrastructure from Operations

Separation of infrastructure from operations has been argued to be an essential prerequisite for non-discriminatory access. Yet it raises important issues that must be addressed if it is to work well. Adequate methods need to be in place to ensure that the infrastructure manager provides an appropriate quality of service, controls its costs, allocates paths efficiently over the network and invests in new capacity where justified. Certainly these issues were not sufficiently thought through before Railtrack was privatised in Britain, although arguably a regulated private infrastructure manager can be established in a way such that these issues are resolved. In the meanwhile, the most successful example of a vertically separated railway seems to be that of Sweden, where the infrastructure remains in public hands, with pricing based on short-run marginal social cost and investment based on social cost–benefit analysis. Nevertheless, we have seen criticisms of both pricing and investment decisions in Sweden, so no solution appears perfect. There is also some evidence that vertical separation raises costs. Nevertheless the strong performance of Sweden since separation indicates that vertical separation can be made to work.

Open Access

Open access so far has had limited effects in Europe; where it has occurred, its effects may still be controversial. For instance, even in Germany – which was identified above as one of the most liberalised rail markets in Europe and has had complete open access for passenger and freight services and competitive tendering of some regional passenger services since 1994 – DBAG still operates the vast majority of services.

In freight, there is complete open access in a number of countries, and a number of small new operators have entered the markets. It appears that these have put pressure on rates, and therefore costs, and quality of service provided by the incumbent operators. In Britain, Sweden and Germany there is evidence of the positive impact of competition in the freight market. For passenger services, it is less clear that open access entry is desirable, since it may worsen the overall pattern of fares and services and increase the need for subsidy (Preston, Whelan and Wardman, 1999). Some argue, however, that even if passenger services are a natural monopoly making them more contestable might be desirable.

Franchising

Given that there is generally a need for subsidy and an argument for government involvement in the level of passenger services and fares, franchising rather than open access appears the obvious way of introducing competition into this sector. However, experience of franchising so far has thrown up some difficulties, with general reductions in cost and improvement in services, but also problems in some aspects of performance (particularly reliability), suggestions of predatory pricing and opportunistic attempts at renegotiations. There appears to be a choice between short franchises, in which public authorities control service planning, fares and in investment, and long franchises in which much more responsibility for these is given to the franchisee (Preston et al., 2000). But on balance, however it is introduced there appears again to be a link between the introduction of competitive tendering and improved performance.

Independent Regulation

EU legislation now requires each country to have a regulator independent of the infrastructure manager (though not necessarily of the government). The key role of the regulator within the new regime in Europe is in regulating and hearing appeals concerning access conditions and charges in order to ensure fair and non-discriminatory access to the infrastructure to all operators. Determination of appropriate infrastructure charges is, however, far from easy. In particular, pure marginal cost pricing requires substantial subsidies which governments may be unwilling or unable to provide and gives inadequate incentive to invest. If high cost recovery is needed, two-part tariffs offer the least distorting option but risk placing barriers on entry. Requiring entrants to compensate incumbents for loss of contribution to fixed costs (as suggested by Baumol, 1983) imposes severe information problems on the regulator.

As is stated above, the current legislation requires regulators to be independent of the infrastructure manager, but not necessarily of government. Indeed, only in Britain is there a specific rail regulator who is not part of a government department, although there is often a right of appeal to a separate competition authority. Where the rail regulator is part of a government department, and often the same one as is responsible for the state owned infrastructure manager and the state owned dominant operator, one may doubt whether this really provides the necessary degree of independence.

In short then, we may conclude that the main elements of rail reform in Europe are heading in the right direction. A combination of competitive tendering, open access and at least a degree of separation of infrastructure from operations does appear to be achieving a significant improvement in performance in European railways, but as always the devil is in the detail and there remain many unanswered questions about the detail of implementation which require further research.

REFERENCES

Alexandersson, G. and Hultén, S., (2003), 'European Regulation and the Problem of Predatory Bidding in Competitive Tenders – A Swedish Case Study, Competition and Ownership in Land Passenger Transport', The 8th International Conference: Rio de Janeiro.

Baumol, W.J., (1983), 'Some Subtle Issues in Railroad Regulation', *International Journal of Transport Economics*, **10**, 241–355.

Cantos, P., (2001), 'Vertical Relationships for the European Railway Industry', *Transport Policy*, **8**, 2.

Cantos, P. and Maudos, J., (2000), 'Efficiency. Technical Change and Productivity in the European Rail Sector: A Stochastic Frontier Approach', *International Journal of Transport Economics*, **27**.

Cantos, P., Pastor, J. and Serrano, L., (1999), 'Productivity, Efficiency and Technical Change in the European Railways: A Non-parametric Approach', *Transportation*, **26**, 337–57.

Commission of the European Communities (1998), 'Fair Payment for Infrastructure Use: A Phased Approach to a Common Transport Infrastructure Charging Framework in the EU', Commission of the European Communities, Brussels.

Commission of the European Communities (2001), White Paper, 'European Transport Policy for 2010, Time to Decide', White Paper, Commission of the European Communities, Brussels.

Cowie, J., (2002), 'The Production Economics of a Vertically Separated Railway – the Case of the British Train Operating Companies', *Transporti Europei*, August.

Crozet, Y., (2004), 'European Railway Infrastructure: Towards a Convergence of Infrastructure Charging', *International Journal of Transport Management*, **2**(1), 5–15.

Evans, J., (2003), 'The Case for Separation of Infrastructure', *European Transport Forum ETF*, June 2003.

Friebel, G., Ivaldi, M. and Vibes, C., (2003), 'Railway (De) regulation: A European Efficiency Comparison', IDEI report no. 3 on Passenger Rail Transport, University of Toulouse.

Gathon, H.J. and Pestieau, P., (1995), 'Decomposing Efficiency into its Managerial and its Regulatory Components: The Case of European Railways', *European Journal of Operational Research*, **80**, 500–507.

IBM and Humboldt University of Berlin (2004), Rail Liberalisation Index 2004, 'Comparison of the Status of Market Opening in the Rail Markets of the 15 Member States of the European Union, Switzerland and Norway', IBM Business Consulting Services and Dr Christian Kirchner, Humboldt University of Berlin.

Link, H., (2004), 'Rail Infrastructure Charging and On-track Competition in Germany – Nine Years Later', *International Journal of Transport Management*, **2**(1), 17–27.

Nash, C.A., (2002), 'Regulatory Reform in Rail Transport – the UK experience. *Swedish Economic Policy Review*', **9**(2).

Nash, C.A., Bickel, P., Friedrich, R., Link, H., and Stewart, L., (2002), 'The Environmental Impact of Transport Subsidies'. Paper prepared for the OECD workshop on environmentally harmful subsidies, Paris, November.

Nash, C.A., Matthews, B. and Smith, A., (forthcoming), 'The European Rail Market: A Survey of Practice', *Experiences of Reform in Britain*, CER, Brussels.

Nash, C.A. and Rivera-Trujillo, C., (2004), 'Rail Regulatory Reform in Europe – Principles and Practice'. Paper presented at the STELLA Focus Group 5 synthesis meeting, Athens, June 2004.

Nilsson, J.E., (2002), 'Restructuring Sweden's railways: The Unintentional Deregulation', *Swedish Economic Policy Review*, **9** (2).

Oum, T.H. and Yu, C., (1994), 'Economic Efficiency of Railways and Implications for Public Policy: A Comparative Study of the OECD Countries' Railways', *Journal of Transport Economics and Policy*, 28–2, 121–38.

Pfund, C., (2003), 'The Separation of Infrastructure and Operations Constitutes a Fundamental Mistake', *Public Transport International* 3/2003.

Pollitt, M.G. and Smith, A.S.J., (2002), 'The Restructuring and Privatisation of British Rail: Was it Really that Bad? *Fiscal Studies*', **23**(4).

Preston, J., (1996), 'The Economics of British Rail Privatisation: An Assessment', *Transport Reviews*, **16**(1).

Preston, J., Whelan, G., Nash, C.A. and Wardman, M., (2000), 'The Franchising of Passenger Rail Services in Britain', *International Review of Applied Economics*, **14**(1).

Preston, J., Whelan, G. and Wardman, M., (1999), 'An Analysis of the Potential for On-track Competition in the British Passenger Rail Industry', *Journal of Transport Economics and Policy*, **33**(1).

Rivera-Trujillo, C., (2004), 'Measuring the Productivity and Efficiency of Railways (An International Comparison)', University of Leeds, Unpublished PhD thesis.

3.   Britain: Competition undermined by politics

Stephen Glaister

INTRODUCTION

Competition was at the heart of the British railways reforms of 1993, and it was competition in an extraordinary number of dimensions: for passengers, for contracts to run trains, for freight customers, for labour, for rolling stock and for engineering services (Foster and Castles, 2004). Although dauntingly complex, imperfectly articulated and implemented in an imprudent hurry, it worked reasonably well for a period of some years: it seemed to be meeting the objectives of the policy.

Unfortunately, compromises were made at the very start that undermined the conditions necessary for effective competition in some parts of the industry. Then, over time, the political sensitivity of the national railways tempted central government into intervening in ways that cumulatively proved fatal to the competitive processes. By 2004 the failures in the administration of the railways had led the whole system to become discredited in the eyes of the general public.

This chapter points out some of the ways in which successive British governments weakened competition. There were important shortcomings under both the Conservative Government that implemented the policy in 1993 and the Labour Governments from 1997 that sought to change it in several ways. This chapter does not seek to argue that competition is a good or a bad mechanism: history shows that delivering railway services can be achieved through an extraordinary range of alternative institutional mechanisms – including, throughout most of its history, competition. Rather, it argues that the recent British experience illustrates that competitive mechanisms can work successfully in national railway systems if, and only if, they are correctly set up and then left unmolested by the political process – a requirement that it is hard to meet in practice.

THE PRIVATISATION OF BRITISH RAIL

When Mrs Thatcher's Conservative Party came into office in 1979 a main concern was to remove barriers to competition: to foster the free market in the belief that it would encourage efficiency. Britain's railways had been in state ownership since 1948, under the day-to-day management of the British Railways Board. By 1988 the Thatcher government, having privatised the bus and coach, telecommunications, gas, water and electricity industries, had considered the railways in sufficient detail to identify five privatisation options:

1. Privatisation as one railway and one company – the option favoured by the Board.
2. Privatisation as a single holding company with a range of subsidiaries – a decentralised version of the previous option.
3. Establishment of a track authority or company to own infrastructure with separate private companies operating the train services.
4. Division into parts based on geography – similar to the six private companies that existed between 1923 and 1947.
5. Division into business sectors on the basis of the then existing management structure: InterCity, freight, parcels, Network SouthEast, Regional Railways.

A sixth was the status quo, favoured by a majority of the public and a large minority of MPs.

The government could not agree but the debate was reopened when the Conservative Party, then led by Mrs Thatcher's successor, John Major, was drawing up its manifesto for the 1992 general election. The government's view, in the words of the Secretary of State for Transport, was that: 'As an organisation, BR combines the classic shortcomings of the traditional nationalised industry. It is an entrenched monopoly. That means too little responsiveness to customers' needs, whether passenger or freight; no real competition; and too little diversity and innovation' (HC Debs, 2 February 1993: 124). Option 3 was eventually selected in spite of the preference of many including, allegedly, the Prime Minister, for option 4.

The original intention was to privatise the train operating companies right away but to leave the infrastructure company, called Railtrack, in public hands at least for 'the medium term' and certainly through the next general election. As a transition, in 1994 Railtrack was established as an internal division of British Rail and in 1995 it became a separate government-owned company.

A decision to accelerate Railtrack's privatisation was made for two reasons: first, due to advice from the financial markets following unexpectedly difficult sales of the freight train operating companies and, second, because of a belated wish to get everything done in advance of the 1997 general election. In turn, that may have been partly in order to give the Exchequer access to the sales proceeds at the earliest opportunity and partly because it was becoming clear that there would likely be a change of government and Labour would certainly not have completed privatisation unless they received it as a done deal. The confusion and poor decision taking caused by the resulting scramble is related in Foster (2005). He demonstrates that the rush, coupled with an inability of the politicians to come to clear decisions about what they wanted and imperfect administrative processes led to an outcome that was much less satisfactory than it could have been. The prospectus for the sale of shares was issued in 1996 (SBC Warburg, 1996) and the privatisation was duly completed before the general election in which, as widely expected, the Conservatives were defeated by Labour.

COMPETITION IN RAIL SERVICES

The problem the government of the early 1990s faced was a familiar one for national railways – how to reduce the demands on the national taxpayer without unacceptable reductions in the scale of railway services. One main way this might be achieved was through generating new user revenues by commercially driven innovation and marketing. The other was by reducing costs, principally through introducing the discipline of commercially driven competition in the labour markets. This last had been seen as one of the major sources of success in the five utilities previously privatised. These included the bus industry, which had been heavily unionised, and in many cases by the same unions as the railways.

The original concept included the following dimensions of competition:

- Competition for passengers by privately owned train operators, each gaining access to a regulated infrastructure company.
- Twenty-five contracts for specific passenger service groups, referred to as 'franchises', to be let by competitive tender and to be competed for again after they expired in seven (in some cases 15) years.
- To facilitate easy entry of passenger train operators, three competing rolling stock leasing companies created to own the existing rolling stock and to acquire and lease out new stock on a commercial basis.
- The rail freight businesses to be sold as a number of competing private businesses.

- The infrastructure owner and operator, Railtrack, to be kept as a privately owned but regulated monopoly. It was to be responsible for central timetabling and coordination of all train movements, signalling, and planning investment in infrastructure and for safe operation of the network under the supervision of the Health and Safety Executive.

Railtrack's sole source of income was to come from access charges paid by the train operators (the Secretary of State retained the power to give direct capital grants for freight facilities if justified on public interest grounds). The company was created with relatively few direct employees (about 12,000) and it was to procure most of the services it needed on the open market including engineering services for maintenance, renewal and enhancement. The existing rail engineering capabilities were broken into 13 companies and sold to the private sector.

It was taken for granted that each of the myriad commercial relationships created between customers and providers needed to be codified in explicit commercial contracts. That these were successfully created in a relatively short time is a tribute to the efficiency, capacity and the inventiveness of the legal services available in Britain – and to the ready availability of the funds necessary to remunerate them. The complex detail is set out in Foster (1994), Lawrence (2001), National Audit Office (2000 and 2004), Office of the Rail Regulator (2000), Helm (2000) and Bartle (2004).

The railway legislation is very similar to that for the telecommunications, gas, electricity and water industries, which created the system we have come to know as the British model of utility regulation. In each case an independent regulator (appointed by the Secretary of State but answerable only to the courts and not to ministers) has public interest duties including a duty to review access charges from time to time. Regulators can carry out a periodic review at any time but a normal pattern has become established on a five-year cycle. At periodic review the regulator will take into account current circumstances – including current asset condition, cost of capital and costs of other inputs and will determine appropriate charges for the next control period.

The Rail Regulator has statutory functions in four main areas: (i) the granting, monitoring and enforcement of licences to operate railway assets; (ii) the approval of access agreements between facility owners and users of railway facilities; (iii) the enforcement of domestic competition law; and (iv) approval of railway line closures. The Regulator's duties are to protect the interests of both providers and users of rail services, to promote competition together with efficiency and economy, to promote the development and use of the network, to safeguard through-ticketing for the benefit of the public, and, crucially for what happened later, to ensure that Railtrack does not find it unduly difficult to finance its activities providing that it behaves in an economic and efficient manner. In fulfilling those duties, the Regulator must also take into account the financial position of the Franchising Director (after 2001, replaced by the Strategic Rail Authority), whose budget was decided by government. The Regulator ensures that arrangements for allocating train paths and settling timetable disputes are fair and reasonable.

Although the Regulator has considerable powers there are many things that he does not control. Some contracts were not regulated, such as the terms of leases for rolling stock and for stations, and the contracts between Railtrack and providers of engineering services (the greater part of Railtrack's expenditure). Most important, and most surprising to the general public, the Regulator has no power to regulate passenger fares. This belonged to the Office of Passenger Rail Franchising (the Franchising Director, OPRAF) through the contracts offered for passenger franchises, on the grounds that fares regulation has direct implications for subsidy and therefore for government expenditure. Hence it could not be left in the hands of a person like the Regulator because he is not accountable to Parliament.

OPRAF, accountable to ministers, was necessary because, unlike the other privatised utilities, the railway could not be expected to become self-financing: public subsidy was inevitable and it was the Franchising Director's job to administer it. Financial support to the railway passed through his office. His function was to define rail passenger franchises and sell them to train operating companies using a competitive tendering procedure. Arrangements for through-ticketing and concessionary fares are enforced through these agreements.

Some people felt from the outset that the roles of the two regulatory offices – the Office of the Rail Regulator and the Office of Passenger Rail Franchising – were confused and poorly understood (Foster, 2005). A recurring proposal over the years has been that they should be combined into the one office.

EXPLICIT POLICY AND POLITICAL RISK

The railways policy ultimately failed because the privatisation legislation was pushed through in 1993 by a Conservative Government (despite considerable opposition within the Party) but the Labour Government elected in 1997 had to administer it. The railway was traditionally an important power base for the Labour Party and Labour had always favoured 'integration', state ownership and centralised control of the railways. It is hard to think of an industry that the traditional Labour Party would have been less willing to see privatised, and less likely to leave alone once privatised, apart from coal mining.

The signal that there were severe political risks was transmitted in particularly simple and explicit terms in the *Prospectus* for the Railtrack Share Offer (SBC Warburg, 1996) which contains a formal statement by the Labour Party, then in opposition. The *Prospectus* reproduced the text of a speech dated 29 March 1996 by Clare Short MP, the Shadow Transport Secretary, which included:

> The Labour Party is totally opposed to the privatisation of the railways including Railtrack and will campaign vigorously to prevent it happening. Should the flotation of Railtrack PLC proceed a Labour Government will make good its commitment to a publicly owned and publicly accountable railway by taking the following steps:
> (1) through regulation, it will seek an integrated railway system. It will amend the Railways Act 1993 to enhance the accountability of the Rail Regulator to the Secretary of State;
> (2) reconstitute British Rail as a fully publicly owned, publicly accountable company holding the public's interest in the rail network; and
> (3) dependent on the availability of resources, and as priorities allow, seek, by appropriate means, to extend public ownership and control over Railtrack . . .
> Labour is confident that its programme for rail can be carried through using the power to regulate, the power of the public subsidy and the power to acquire ownership. We do not believe that the public will or should be willing to continue to provide an annual input of public funds of as much as £2 billion without proper public accountability and a fair return on public investment.

COMPETITION IN LABOUR MARKETS

Competition in the labour market had been an explicit part of the 1984 policy on privatising and deregulating urban bus services. Earnings for drivers in the regulated bus industry were higher than drivers in comparable, competitive industries. The White Paper (Department of Transport, 1984) insisted that to achieve the labour market competition it was necessary to break up, privatise and deregulate the government owned monopoly bus companies in each metropolitan area. This was done immediately outside London and more gradually in the London metropolitan area by the progressive introduction of competitive tendering for routes.

The impact of privatising and deregulating the bus industry is shown in Figure 3.1, which graphs the full-time average hourly manual earnings for male bus drivers and for all male manual workers. Before the reforms went

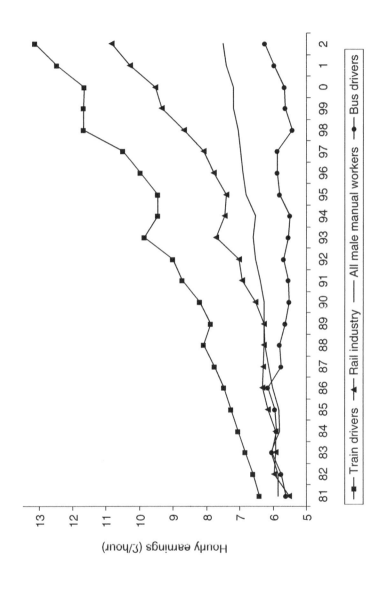

Figure 3.1   Hourly earnings of full-time male railway workers, train drivers, bus drivers and all full-time males (1997 prices)

into effect in 1985 the average hourly earnings of bus drivers were slightly higher than those for manual workers as a whole. Afterwards there was an immediate fall and the gap has widened since (although bus pay rates have accelerated in recent years as general labour market conditions have tightened). This undoubtedly contributed to the reduction in real unit bus costs of over 40 per cent that was achieved after bus deregulation.

This pattern was not repeated in the case of the railways, as also shown in Figure 3.1. In the 1980s the average hourly earnings in the rail industry were close to the average for all manual workers and those for train drivers and assistants were about 10 per cent higher. After the structural change of 1993, rail industry earnings rates moved ahead of general earnings and by 2002 they were nearly 50 per cent higher. Real earnings of train drivers increased even more, so that by 2002 they stood 80 per cent above general manual earnings..

The greater ability of the rail unions to protect their members may be due to the lower flexibility and the higher political salience of rail service. Bus routes come and go. If a bus company runs into financial difficulty with a route it will quickly withdraw and the route may or may not be taken over by a competing company. In short, the forces of competition are effective at punishing attempts to extract returns to labour or capital over and above the going competitive rate. Jobs are genuinely at risk. Railways are different. Experience over decades has demonstrated repeatedly that when a rail service gets into financial difficulty then the chances are good that some political authority will intervene to rescue it, whatever the cost.

PASSENGER TRAIN OPERATING COMPANIES

Competition Among Operating Companies

Soon after the passage of the Railways Act in 1993 the government began to retreat from the idea of competition among train operating companies. One reason was the realisation that the degree of on-rail competition originally envisaged might not be technically feasible. Foster (2005) comments that

> Extensive competition was introduced to the railway through franchising and outsourcing, but on-rail competition between different train companies competing on the same route was practically impossible, except in a few areas. However, differences of opinion within cabinet, and ideological prejudice, made it impossible to be open about this . . . the only competition in this area was between participants in the policy process vying to delay admitting there could be no such competition.

An equally important consideration was the Treasury's realisation that under the old regime some of the rail routes had been highly profitable and their profits had been used to cross subsidise the loss making parts of the railway. Open competition would annihilate those monopoly profits. Since the government was committed to not allowing privatisation to lead to any service reductions or withdrawals the implication was that direct subsidies from the Exchequer would have to increase substantially. Indeed, John Smith[1] has argued that there was a clear conflict between competitive franchising and encouraging the development of on-rail competition. The former requires an element of monopoly – particularly where bids are based on subsidy minimisation.

The upshot was that the government announced a policy of 'moderating' train-on-train competition (Department of Transport, 1993). The Rail Regulator responded with a horribly complicated set of rules (Office of the Rail Regulator, 1994) designed to allow train operating companies (TOCs) to protect what they declared as the core of their businesses while exposing them to competition on non-core activities. In effect one TOC could compete on fares and service quality with another primarily in situations where there are distinct lines of route between an origin and a destination. In some cases this competition has been active and effective. Additionally, TOCs could trespass onto the margins of each other's territories. But competition among the TOCs fell far short of the scale that the original policy had envisioned.

Competition for Franchises

If there was to be little competition among the TOCs, at least there would be competition for the award of the 25 TOC franchises. The TOC contracts had two components: a minimum guaranteed level of services to be provided by the operator, and a degree of flexibility above this level which allowed the operator room to develop and improve services. Franchise agreements allowed for adjustments of the service minimum over time, subject to consultation and a veto held by the Franchising Director. The Franchising Director hoped operators would find it in their commercial interests to offer a better service than the minimum specified. But the competition was primarily over who would sign a normal commercial contract to meet the specifications for the smallest payments by government.

Competition for the contracts was strong and seemed to become more aggressive over time as bidders gained confidence. The first contract was completed in February 1996 (South West Trains, just before Railtrack's floatation) and the last in April 1997 (Scotrail, just before the change of government). Most of the contracts had a seven-year term, but five had a 15-year term.

Some commentators at the time wondered how the companies could meet their commitments but, in keeping with the overall philosophy of transferring commercial risk, OPRAF accepted the bids at face value without second-guessing the commercial wisdom of the bidders. In many cases the bidders – especially the bus companies that won 15 of the franchises – were confident they could run the services with fewer staff. In others it was anticipated that large increases in passenger revenues could be generated by increasing both running speeds and service frequencies. Some were planning both to cut staff and to increase services.

Figure 3.2 shows the total subsidies contracted for and the total subsidies actually paid between fiscal years 1997–98 and 2003–04. Had the contracts been honoured the subsidy would have fallen from £1.8 billion per year to £0.7 billion per year, which would have been a major triumph for the policy. Things did go reasonably well for the first few years. Total subsidies fell only slightly less rapidly than anticipated. Moreover, as Figure 3.3 shows, train kilometres grew from 1993 at a sustained rate which is without precedent in the last 100 years – again, a major triumph.

But behind these figures there were the beginnings of problems. Quite early on some of the TOCs discovered that they had been over-ambitious in reducing employee numbers and that they could not run the service with the numbers they had planned. Service deteriorated significantly on

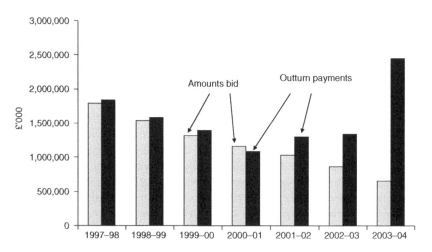

Source: OPRAF and SRA Annual Reports, various years.

Figure 3.2   *Train operating company total agreed bids and outturn*
                payments (current prices)

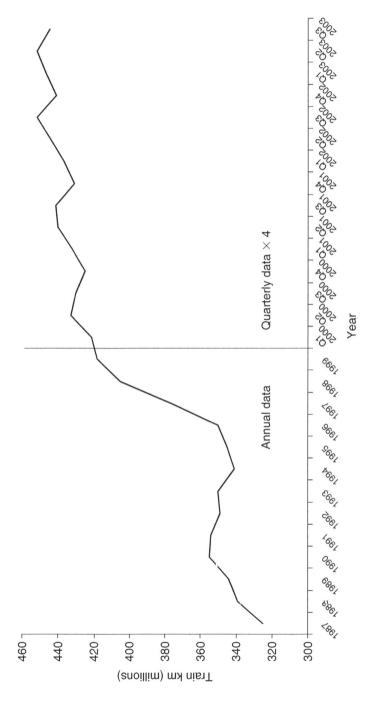

Figure 3.3   Railways in Britain: train kilometres (millions) 1987–2004

some commuter routes into London: the public quickly blamed 'Tory privatisation'.

Then trains began to impede one another. When privatisation was designed the conventional wisdom was that there was spare capacity on the tracks and the big problem was to reduce subsidy while preventing further decline. The charging regime for access to the infrastructure was deliberately designed to enable new services to be offered at low incremental cost. As Figure 3.3 shows, the TOCs made the intended response to the price incentive: they began to put on many more trains, to the point where congestion began to interfere with train reliability. While congestion was serious only in relatively few places, they included many of the approaches to the London termini and commuter routes for some other major cities. These accounted for a substantial proportion of passenger trips and they are the politically salient ones. The public found the declining reliability – once again, inevitably 'the fault of Tory privatisation' – to more than offset the benefits of more frequent and more varied services. This was notwithstanding the fact that patronage continued to grow rapidly as shown in Figure 3.4. The added trains led to a modest decline in punctuality after 1997, as illustrated in Figure 3.5, although that decline would pale into insignificance when compared with what was to follow.

Some of the TOCs began to allege that they had run into difficulty in their negotiations with Railtrack to provide the new, high quality infrastructure they needed if they were to achieve the revenue growth they had implicitly committed to in their contracts. The original expectation was that Railtrack would undertake enhancements on a commercial basis in return for increased track access income from train operators. It increasingly became apparent that few, if any, major upgrades were commercially viable but required subsidy if they were to proceed. Railtrack was accused of being unresponsive and unwilling to take reasonable commercial investment risks. Ironically, while this may have had some validity, Railtrack did enter into a monumentally risky agreement with Virgin to upgrade the West Coast Main Line infrastructure beyond what had been envisaged in the original reconstruction project, in order to provide for running at 140 mph rather than 125 mph and for the extra capacity Virgin had assumed it could achieve when it made its bid for its franchise. This contract ultimately helped to precipitate Railtrack's commercial failure.

Finally, there was the change of government in May 1997 that brought to power the party that had made its distaste for rail privatisation very clear. In the first instance it decided to change nothing, perhaps because the national budgets were unusually tight, the financial position of the railway was improving rapidly and the government had other problems to

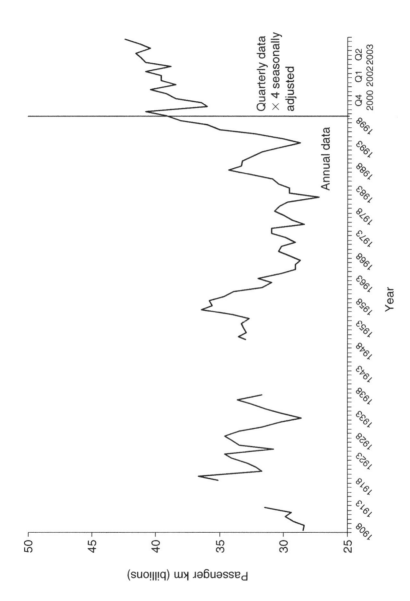

Figure 3.4   Passenger kilometres (billions) Britain, 1908–2004

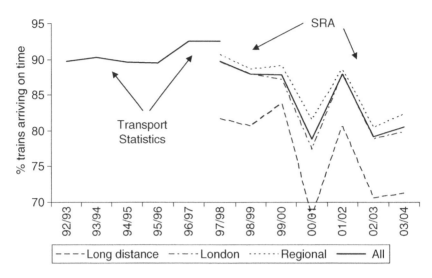

Sources: *Transport Statistics* and SRA, *National Rail Trends*, various years.

Figure 3.5   Passenger train punctuality, 1992/93 to 2003/04

attend to. However, there was a propensity on the part of the members of
the new Labour Government to draw attention to failings and to promise
'action', rather than to take the line that the industry was now the responsibility of the private sector providers and the independent, public interest
regulator, and that government should leave the industry to sort itself out
like any other.

Renegotiating the Franchises

The perceived failings eventually led the government to take action by
replacing OPRAF with a new Strategic Rail Authority (SRA). The idea,
as explained in the Transport White Paper of 1998, was that the SRA
would 'provide a clear, coherent and strategic programme for the development of our railways . . . [and] will provide a focus for strategic planning of the passenger and freight railways with appropriate powers to
influence the behaviour of key industry players' (paragraphs 4.12 and
4.14).

Although strategic planning was generally accepted as a shortcoming of
the privatised rail system, creating the SRA was not a high priority for the
government and it took all of two and a half years for legislation firmly
promised in the White Paper to reach the statute book. While the Transport

Table 3.1   Numbers employed by the train operating companies

£000s	1996	1997	1998	1999	2000	2001
Number employed	46,845	44,577	37,108	36,392	37,095	38,234

Source: Shaoul (2004).

Bill became ensnared in Parliamentary bureaucracy and feeling under pressure to be taking some action on railways policy, the government frequently complained about the performance of the railway. On more than one occasion Deputy Prime Minister John Prescott, the Secretary of State for Transport, held railway 'summits' to which he summonsed the leaders of the industry and insisted that something must be done. He spoke frequently of his intention to 'renegotiate the contracts' under which the TOCs were operating in order to achieve greater public accountability.

Once the SRA was instructed to commence renegotiation of the contracts, however, the progress of negotiating changes proved slow. No contracts changed during the first Labour government. Meanwhile, in late 2001 it began to transpire that several TOCs were in serious financial difficulty and had been rescued from the prospect of company failure by subvention from government. This shows up in Figure 3.2 where, for the first time contract payments for fiscal year 2001–02 were significantly above what had been specified in the agreed contracts.

One explanation for the decline in the financial position of the TOCs was that, as noted earlier, labour costs had not been cut as much as hoped. Table 3.1 shows that the numbers employed by the TOCs had fallen markedly between 1996 and 1999. They then increased but probably less rapidly than the volume of train service provided, so it is likely that improvements in productivity only offset the increasing pay rates to some degree. If the TOCs had been also counting on the competitive reduction in pay rates that they had enjoyed with bus deregulation, they were disappointed. By July 2003 nine of the franchises had failed financially and had been allowed to continue on some kind of cost-plus basis (Transport Select Committee, 2004, paragraph 123). A crucial policy decision had been taken that the normal mechanism for enforcing commercial risk transfer – namely bankruptcy – was not going to be enforced.

It is possible that some of the bidders for the franchises were overly aggressive because they assumed that renegotiation would be possible. The legislation made provision for special arrangements in order to keep services going in the event of bankruptcy of a train operator. But the bidders may have correctly anticipated that government would not, in practice, be able to stomach bankruptcy of a public passenger rail service should things go badly. It is also possible that some of the TOCs were victims of the 'winner's curse'. This can occur in auctions where there is uncertainty about the future value of the item being bid for. The bidder who has the most optimistic estimate of the value will be the one that wins the auction and may therefore pay too much, unless bidders are sophisticated enough to anticipate the problem and shade their bids accordingly.

Over the years the SRA struggled with the issue of how long franchise contracts with the TOCs should be. The experience of London's buses had illustrated that relatively short contracts (three to five years) favoured the commercial discipline that goes with active competition for contracts. But at one stage the SRA seemed convinced that the need to secure long-term investment made it advantageous to agree to long tenures for the rail contracts. As Chairman, the late Sir Alistair Morton perceived a need for large-scale investment in expanding the capacity of the network to meet government growth targets. He believed that Railtrack had neither a big enough balance sheet nor the programme management skills to undertake the necessary investment – hence the need to encourage investment by the TOCs. This was to be facilitated by long-term franchises: 20 or 30 years were favoured at one time. The SRA encouraged the TOCs to come up with their own ideas for network enhancement that led to a range of propositions. It was ironic that the administration that was so frustrated by their inability to alter the seven-year contracts it inherited was simultaneously determined to commit to contracts as long as 20 years. Few new franchises were actually let.

The government eventually overruled the SRA and insisted that, at least for a while, only short-term extensions were negotiated – and, note, not competed for. Extending contracts, rather than recompeting them, obviously upsets the incentives hoped for from competition for the market.

THE ROLLING STOCK COMPANIES

In order to keep barriers to entry to the train operating business low, the government created three companies (ROSCOs) to own, lease out and to invest in new passenger rolling stock. They were, and remain, unregulated. It is unclear to what extent these companies competed among themselves: there are important technical restrictions on the transfer of rolling stock between different lines. It was always open to TOCs to procure rolling stock in other ways, which put its own competitive pressure on the ROSCOs – although few have done so.

At various times, complaints have been made that the ROSCOs were earning excessive returns (see, for example, Shaoul, 2004) and that the companies were resold for much more than they had initially sold for at privatisation. The Rail Regulator investigated the ROSCOs under his competition powers and the National Audit Office investigated the original sale. In neither case was any major problem discovered, though the companies agreed on a code of practice with the Regulator. Nevertheless, the government in its 2004 White Paper, *The Future of Rail* (paragraph 4.3.30) expressed its intention to intervene to 'see how the operation of those markets can be improved'.

RAIL FREIGHT

Freight services on the privatised railway were always intended to be provided by competing companies, with open access to the track network. There was no attempt to create any analogous arrangement to the subsidised passenger rail franchises. The first intention had been to offer the existing freight business for sale as a number of companies. However, having tested the market only two companies were created. There has since been significant competitive entry by other carriers.

Access charges for freight were set to cover rather modest estimates of variable cost alone, in order to maximise the chances of viable rail freight developing, and on the argument that much rail infrastructure was maintained primarily for the benefit of passenger services. This strategy proved to have two failings. First, as the volume of heavy freight usage increased it became apparent that the cost of track wear and tear from freight was significantly higher than had been assumed. An industry insider commented that:

> the real problem was the nature of the access agreement with EWS [the main freight operator] which allowed freight to roam across the network. New flows, such as coal traffic from Hunterston to power stations in Yorkshire and the Midlands, brought heavy coal trains onto the Carlisle and Settle line which for 20 years had been maintained only for light passenger trains, and gave rise to a bill of more than £100 million for track repairs, ultimately paid for by the taxpayer. Freight flows, unlike passenger, can be relatively short term.[2]

Second, as track became congested the failure to price in long-run capacity costs meant that rationing had to be enforced and the price signals were not capable of bringing about efficient use of the network.

Notwithstanding these weaknesses, competition for rail freight services has worked reasonably well. There has been significant innovation in both the nature of the services offered and in the methods used to deliver them.

For instance, the freight operators purchased a quantity of cheap and reliable locomotives from General Motors of America, something that had not happened under nationalisation. Rail freight has not grown as fast as the government had hoped, but that was largely because the relatively short lengths of haul in the UK give trucks an important advantage. Such growth as there has been has largely been in traditional sectors, such as moving coal to power stations over longer distances; there has been less success in winning new markets.

RAILTRACK

The failure of Railtrack is the best known of the difficulties experienced by Britain's rail privatisation. In fact, the policy would have run into difficulty in any case because of the severe problems experienced by the TOCs and the unrealistic political aspirations and inadequate funding to meet them. But Railtrack attracted by far the greatest public attention. Recovering from its demise continues to be extremely difficult to this day.

Railtrack was deliberately put beyond the direct control of government, on the grounds that experience had repeatedly shown that government interference had been damaging to the successful running of rail businesses. At first things certainly seemed to go well. The shares were over-subscribed at flotation at a price of £3.90. That valued the company at £1.9 billion, less than half the historic cost book value of the assets. The share price reached a peak of £17.68 in 1998, *after* the change of government. Financial analysts were clearly unconcerned by the signals that policy and political risks were lurking in the background. They must have perceived a relatively low risk public utility with the potential to expand its capital base and to increase and preserve profits. This view was reinforced by the conventional wisdom of the early 1990s: that British Railways had always been dominated by engineers who were unable or unwilling to respond to the pressures to make the railway sufficiently efficient and modest in scale for it to be affordable in modern economic circumstances.

Robert Horton the first Chairman of Railtrack and, from 1997 Gerald Corbett, a powerful Chief Executive, were both recruited from other industries. It is alleged that many of the best senior engineers were lost to the company during the restructuring of the industry in the mid-1990s, other managerial skills being preferred over theirs (see, for example, National Audit Office, 2004, paragraph 2). All this may have contributed towards a tendency to underestimate the extreme complexity of a large railway, having heavy, long-lived, safety-critical assets of many types, all working together in an interdependent system.

Another problem that, in the long run, turned out to be just as significant was that Railtrack's senior management seemed to find difficulty with the special public service and public accountability dimensions of their new industry. They regarded the Rail Regulator as an adversary. His legitimate function in representing the public interest, those of Railtrack's users and ultimately those of taxpayers who were liable for Railtrack's charges, was not understood. It was wrongly assumed that the long-term interests of shareholders would be best served by keeping the Rail Regulator as far away from the company's affairs as possible: anything seen as an intervention was resented; information was not supplied willingly. Both economic and safely regulation were regarded as intrusive.

The West Coast Main Line

An early incident, which was to prove a main cause of the commercial failure of Railtrack, was the negotiation of a contract with Virgin for the upgrading of the West Coast Main Line. The Regulator had to approve the contract, and he did so even though he may have had doubts about whether the project could be delivered at the agreed price, taking the view that Railtrack's shareholders should be left to bear the commercial risks. He did make his approval conditional on Railtrack creating major increases in the capacity beyond their proposals in order to cater for the legitimate needs of freight and other track users who had been rather forgotten in the rush to cater for Virgin's requirements.

In the case of the West Coast Main Line, Virgin had committed to turning a subsidy of £77 million in the first year to a small payment (that is a negative subsidy) by 2002–03 and a payment of over £200 million a year by 2008–09. Similarly their winning Cross Country bid was to convert an annual subsidy of £12 million into an annual payment of £10 million by the end of the 15-year term. It seems likely that these bids were always over-optimistic and by 2001–02 both Virgin franchises had already run into serious difficulties with the level of service they were able to secure from Railtrack. In later years the discrepancies became much larger.

Alistair Osborne gives an account of the West Coast Main Line debacle (*Daily Telegraph*, 25 September 2004):

> With typical razzmatazz, Branson [Virgin] said he would order 140mph trains, capable of tilting round corners. . . . For this, Branson needed a guarantee from Railtrack that it could provide the high-speed line. . . . The contract contained a clause compelling Railtrack to pay Virgin £250 million compensation should it fail to deliver the railway – a vast sum for a company floated with less than £2 billion of equity. In December 1999, Railtrack admitted that moving block [signalling] technology, as proved on the Jubilee Line extension, simply didn't

work. . . . Says Chris Green, the Virgin Trains chief executive who steps up to chairman on Monday: 'Had Railtrack waited and got a proper technical report, they would have found out moving block was not the answer and that the costs were going to be massively more than they thought.' . . . As Railtrack belatedly got to grips with the west coast project, the forecast cost rocketed – to £5.8 billion in 1999, and £7 billion in 2001.

Long aware of the risks, Branson showed typical acumen in June 1998, selling bus and rail group Stagecoach a 49 per cent stake in Virgin Trains. Two years later, he renegotiated the franchise, legitimately arguing that while he had committed himself to the trains, the upgrade was in disarray.

The negotiations continue to this day . . . Meantime, Virgin runs the franchise as a management contract, making a small profit margin. In the year to March 31, 2003, when the original franchise agreement envisaged a £4 million return to the taxpayer, Virgin received £189 million. In the most recent financial year, Virgin got £332 million instead of paying back £59 million, with subsidy per passenger for each mile travelled almost doubling to 20 pence.

Railtrack had committed to this commercial contract on the basis of optimistic engineering cost estimates, and on an imprudent view of the ease with which a modern electronic signalling system could be used. It is said that among the main causes of the huge cost overrun were frequent changes of specification as more TOCs and more freight operators were given access and too many changes of project manager.

It is hard to believe that a prudent company would have committed itself to such a large engineering project on the basis of improperly quantified risks, had they not implicitly been assuming that if things should go wrong then the government would come to the rescue, as they had so often under the old regime and, indeed, as they did subsequently, for a limited period.

Maintenance and Safety

Another matter of significance was a familiar one for regulated private utilities. The regulated access charges were set on the basis that they would be sufficient to pay for adequate maintenance and renewals work and to pay a proper return on equity and debt. The accusation was made that Railtrack was spending too little on maintenance and renewals and too much on dividends to shareholders: one of the reasons for the rise in share price. Even though Railtrack did achieve higher rates of investment in their infrastructure than had been achieved before, the National Audit Office (NAO, 2000, Figure 2) confirmed the view that there had been a decline in some aspects of the health of the network and, in particular an increase in the number of broken rails. The Regulator had become concerned that the network was not being adequately maintained and warned specifically that the increase in the number of broken rails was not acceptable. Arguably, the decline in track quality and increase in broken rails were mainly the consequence of traffic growth on the system. Ironically, the number of broken rails was falling by the time of the accident at Hatfield in October 2000. The government promised action, but did very little beyond holding a few conferences at which ministers berated the industry and told it to improve.

The Regulator was also concerned about the inadequacy of Railtrack's knowledge of the volume and condition of its assets. British Rail had full data before privatisation, but this stayed with the several British Rail engineering companies when they were sold to the private sector. Railtrack was slow to extract enough information to create a comprehensive, central asset register, even though one would have thought that the company would need this information to protect the long-term interests of its shareholders, and the Regulator was insisting that the effort be speeded up. One should not underestimate the size of this task. There are some 700 asset categories for the railway reflecting a whole range of technologies. To be effective the register has to be tied into a work management system so that the information is continuously updated with activity undertaken on the network. Hence, the contractors had a key role in operating the system. Few continental railways have yet succeeded in developing such systems.

Finally there were two major accidents, both in West London: one in 1997 at Southall which seven people were killed and one in 1999 at Ladbroke Grove in which 31 people were killed. Both accidents involved trains failing to stop at red signals. The extent to which privatisation may have been a factor remains controversial but the general public, encouraged by ministers, immediately laid the blame at the door, once again, of 'Tory privatisation'.

The Ladbroke Grove accident in particular was a crucial turning point: government could have taken the line that this was now a private industry and it was a matter for the independent safety and economic regulators to sort out. Government routinely takes this line, for instance, in the cases of aviation and gas accidents. But Railtrack was heavily criticised in the press and by senior members of the government. This greatly heightened the general public's perception that privatisation had made the railways less safe despite clear evidence that safety was improving before privatisation and it continued to improve at much the same rate afterwards (see Evans, 2004).

All these factors came into play after a third accident at Hatfield in October 2000. A train travelling at speed was derailed because of the failure of a decaying rail. Four people were killed. Investigators quickly established that the rail in question had exhibited symptomatic cracks before failure.

The accident may have been a consequence of avoidable negligence, but it was not as serious as some railway accidents and it did not take the accident rate outside of what was to be expected on the basis of historical trends.

However, the way Railtrack managers responded did immense damage to the industry (see Foster and Castles, 2004). They feared the worst possible response from the press and from government, felt they had to avoid another similar accident at all costs, and jumped to the conclusion that cracks might exist at many other places on the system. It was later established that, while gauge corner cracking did indeed exist in other parts of the network, there were no problems comparable to those at Hatfield and none that could not have been handled in the ordinary way.

Railtrack all but closed the system by imposing very wide and restrictive train speed limits that caused many train cancellations. The disruption was compounded by one of the wettest autumns of recent years, leading to embankment slips and flooding. Under pressure from government Railtrack embarked on a hopelessly ambitious and expensive programme of emergency track replacement. At first they promised government and the public that the work would be complete in time for Easter 2002 – presumably because they thought that was what government wanted to hear – even though the simplest calculations of the volume of work and the labour and materials available to do it showed that this deadline could never have been met.

All this lead to the catastrophic decline in passengers displayed earlier in Figure 3.5. Naturally, Railtrack lost income through failing to provide contracted train paths to the TOCs, and it suffered financial penalties under the performance regime. The episode highlighted that with the new privatised railway no one was responsible for managing the critical wheel/rail interface: the cracking phenomenon was attributable in large part to changing wheel profiles.

Financial Crises

Coincidentally the Regulator's periodic review of Railtrack's charges was published just after the Hatfield accident, having been in preparation for many months. During the proceedings for the review it had become clear that Railtrack was facing a second, major financial problem because of the commercial agreement concerning the West Coast Main Line.

Government had already made substantial special grants available to Railtrack to rescue it. The situation was taken into account in the periodic review, but in the months following the review's publication Railtrack's finances deteriorated. In April, Railtrack, the government and SRA agreed to bring forward revenues which, as part of the periodic review, had been deferred until 2005. They also agreed to a statement of principles that redefined Railtrack's role in relation to the network. The government endorsed Railtrack's role as the national infrastructure provider but the company acknowledged that responsibility for funding and delivery of major enhancement schemes could rest with other companies or consortia. Future enhancement projects were subject to competitive procurement – a new competitive dimension.

The situation stabilised for a while until a new Railtrack chairman was appointed who was intent on new negotiations – and perhaps lacked an appreciation of what went on before. The independent Rail Regulator later said that Railtrack made a mistake in attempting to negotiate privately with the government for yet more grant, rather than making a proper application to him (Winsor, 2004a, 2004b). He would have been bound to consider it under one of his primary duties in the Railways Act 1993: to enable Railtrack to finance its activities.

In October 2001, without warning, the Secretary of State for Transport (by then Mr Byers) used the excuse of the further grant requests to put Railtrack into Railway Administration, a special form of bankruptcy provided for by the Railways Act. This made the shares worthless and the Secretary of State stated that there would be no compensation for the shareholders. Some months later, under pressure from City institutions, the government relented and found a way to increase borrowings in order to pay approximately £2.50 per share, a little less than the share price before the administration was announced. Debts to bond holders were honoured.

The government might have encouraged a conventional take-over of Railtrack and there were companies that showed an interested in this. The normal competitive market for corporate control would have acted to change the management and rebuild the company. That would have kept the structure intact and avoided the damaging hiatus that, in fact, occurred. But Mr Byers was apparently determined to take the opportunity to destroy the privatised, shareholder ownership structure that the Labour Government had inherited in 1997 – thereby fulfilling one of the promises made by Clare Short in the privatisation *Prospectus*. Moreover, Byers indicated to the Regulator that if he should consider a request from Railtrack for a rescue, then the government would immediately introduce summary legislation to overrule him (Winsor, 2004a, 2004b). This compromising of the Regulator's independence is of considerable significance, not only for the future of the railways, but also for the other British privatised utilities.

If the Left of the Labour Party saw Railtrack's bankruptcy as the opportunity to completely renationalise the railway, they were quickly disappointed.

The Treasury was unwilling to find the funds necessary to buy out the TOCs' contracts and other surviving private interests. In addition and more importantly, Railtrack had considerable and rapidly increasing debt that the Office of National Statistics had classified as private debt on the grounds that the company was not under public control. The Chancellor was absolutely unwilling to countenance any move that would bring that debt onto the public balance sheet. Railtrack would linger in administration for about a year at considerable cost (Winsor, *Spectator*, 3 July 2004; NAO, 2004, paragraph 3.13).

NETWORK RAIL

When the government put Railtrack into administration, it announced that it wished to reorganise Railtrack as a special and rarely used form of company called a Company Limited by Guarantee. The new company, eventually named Network Rail, would be 'non-profit' in that it had no shareholders and was financed entirely by debt. In lieu of shareholders, it would be run by an executive board accountable to about 120 'members', many chosen to represent one of a large number of public and private interests including train operators, railway employees and passengers.[3]

Major new investments would continue to be undertaken by 'Special Purpose Vehicles' (SPVs): contractual arrangements with private sector providers. This idea predated the creation of Network Rail and was intended to harness private sector project management skills and to benefit from the stronger balance sheets of outside companies. Ironically, these SPVs would be financed by both equity and debt, so even the claimed elimination of 'for profit' equity was illusory. It is unclear how SPVs would be constituted, or whether they would prove to be a practical proposition in the highly complex and interconnected system that is an operating railway. The determination of both incremental cost and incremental revenues attributable to a new project would have been difficult and likely contentious.

The result is considerable confusion about the governance of Network Rail. Under the original privatised structure everybody understood that the board of Railtrack, like the board of any corporation, had a legal duty to serve the long-term financial interests of shareholders subject to the constraints defined by normal legislation and by the Rail Regulator. The accountabilities and incentives under the new structure for Network Rail are much less clear. Although Network Rail documentation says that 'members will perform the corporate governance role normally carried out by shareholders in companies which have a share capital', it also states that members 'are not liable in any way for the activities or finances of Network Rail and any of its subsidiaries' and 'it will not be the role of members to set the strategic direction or engage in management of Network Rail.' In any case, it remains to be seen whether, in practice, the membership of over 100 individuals is able to formulate a coherent set of policies and get the executive board to implement them.

Arguably, the restructuring of Railtrack into Network Rail did little to address whatever were the fundamental failings of the railway structure after privatisation and yet it weakened and obfuscated the infrastructure company's objectives and created weaker incentives to look after the interests of the taxpayer. Ironically, recent and careful statistical analysis by Kennedy and Smith (2004) confirms that despite the weaknesses in the initial management, 'Railtrack delivered substantial real unit cost reductions in the early years after privatisation (between 5.9 and 7.9 per cent for maintenance activity; and 6.4 to 6.8 per cent for overall maintenance and renewal activity) . . . However, these improvements were largely offset by the post-Hatfield cost increases, which resulted in unit cost increases of 26 and 38 per cent for maintenance and overall (maintenance and renewal) activity respectively.'

There is little doubt that Network Rail now has better senior management. They are successfully reintroducing sound engineering practice, and committed to bringing the runaway costs back under control. It is an open question whether the incentive structure they are working with will enable them to succeed in the long term.

RAILWAY ENGINEERING

As noted earlier, the original design for rail privatisation conceived of Railtrack as a small organisation with the job of competitively procuring the repair, maintenance and enhancements services it required from separate engineering companies. The old British Rail engineering operation was divided up into several separate, territorial organisations, which were sold to the private sector and bought by general civil engineering concerns, many of them large, well known companies.

Unfortunately, two elementary and damaging errors were made during privatisation. The first was that the engineering companies were sold with negotiated procurement contracts already put in place by government. In other words, there was not an open competition to determine the terms on which Railtrack would procure. This may have been done because the outgoing Tory government was determined to complete the rail privatisation in the little time they had before the 1997 general election, leaving inadequate time for a proper competitive tendering exercise. Another view was that the pre-arranged contracts had been struck on generous terms in order to inflate the sale price of the engineering companies at a time when the Exchequer was in particular need of funds. Whatever the reason, the result was to deny Railtrack the benefits of fully competitive procurement at the crucial start of the new regime. This was unfortunate, given that one of the largest gains from privatisation is often a 20 per cent or so reduction in unit costs from replacing in-house procurement within the public sector with competitive procurement (see Domberger, 1998 and Glaister, Kennedy and Travers, 1995).

The second error was that Railtrack failed to put in place adequate contract management arrangements. It was not understood that active contract management is an absolute necessity in situations like this in order to affirm that the work being paid for is being done to the agreed standard. Railtrack allowed the competencies of its own engineering staff to atrophy so they lost the ability to be an intelligent purchaser (National Audit Office, 2004). The maintenance companies recruited new staff of varying degrees of experience in the railway business and gave them variable amounts of training. There were some highly visible failures, some of them safety-critical. It is alleged that poor communication and defective workmanship contributed to several accidents including Hatfield (maintained by Balfour Beatty) and some defective track components at Potters Bar (maintained by Jarvis).

A new generation of track maintenance contracts was introduced from 1999 with a retendering process. These moved away from fixed price contracts towards cost reimbursable, open book pricing, and they were intended to provide greater transparency and improved information on costs and outputs. Unfortunately, the benefits of these new arrangements did not have time to show through before the Hatfield accident in October 2000.

Eventually, in 2003, Network Rail made the decision progressively to terminate its outstanding maintenance contracts and to bring the function back in-house, while continuing to procure enhancement work from the private sector. Some of the private sector providers (notably Jarvis) decided to leave the railway maintenance sector. In the long run Network Rail may succeed in reducing their engineering costs by bringing the maintenance function in-house, but no evidence has been presented to demonstrate why this would be the case. What is certain is that there will be substantial costs of buying out the existing contracts and transferring a large number of employees onto the books of what was a relatively small employer, and thereafter managing the employment and the labour relations in what is a notoriously difficult industry. The overall conclusion is that one of the major potential sources of efficiency gain from rail privatisation – competition in the market for civil engineering work – was never achieved.

THE LATEST NEW RAILWAYS POLICY: *THE FUTURE OF RAIL*

In July 2004 the government published its latest review of railway policy, *The Future of Rail* (Department of Transport, 2004). The review was precipitated in part by the political imperative 'to do something' in response to the general public dissatisfaction with both the performance of the railway and the principle of privatisation. But the most immediate impetus was the Rail Regulator's special review of Network Rail's access charges, undertaken in the aftermath of Railtrack's failure, published in December 2003 and coming into force in April 2004.

The review contained bad news for the government because the Regulator judged that the basic costs of Network Rail were going to be higher than had been thought before Hatfield (NAO, 2004). In 2004 public funding for the railway would rise to £3.8 billion, up from £1.8 billion in fiscal year 1997–98 (Department of Transport, 2004, paragraph 2.2.1). In addition, the year in which Railtrack rotted in administration contributed towards a very rapid increase in Network Rail's debt, which rose from £585 million at privatisation to £9,404 million by March 2003 (see NAO, 2004a, paragraph 3.10). The increased annual bill for running the railway flew directly in the face of everything the Treasury had been trying to achieve for the railway for decades.

The government sought to blame the cost increase on the independent Regulator, complaining bitterly that he was high-handedly setting taxpayer-funded levels of public expenditure, which he had no constitutional right to do. But the Regulator (Winsor, 2004a, 2004b) argued that he had simply done what the law required of him, namely to determine how much an efficient infrastructure company in current economic circumstances should be paid for delivering the outputs that the government had asked for. At the core was a problem that has bedevilled government involvement in railway policy for decades. On the one hand, the Treasury was unwilling to find the relentlessly increasing money the railway demands of the Exchequer and, on the other hand, the government was unwilling to face the political difficulties of contracting railway services.

The government's confusion is confirmed in *The Future of Rail*, a rather vague document that proposes remarkably little fundamental reform. The basic structure of the industry is to remain unchanged. Network Rail will remain as the regulated monopoly infrastructure provider and privately owned passenger and freight train companies will continue to operate on either a contracted or open access basis. The one major change proposed is to abolish the Strategic Rail Authority and transfer its functions to the Department for Transport. This may not seem to be a very radical change since the SRA has always been a 'non-departmental public body', subject to direction from the Secretary of State.

The major reason that the SRA came to be perceived as having failed – and was always bound to fail – was that it was never given enough money to deliver the task that government expected of it. From the first the Chairman of the SRA emphasised the problem of insufficient funding. But the SRA's funding problems became greater, first as the TOCs ran into financial difficulty and had to be rescued and later as track access charges increased in response to Railtrack and Network Rail's cost problems.

Another reason the SRA came to be perceived as a failure was that it seemed neither strategic nor authoritative. In the earlier years strategy documents were promised and then repeatedly delayed. There was much confusion over franchising policy with indecision about what an appropriate franchise length might be. More recently the SRA, under the chairmanship of Richard Bowker, attempted to promote the case for more railway funds to government and the general public, but this was perceived as unconvincing special pleading.

Aside from the SRA, *The Future of Rail* leaves the problems of the industry unresolved. In the foreword the Secretary of State speaks of 'an inefficient and dysfunctional organisation coupled with a failure to control costs'. The document claims that 'the attempt to create a commercial market relationship between the train and track companies failed' (paragraph 1.2.1), and speaks of 'misaligned incentives' (paragraph 1.4.12). But while 'The weakness of the current structure . . . is the complex and adversarial relationships between the different parts of the industry. The Government believes that these will be better remedied without moving to common ownership' (paragraph 4.2.9). In short, the government's new proposals do not seem very different from the current situation.

The accountability of Network Rail presents an important unresolved problem. To keep the debt off the public balance sheet, Network Rail *must not* be under the control of the public sector. But the financial press has repeatedly reported that the interest cost of Network Rail's borrowings are being reduced by the comfort offered by the underlying government support. If the government is perceived as supporting the debt in any case, one has to wonder why the government does not borrow directly in order to enjoy the low rates available to direct sovereign debt. The government is in danger of paying risk premia to others while actually bearing all the risks itself.

It is unlikely that the structure now proposed for the railway can operate successfully for very long. Railtrack's year in administration, the subsequent increases in costs, the realisation that more needs to be invested, the borrowing at the request of government in order to reduce current taxpayer funded grants, government's aspirations to carry more rail traffic and its refusal to countenance large-scale closures all lead to one place: rapidly increasing debt for Network Rail. The original intention was that Network Rail would earn profits and would retain these in order to build up a buffer fund designed to cushion commercial risks, the function normally performed by equity. In fact, no such profits have been earned and none look likely. Rather, debt has escalated. Given the unprofitability of many passenger services and the reluctance of the government to greatly increase its recurrent grant, it is very hard to see how Network Rail will ever repay – or even bring under control – debt on this scale.

CONCLUSIONS

The fundamental principle driving the British railways policy of the 1990s was not change of ownership (that is, privatisation). It was the establishment of competition in every aspect of the business in order to achieve cost efficiency and transparency of policy. Ministers were slow to make up their minds about exactly what they wanted, and execution of policy was unduly rushed because of a late decision to privatise Railtrack in advance of an impending general election. But it was successfully, if imperfectly implemented and it started to produce some remarkably good results.

We shall never know what the long-term outcome might have been if the policy, once implemented, had been left alone. It soon fell foul of two phenomena. First, policy risk: the Treasury proved to be unwilling to provide the public funds necessary to allow competition to operate as originally envisaged. Competition for passengers had to be 'moderated' and competitive procurement of engineering services for Railtrack was also abandoned, allegedly because that might have reduced the privatisation sale revenues for the Treasury.

Second, political risk: governments proved, in practice, to be unwilling to tolerate the criticism that they feared they would attract if they had allowed the company failures that are essential to an effective competitive processes. When the TOCs failed, government bailed them out. When Railtrack made a fatally bad investment and mismanaged its information systems, government again rescued it for a while, before intervening in a way that destroyed the normal competitive market for corporate control. This unwillingness to allow rail firms to fail helped also to undermine the introduction of a competitive market for railway labour.

Crucially, there was a change of government soon after rail privatisation had occurred. The Labour Party had been explicit while in opposition about its deeply felt commitment to reverse the rail privatisation. Once in power the new Labour Government seemed to be uncomfortable with the notion of competition in the railway industry. It did nothing much for a while beyond loud criticisms from the sidelines. Then, when Railtrack ran into terminal financial difficulty, the government took its chance to give the public the appearance of recovering control of the industry. But here again policy risk asserted itself: Treasury fiscal and national debt policy prevented renationalisation. Instead, both the new infrastructure company, Network Rail, and the TOCs now sit precariously on an indistinct boundary between public and private sectors with foggy corporate objectives and ill-defined duties towards the public interest.

No evidence or experience has demonstrated that one cannot separate rail infrastructure from operations if that is what is desired. Indeed, contrary to what the public may have been led to expect, the 2004 review of railways policy clearly reaffirms this division for the future. Separately, and slightly surprisingly, the Labour Government itself created just such a division (differently configured) with its new structure for the London Underground, implemented a full six years after reaching power. Foster (2005), who was a close and authoritative observer of events both before and after rail privatisation is of the opinion that:

> in practice [separation of train from track ownership] has lead to compara-
> tively few problems. I believe the best evidence that the vertical separation
> of train from track was feasible, is not only that rail privatisation continues
> on that basis, but that it has become central to rail regulation and interoper-
> ability of rail systems throughout Europe. Furthermore its retention was
> among the few givens when the Labour government reviewed the railways in
> 2004.

The practical experience of Britain demonstrates that it may or may not be the best way of proceeding but that it can be done.

That being said, rail privatisation on the British model can only be made to work in a stable and fairly predictable way on three crucial provisos. First the legal system must be sufficiently competent, robust and respected to put in place the necessary contractual arrangements: there has never been any doubt about this in the British context. Second, it must be possible to specify an appropriate performance regime that will provide the incentives to induce the required behaviour. This is open to question: there are both analytical questions (for example what are the right financial penalties to use?) and legal questions (for example can they be successfully drafted into contracts that are enforceable in practice?). Finally, once created, these arrangements must be left alone to mature, without the fatally damaging consequences of interventions by government or others that undermine the incentives carefully designed into the 'fragmented' structure.

The 2004 review of railways policy leaves most fundamental questions unanswered. There is ambivalence about the role and meaning of enforceable commercial contracts, and the associated performance incentive regimes. There is ambivalence about whether Network Rail is or is not private, whose interests it serves and whether it is or is not under government control. Most importantly of all there is little sign of the fundamental issue being addressed: how big a railway the nation is willing to pay for over the long term. If the government is not willing to pay the likely cost of the present scale of operation, what is to be cut? Network Rail's debt is already much higher than Railtrack's was and it has recently been further increased at the government's request by deferring some of the increased access charge payments as determined by the Rail Regulator.

The British experience illustrates that the financial and political costs of introducing competitive forces and private ownership into previously nationalised railways are likely to be immense. But the cost to the public purse of the railways is also immense. Competition, if allowed to be effective, may offer much more than enough gain to offset the costs of introducing it. Arguably this has been demonstrated several times with the privatisation of the other major British utilities.

Unfortunately, the British experience may also illustrate the possibility of ending up with the worst of all worlds: to incur the costs of introducing competition but then to intervene to prevent that competition from delivering its benefits. If competition is to be the driving force for policy, government intervention is still necessary: but it must be intervention to promote genuinely competitive procurement and effective contract management. The moral of the British experience is that effective competition is possible in many dimensions of the provision of railway services, but that it is pointless for governments to introduce it unless they can deliver on the commitment to allow it to function.

NOTES

1. Director of Regulation and Government, Railtrack. Personal communication.
2. Personal communication.
3. In choosing this preferred model the government was greatly influenced by Glas Cymru, a relatively small and simple Welsh water company that had been set up as Company Limited by Guarantee in 2001 (see Gómez-Ibáñez, 2002 for an account). On close inspection it is apparent that these companies are in fact 'not for dividend' as distinct from 'not for profit' as was made clear in the Department for Transport's notices to the Press at the time. There are no conventional shareholders but profit on operations must be earned in order to pay the required return to debt holders.

REFERENCES

Bartle, I., (2004), *Britain's Railway Crisis – A Review of the Arguments in Comparative Perspective*, Centre for Regulated Industries.

Department of Transport (1984), *Buses*.

Department of Transport (1993), *Gaining Access to the Railway Network*, February.

Department of Transport (2004), *The Future of Rail*.

Domberger, S. (1988), *The Contracting Organisation*, Oxford: Oxford University Press.

Evans, A., (2004), *Rail Safety and Rail Privatisation in Britain*, Inaugural Lecture of Imperial College London.

Foster, C. D., (1994), *The Economics of Rail Privatisation*, CRI Discussion Paper 7, April, reprinted in *The Development of Rail Regulation*, CRI collections Series 2, November 2003.

Foster, C. D. and Castles, C., (2004), 'Creating a Viable Railway for Britain – What has gone Wrong and How to Fix it', typescript.

Foster, C. D., (2005), *British Government in Crisis*, Oxford: Hart Publishers.

Glaister, S., Kennedy, D. and Travers, T., (1995), *London Bus Tendering*, Greater London Group.

Gómez-Ibáñez, J. A., (2002), *Glas Cymru and the Debate Over Non-Profits*, Teaching Case, Kennedy School of Government, Harvard.

Gómez-Ibáñez, J. A ., (2003), *Regulating Infrastructure*, Harvard.

Helm, D., (2000), *A Critique of Rail Regulation: The Beesley Lectures in Regulation*, IEA and London Business School, October.

Kennedy, J. and Smith, A. S. J., (2004), 'Assessing the Efficient Cost of Sustaining Britain's Rail Network', *Journal of Transport Economics and Policy*, May.

Lawrence, G., (2001), *The Rail Industry in Great Britain, Institutional and Legal Structure 2000/2001*, Centre for the Study of Regulated Industries, Bath.

National Audit Office (2000), *Ensuring that Railtrack Maintain and Renew the Network*, HC 397 Session 1999–2000, April.

National Audit Office (2004), *Network Rail: Making a Fresh Start*, HC 532.

Office of the Rail Regulator (1994), *Competition for Railway Passenger Services: A Policy Statement*, December.

Office of the Rail Regulator (2000), *The Periodic Review of Railtrack's Access Charges: Final Conclusions*, Vols I & II, October.

SBC Warburg (1996), *Railtrack Share Offer, Prospectus*, 1 May.

Shaoul, J., (2004), 'Railpolitik: The Financial Realities of Operating Britain's National Railways', *Public Money and Management*, January.

Transport Select Committee (2004), *The Future of the Railway*, HC145, March.

Winsor, T., (2004a), 'The Relationship Between the Government and the Private Sector: Winsor v Bloom in Context', *Incorporated Council of Law Reporting*, 5 April (also available at http://www.rail-reg.gov.uk/upload/pdf/ICLR-annual-lec-050404.pdf).

Winsor, T., (2004b), '2004 DfT Rail Review – Submission by the Rail Regulator', *Office of the Rail Regulator*, 6 May.

4. France: Avoiding competition

Emile Quinet

INTRODUCTION

France, like other countries, has special characteristics that have affected its approach to railway reform. This chapter begins by examining the similarities and differences between the French and other European railways in the early 1990s, on the eve of the European push to restructure. It then describes two rounds of reforms. The first round, adopted during the 1980s and 1990s, largely avoided the issue of restructuring and focused instead on strengthening the French railways by improving services in various ways. The second round of reforms, initiated at the end of the 1990s, responded to the restructuring requirements of European Commission Directive 91/440 and changed fundamentally the relationships between the various actors in the railways system. The chapter concludes by speculating about the likely effects of both rounds of reforms, focusing particularly on the question of whether the latest round is likely to result in effective competition and whether the French public railways will be ready for that competition if it arrives.

SIMILARITIES AND DIFFERENCES ON THE EVE OF REFORM

Similarities

In the early 1990s, the French railways shared many features in common with other European railways. As in most of Europe, the French railways were operated by a single integrated firm, the *Société Nationale des Chemins de Fer Français*, or SNCF. The SNCF was, and still is, a government owned firm belonging to the French legal category of an *Etablissement Public Industriel et Commercial*. At the time the SNCF had a legal monopoly to operate all intercity passenger and freight railway services. Traffic trends were also similar: SNCF's passenger traffic was increasing and freight traffic decreasing at roughly the average European rates. Freight was a bit

Table 4.1   Goods market share in some European countries

	D	E	F	I	UK
1970	0.405	0.259	0.361	0.234	0.231
1980	0.356	0.190	0.280	0.133	0.163
1990	0.269	0.128	0.201	0.098	0.105
1991	0.213	0.116	0.200	0.098	0.105
1992	0.189	0.101	0.189	0.094	0.109
1993	0.177	0.086	0.179	0.092	0.093
1994	0.174	0.089	0.182	0.098	0.083

Source: DG TREN statistics.

of an exception in that SNCF's share of the market, although declining, was one of the highest in Europe, as shown in Table 4.1.

The financial situation was roughly comparable as well. SNCF received relatively fewer operating subsidies from the government than its other European counterparts. In 1994, for example, subsidies accounted for 32 per cent of SNCF operating expenses, a figure lower than that of any other major European railway and almost half the rate of subsidy enjoyed by the Spanish and Norwegian national railways, as shown in Table 4.2. But SNCF was also relatively heavily indebted. By 1998, SNCF debt amounted to 2.6 per cent of the French GDP, while most other European railways had debts of between 1 and 2 per cent of their national GDPs, as shown in Table 4.3. The high debt was largely due to the fact that investments in the French railways during the 1980s and 1990s had been financed almost exclusively through loans rather than government grants, and that huge investments had been made in the first three high-speed rail lines during this period.

Productivity was similar to that in other European railways, although here too there were some slight differences. A number of scholars have compared the productivity of the European railways during the 1990s, and most found that SNCF productivity was higher than that of other railways but increasing more slowly, so that the other European railways were gradually closing the productivity gap. To the extent that French railway productivity was increasing, moreover, it was largely due to capital rather than labour productivity gains[1]. Only one group of researchers, Briard, Rémy and Sauvant (2001), compared the productivity trends for SNCF's different major service types (high-speed passenger, other passenger and freight). They concluded that the company's overall productivity gains were due less to improvements in productivity of individual services than to a shift in output mix from the relatively less productive services (other passenger and freight) to more productive ones (high-speed passenger).

Table 4.2   Railway debts in Europe

	Railway debts (million ECU)	Rail debt in % GDP	Public debt in % GDP	Public borrowing in % GDP
Austria, OBB	2892	1.7	65	4.4
Belgium, SNCB	3539	1.8	136	5.3
Denmark, DSB	2782	2.3	76	3.5
Finland, VR	166	0.2	59	6.3
France, SNCF	28 731	2.6	48	5.8
Germany, DB AG[1]	5795	0.3	50	2.5
Greece, CH	937	1.1	110	12.1
Ireland, CIE	323	0.7	91	2.0
Italy, FS	42 067	4.9	126	9.0
Luxembourg, CFL	168	1.4	6	2.2
Netherlands, NS	2807	1.0	78	3.2
Portugal, CP	1529	2.1	72	5.8
Spain, RENFE	8140	2.0	63	6.9
Sweden, SJ + BV	1958	1.2	80	10.8
UK, BR+Railtrack	10 709	1.2	54	6.8
Slovenia, SZ	153	1.29	18	2.3

Notes: After recapitalization; DB debt in 1993 was 33 788 MECU.

Sources: ECMT 1998; Mercer Management Consulting; SZ: Ministry of Finance of Slovenia.

Table 4.3   Support from governments and other state bodies related to operating incomes (1994)

	1994		
RENFE(Spain)	0.616	NSB (Norway)	0.618
SNCB (Belgium)	0.460	OBB (Austria)	0.513
SNCF (France)	0.318	DB (Germany)	0.363
CFF (Switzerland)	0.360	FS (Italy)	0.367

Source: Henry and Quinet, 1998.

Differences

Although the traffic, financial, and productivity figures were roughly similar, French history and geography have given its railways some special features which, while found in other European countries, are present in

France to a greater degree. The first and most important of these is a long tradition of public sector involvement in industry that dates back to the 17th century and the *Manufactures royales* created by Colbert. This involvement increased sharply after 1945, with the nationalization of many industries (power, coal mining, several banks, some car and aircraft makers), and again at the beginning of the 1980s with another wave of nationalizations (of banks and some chemical and petrol firms). The privatization process started in the 1990s, but grew only slowly. In the case of the railways, France had six main companies – one state owned and five private regional railways – until 1937, when the government merged them into a single state owned and operated public company, SNCF. Due to the strength of the public sector, most public sector managers in the SNCF and elsewhere have an ethos of planning and command-and-control procedures. Many public sector managers have an engineering background, and are oriented more towards technical achievements than the search for profit.

A second important difference is that the concept of public service is deeply rooted in French attitudes. It is extensively defined in French legislation: there is a special body of laws for public service and special courts to interpret them. The French view public service as a tool not just to address the basic needs and failures of markets, as seen from an economic point of view, but also to achieve equity or distributive goals. The importance of these distributive concerns is signalled by the famous revolutionary slogan that became the nation's motto: *liberté, égalité, fraternité* (freedom, equality, and fraternity).

The extensive involvement of government in industry and the broad conception of public service and responsibilities mean that trade unions wield enormous influence. At SNCF, the unions have representatives on the company's board of directors, where they advance their members' interests in such matters as wages, employment, and working conditions. Work rules at the railway are strict and complicated, limiting flexibility and productivity. Employment rights are also very strong: layoffs are prohibited, for example, so that it is impossible to reduce staff except through retirement. It is difficult to move employees quickly from one post to another as the relevant procedures are complicated and lengthy. Given these constraints, the SNCF cannot adapt to change nearly as quickly as other rail operators. In the short run, SNCF's costs are almost fixed, a drawback in markets where customer requirements often change and where there is fierce competition from other modes of transport.

Finally, the French railways are also profoundly affected by the country's population density, which is half that of its northern neighbours (Germany, Britain, Switzerland or the Benelux). France is composed of large agglomerations (Paris, Bordeaux, Lyon, Marseille, Lille), with few settlements in between. This geography is well suited to intercity passenger service, and the French railways have always competed fairly well with air and auto. In domestic freight, however, the railways are hampered by relatively low traffic volumes and short lengths of haul compared, for instance, with North America. The railways should be reasonably competitive for international freight service but, unfortunately, coordination with foreign operators has been historically very bad. The coordination problems, found in other European countries as well, have been both technical (due to differing equipment standards) and managerial (due to a lack of commercial coordination and excessive red tape at border crossings).

REFORMS PRIOR TO RESTRUCTURING

The TGV

The French government and SNCF adopted a series of policies designed to strengthen its railways that were independent of, and in some cases predated, the European Commission's push to restructure. One of the most important of these was the decision to develop an extensive network of high-speed passenger services called the TGV (*Train à Grande Vitesse*). The SNCF built the first special high-speed track between Paris and Lyon in the 1970s, and the service began operation with top speeds of 270 km/h in 1981. Five more main lines were opened in the 1980s and 1990s, and top speeds were increased to almost 350 km/h. Although other European countries have begun building high-speed lines, France remains by far the leader, as shown in Table 4.4. An important feature of the TGV trains is that they can operate on normal as well as special high-speed track, although they are restricted to normal speeds when on normal track. This means that the TGV offers direct service (without transfers) between many French cities and towns as well as to neighbouring countries, as shown in Figure 4.1. As a consequence, the TGV services carry more than half the total rail passenger traffic in France.

Cooperation in International Services

SNCF's strategy has been to cooperate rather than compete with other international railways. Its website explains that 'SNCF believes in developing partnership with other railways rather trying to compete with them. SNCF has been operating with its partners several projects which have led to an increase of rail market share compared to other means of transport. Those schemes benefit each partner.'

Table 4.4   Evolution of the European High-speed Rail networks (Length (km))

	B	D	E	F	I	EU-15
1981	–	–	–	285	–	285
1983	–	–	–	402	–	402
1988	–	–	–	402	–	402
1990	–	n.a.	–	667	n.a.	n.a.
1995	–	n.a.	376	1124	n.a.	n.a.
1996	12	434	376	1152	237	2211
1997	71	434	376	1152	259	2292
1998	71	486	376	1147	259	2339
1999	73	491	377	1147	259	2347
2000	73	510	377	1147	259	2366
2001	73	510	377	1395	259	2614
2002	135	687	377	1395	259	2853

Notes:
Lines capable of speeds of 250 km/h or more.
In this table, as in other tables and figures, B means Belgium, D Deutschland, E Spain, F France, and I Italy.

Sources: Union Internationale des Chemins de Fer; DG TREN.

During the 1990s, the main focus of SNCF's cooperative efforts was in international passenger services, particularly as a part of its TGV strategy. The best known example of cooperation is the Eurostar service between London and Paris through the Channel Tunnel. But SNCF has also created joint ventures with neighbouring rail operators in conjunction with most of its other high-speed rail lines. These joint ventures operate international services such as the *Thalys* with SNCB and DB or the *Ligne de coeur* with CFF.

In freight transport, SNCF set up alliances with other potential partners through joint ventures, such as *GoVia* with a British transport company and *Go Ahead* for the railway concession for the South Central, South London railway network. It signed bilateral agreements with Germany to improve rail freight flows between the two countries, in a service called the 'Rail Euro Concept'. SNCF also signed a partnership agreement with Italian and Belgian railways in a joint venture called *Ifrabel*. In addition, SNCF is currently negotiating with the Polish State Railroad regarding freight operations. Nevertheless, SNCF's cooperative efforts fall short of the alliances developed for freight traffic by other foreign operators, particularly DB which took over the Dutch and the Swiss railways.

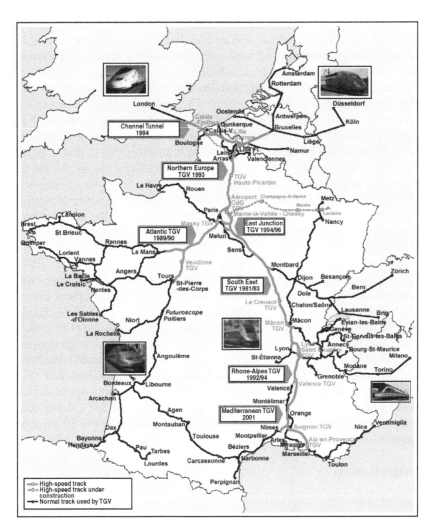

Source: SNCF.

Figure 4.1   The TGV network in 2004

Regional Decentralization

France is divided into 21 *Régions*, which are governed by elected assemblies and are empowered to manage certain public services. The Reform Law of 1982 authorized an experimental transfer of authority for regional rail services from the national government to the regional councils. Seven regional councils volunteered to participate from 1997 to 2001, and were given the responsibility for regional rail service together with the relevant subsidies the national government had previously given to the SNCF. The experiment was deemed a success, and in 2000 the government passed a law that mandated the transfer of responsibility for regional rail services to all regional councils as of 1 January 2002. The regional councils now negotiate contracts with SNCF that stipulate the nature of the services SNCF is to provide, the prices it can charge passengers, and the subsidies it will get from the regions. The Ile de France region is an exception in that it is not as autonomous as the other regions: Transport decisions in the Ile de France are made by a special transport authority, the *Service des Transports en Ile de France* (STIF), which is governed by a board composed of representatives from the national government, the region and the *départements* (France is divided into 100 *départements*). STIF contracts for local services from SNCF.

Most observers believe that the regions have been unable to put effective pressure on SNCF to reduce costs so far, perhaps because the regions still lack expertise in procuring railway services. As one regional official put it, 'the SNCF considers us just a money pump'. This situation is likely to change over the years, however, as regions become more demanding and more skilled at drafting contracts. As of 2004 there were already some encouraging signs. Most contracts now specify a fixed annual fee instead of reimbursing costs and the regions that first experimented with rail responsibilities, and thus have more experience, have been able to negotiate large increases in service relative to subsidies. For example, recent contracts call for a 4 per cent increase in service and a 3.4 per cent increase in traffic but only a 2.3 per cent increase in subsidies (according to *Conseil Economique et Social*, 2004).

Freight Reforms

Policymakers have long been concerned about the railways' low share of freight traffic because of their desire to slow or halt the growth in truck traffic and the highway congestion and air pollution that trucks create. The government and SNCF have made several efforts during the 1990s to become more competitive in freight, but none succeeded. In 1999, for example, the government set the ambitious goal of doubling freight traffic within ten years but never supplied the railway with the necessary means; as a result, freight traffic continued to decline and freight deficits increased. In 2004, SNCF estimated that it lost money on 80 per cent of the freight it carried (*Assemblée nationale*, 2004).

In that same year, the SNCF adopted a dramatic plan designed to enhance quality of service and to restore financial profitability of freight traffic. The goal is to eliminate unprofitable market segments within three years and to maintain a traffic growth of 3 per cent per year in subsequent years. The plan calls for SNCF to improve the quality of its services by focusing its attention on five priority corridors and by developing closer commercial relationships with shippers. In addition, it calls for SNCF to cut unit costs by 20 per cent through a combination of longer trains, higher load factors, eliminating poorly used intermodal container terminals, and 600 million euros in new capital improvements financed by a grant from the government. It is clear that the plan implies a sharp initial reduction in SNCF's market share, particularly for intermodal containers and from the cancellation of services with small flows, although neither the railway nor the government emphasizes these points. Early results suggest that quality of freight services has improved, although traffic has fallen off more than expected. In any event, it is still too soon to know whether the plan will succeed.

RESTRUCTURING INFRASTRUCTURE AND OPERATIONS

European Directives and Norms

France's efforts to separate infrastructure from operations and introduce competition were not taken on the government's own initiative but in response to the directives of the European Commission. As Nash explains in Chapter 2, in 1991 Directive 91/440 called for separate accounting for railway infrastructure and rail transport operations. The subsequent 'first railways package' of 2001 required, among other things, open access to the Trans European Rail Freight Network (TERFN) by 2003, the splitting of train operators and infrastructure into separate divisions with separate accounts (if not in separate companies), non-discriminatory allocation of paths, and the setting of paths and charges by an authority independent of any train operator. The second railway package of 2002 introduced measures to promote interoperability of rolling stock and to open access for freight operators to all parts of the rail network by 2007. A third railway package was under discussion in 2005 that would set a schedule for opening competition in international passenger services.

France's railway restructuring was also influenced by the European Union's Maastricht norms, which, although not dealing directly with railways, establish certain financial requirements for staying and becoming a member of the European Union, including that public debts should not exceed 50 per cent of a member's gross domestic product (GDP). This norm has caused each national government to seek ways to decrease its debt, sometimes artificially, through accounting and legal devices.

The French Response

Directives do not mandate specific means to achieve the goals they set. Therefore, each country must decide how to make the changes in national legislation needed to comply with these directives. France has complied on schedule with the requirements of all the European railway directives. It has split the accounts for infrastructure and operations and established rules for access by international freight operators, and for the allocation and pricing of routes, as demanded by the 1991 directive and the first railway package. But France was probably one of the most reluctant countries to provide open access to the TERFN lines by 2003 and to all freight lines by 2007 as required by the first and second railway packages, respectively.

France's policy on restructuring has been shaped importantly by the strong union opposition to any breakup of SNCF. The railway trade unions demonstrated their power in December 1995, with a month-long strike over a bill that would have reduced public sector pensions. The government backed down on the pension issue, and soon after, in a presumably weakened bargaining position, it reached an agreement with the unions that SNCF would remain a unified firm and a public service.

The agreement with the unions helps to explain the peculiar features of the railway reform law passed in 1997. That law created a public undertaking named *Réseau Ferré de France* (RFF), charged with the responsibility for infrastructure construction and maintenance and with the goals of promoting rail transport in France and to developing and enhancing the national railway network. Despite its broad responsibilities, however, RFF was designed to be a very small agency of only about 500 employees, whose decisions would be implemented by the infrastructure division of SNCF. The 1997 reform law requires that RFF contract with SNCF to operate its railway infrastructure. The RFF received the property of the national railway network and in return assumed roughly two-thirds of SNCF's debt.

The 1997 reform was designed to meet various European mandates while respecting French concerns. The creation of RFF met the requirement to split responsibilities between railway operators and infrastructure managers. Similarly, transferring some of SNCF's debt to RFF reduced the public debt and made France less vulnerable to the Maastricht norms, since, for obscure reasons, RFF debt was considered to be private debt. At the same time, SNCF was left pretty much intact – which appeased the trade unions opposed to liberalization and fragmentation – and the fact that

SNCF would continue to maintain the infrastructure and operate the trains reassured French railway specialists, many of whom thought it desirable to maintain a close connection between infrastructure and services.

With the RFF in place, the first railway package was implemented by a 7 March 2003 decree that opened the TERFN tracks to all international freight operators as of 15 March 2003 and the whole railway network to international and domestic freight operators as of 15 March 2008. The decree also established a set of non-discriminatory rules for network access.

Actors in the French System

The two main operational agencies are SNCF and RFF. Before the 1997 reforms, SNCF's status was defined by the Act No. 82-1153 dated 30 December 1982 which gave it the exclusive right to operate railway infrastructure and trains in France. Under the Reform Law of 1997, SNCF is to operate railway services over the national railway network, to manage the railway infrastructure on behalf of RFF, and to pursue both responsibilities in accordance with the principles applicable to public services. SNCF is empowered to carry out all activities directly or indirectly connected with its objectives. Railway infrastructure management involves responsibility for traffic regulation, security of the network and good state of infrastructure repair and maintenance. SNCF may create subsidiaries or invest in other companies, groups or entities, the purpose of which is related or contributes to that of SNCF.

The RFF assumed the portion of the old SNCF debt that, in theory, corresponded to the capital value of infrastructure transferred from SNCF to RFF. (In practice, the complete list of the infrastructure assets transferred to RFF was not fully documented until 2002.) Financial exchanges between the two firms go in both directions: RFF pays SNCF for infrastructure maintenance and operations, while SNCF pays RFF access fees. RFF is also in charge of investment policy, and must earn an adequate return on any investments it undertakes; if the government, or any other body, wants unprofitable investments to be built, it must subsidize them. The national and regional governments had to subsidize the recent construction of the new high-speed track between Paris and Strasbourg, for example, because the forecast rate of return was only 2 per cent[2]. Although SNCF is in charge of giving advice on timetables, path allocation is the responsibility of RFF, with a possible appeal to the Ministry of Transport in case of disagreement.

The national government has two main roles, both of which it exercises through the Ministry of Transport. First, the Ministry is the shareholder of RFF and SNCF, providing finance to both firms and establishing the broad goals for their management. In its shareholder role, the Ministry also names the main managers of the two firms, and has power to intervene in major budget decisions such as subsidies and borrowing. Second, as a regulator, the Ministry must approve the infrastructure charges and is the last appeal body for disputes over path allocation.

The Ministry of Transport is advised by the High Council for Railway Public Service (*Conseil Supérieur du Service Public Ferroviaire*, or CSSPF). The CSSPF is charged with promoting 'a balanced development of the rail system, in order to maintain the unity of the public rail service and to ensure coherence between the orientations of the two public firms, RFF and SNCF, and the compliance of these two firms to public service objectives'.[3] The Council was created in 1999 as the result of widespread concern that the reform creating RFF might endanger the achievement of public service objectives. It is composed of 37 members including members of the Parliament, local politicians, members of trade unions and rail users. The head of the CSSPF is named by the government.

Financial Relationships among the Actors

Restructuring of past debt

The debt restructuring during the reforms was affected by subtle legal considerations that determine whether the railway debt must be classified as public debt or not. The classification has both macro-economic consequences (in that public debt is governed by Maastricht norms) and micro-economic consequences (in that the classification affects perceived risks and thus the cost of borrowing). A related concern is whether government financial participation should be considered as an asset of the firm or as a subsidy, especially when the participation is caused by an operating deficit (see Figure 4.2).

The total debt of the railways system on the eve of the 1997 reforms amounted to 35.5 billion euros.[4] Of that, 20.5 billion euros was effectively transferred to RFF, 5 billion euros to another organization called SAAD, and the remaining 10 billion euros left with SNCF. The 20.5 billion euros of SNCF bonds that RFF assumed responsibility for actually still remain in SNCF's name for various legal reasons, but the RFF's balance sheet incorporates a debt due to SNCF that corresponds to the payments of interest and principal on those bonds. SAAD is a special organization originally created in 1991 to strengthen SNCF's balance sheet and reduce the direct subsidies it needs by assuming the debts it had accumulated at that time. SAAD interest and principal payments are paid directly by the national government.[5]

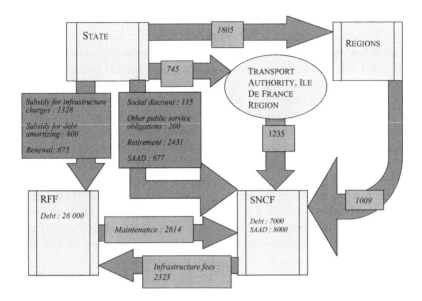

Source: Adapted from *Assemblée Nationale*, 2004.

*Figure 4.2   Financial flows concerning the French railway system for 2004
(€ millions)*

Maintenance payments to SNCF
The financial flows underlying the contractual relationships are summarized in Figure 4.2. One of the main flows is the payment from RFF to SNCF for infrastructure management activities. This fee amounted to 2.6 billion euros in 2003, and is expected to remain at about that level for the years to come. The maintenance contract is generally regarded as too vague, without incentives or clear quality objectives. It excludes renewals, which are paid separately. The amount of funding for renewals is decided by the national government rather than the RFF, but the RFF decides what specific renewal projects to pursue with the funds made available.

Infrastructure access fees paid to RFF
The second key flow is the access payments made to RFF by SNCF. These access fees were set very low initially and have been increased gradually, rising from 890 million euros in 1997 to 1.9 billion euros in 2003. Until 2004, the fee was essentially a lump sum designed to cover the entire year and usually negotiated in the middle of the year, when SNCF costs for the year were

known. The negotiated amount was then divided by actual and expected traffic flows and expressed in euros per ton kilometre, but the total amount paid did not vary with the amount of service SNCF actually operated.

In 2004 the access fee system was changed in several important ways. First, the access fees per unit of traffic were set two years in advance instead of essentially being negotiated after the fact. Second, the structure of the fees was changed to sharply increase fees for local passenger trains, freight and ancillary services (such as stops in stations or the use of marshalling yards). Third, the projected total volume of fees was forecast to increase more gradually at a rate of about 300 million euros per year.

The past and forecast trends in access fees are summarized in Table 4.5. The largest increases in fee revenue have come from the TGV (before 2004), local trains, and, to a lesser extent, freight. These changes reflect French policy of setting access charges to reflect a combination of willingness to pay (for example, for the TGVs, which pay above their marginal costs), scarcity of capacity (for example, for links inside or close to large conurbations, especially the commuter trains in the Ile de France), and marginal infrastructure maintenance costs (for example, for freight, whose heavy axles increase track wear) (Quinet 2002). The growth in total access fee revenues has been advantageous for many railway stakeholders: first, it reduces the need for government subsidies for RFF[6]; second, it puts some pressure on SNCF to lower costs and increase productivity, and finally, though this argument is never made explicitly, it is a means of discouraging the entry of potential competitors to SNCF.

Table 4.5   Evolution of infrastructure fees revenues

	Revenue (€ million)								
	1997	1998	1999	2000	2001	2002	2003	2004	2005
TGV	211	139	616	635	752	897	934	993	1,039
Long-distance passenger trains		126	154	156	154	165	151	198	209
Local trains	85	94	130	134	143	215	224	459	467
Île-de-France trains	430	462	457	472	481	488	506	545	556
Freight	132	150	148	151	155	143	125	225	264
Miscellaneous	34	–	–	–	–	46	38	41	44
Total	892	971	1505	1548	1685	1954	1978	2461	2579

Source: RFF.

The structure of the access fees is summarized in Appendix 1. As in most European countries, the fees are assessed on the basis of the number of ton-kilometres operated. There are four different fees: for access to tracks, path reservation, access to stations and track wear (or circulation). The access and reservation fees vary by track type (high speed versus normal speed), the reservation fee also varies by peak versus off-peak service, and the track wear fee varies between passenger and freight service.

Infrastructure investments by RFF
RFF is responsible for investment in infrastructure improvements but RFF investments must earn a reasonable rate of return, currently set at 8 per cent, or be subsidized by public bodies (the national government, the regions, international organizations). SNCF is responsible for building the improvements, which it subcontracts to civil engineering firms. SNCF also participates in the appraisal of proposed infrastructure investments and may make commitments to operate some services on the new or improved lines to facilitate the acceptance of the project either by the public or investors.

Contracts between the regions and SNCF
As explained earlier, the regional councils now contract with SNCF for all regional train services. The contracts often call for some small infrastructure investments on secondary tracks, which are partly financed by the regions. It is important to note that the funds that the national government transfers to the regions to compensate for their responsibility for regional train services[7] can be used by the regional governments to support other government services instead. In theory (but perhaps not in practice), this will put some pressure on SNCF to control costs since a region can spend its funds on other things if the regional train service is perceived as poor value for money.

National government subsidies to the SNCF and the RFF
The national government provides subsidies to SNCF to compensate for tariff reductions offered for social reasons (for example, to large families or the unemployed) or because of public service obligations (for example, discounts for members of the armed forces and the police). In addition, the government provides payments to compensate for SNCF's unusually high pension costs (since SNCF has a particularly high ratio of retirees to current workers) and to pay off the old debts accumulated in the SAAD account. Finally, occasionally the national government grants SNCF specific subsidies which are classified as increases in equity capital. One example is the plan to revitalize freight described earlier; the government is providing support of 800 million euros a year for three years, and the

European Commission has agreed to this subsidy provided that the plan delivers the results forecast.

The national government provides three forms of financial support for the RFF. The first is the subsidy for track renewals mentioned earlier. Second is a capital increase of around 1 billion euros per year to alleviate the financial burden of the 20 billion euros of debt assumed from SNCF in 1997. This sum is only for the pre-1997 debt; debt on more recent investments should be recovered from SNCF and other train operators through access charges. Finally, the government also makes a contribution to infrastructure charges, designed to cover the gap between the infrastructure fees and the cost of the maintenance contract between RFF and SNCF.

THE RESULTS OF REFORM TO DATE

Assessing the results of the railway reforms is difficult for several reasons. First, so many different reforms have been attempted over the last two decades that it is difficult to disentangle their separate effects. Moreover, some of the most interesting reforms, particularly the separation of RFF from SNCF and the opening of entry for international freight services, are so recent that their full effects will not be apparent for many years. Finally, there is the fundamental difficulty of estimating what the counterfactual is; in other words, how the railways would have performed in the absence of the various reforms.

Nevertheless, it is possible to get a rough sense of the results of the earlier reforms by comparing the basic trends in railway traffic, productivity and finances in France with those in other European countries. But for the most recent reforms, including the restructuring, one can only speculate about the likely effects in qualitative terms.

Trends in Traffic, Productivity and Finances

Traffic

The French railways record in passenger traffic was unimpressive for the first half of the 1990s, but then picked up substantially at the end of that decade and the beginning of the next. During the 1970s and 1980s passenger traffic had grown steadily in France while it stagnated in other major European countries, as shown in Figure 4.3. But for the first half of the 1990s the situation was reversed with French ridership stagnating at about 60 billion passenger kilometres per year while German and British ridership was growing. French ridership began to pick up again in 1996 and reached 72 billion passenger kilometres by 2003.

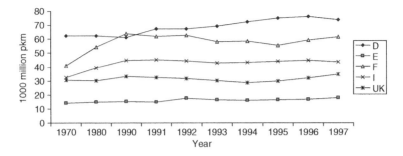

Source: DG TREN statistics.

Figure 4.3   Passenger traffic evolution

Table 4.6   Evolution of passenger traffic

	Billion passenger × km					
	1998	1999	2000	2001	2002	2003
Intercity	47.5	49.1	51.7	52.8	54.3	53.2
TGV	30.0	32.3	34.8	37.4	39.9	39.6
Other intercity	17.5	16.8	16.9	15.4	14.4	13.5
Local services out of Ile de France	7.7	8.0	8.5	8.8	9.2	9.1
Ile-de-France	9.3	9.1	9.7	9.9	10.1	10.0
Total passenger traffic	64.5	66.2	69.9	71.5	73.5	72.3

Source: Commission des comptes de transports de la nation, 2004.

All of the recent ridership growth is on the TGV and the regional train services, as shown in Table 4.6. The TGV gains are due in part to the increase in high-speed tracks (from 1,147 kilometres in 2000 to 1,395 kilometres in 2002). The new yield management introduced by SNCF probably played a role as well. Yield management attempts to increase patronage through carefully differentiated tariffs and has helped keep the load factors on the TGV twice as high as the load factors on other long distance trains (Briard, Rémy and Sauvant, 2001).

The increase in regional train passengers is thought to be a consequence of the regionalization policies (*Conseil Economique et Social*, 2004). It is instructive to compare the six regions that have experimented with regional responsibility for rail since 1997 with the remaining regions which did not assume responsibility until January 2002. In the period of the experiment, patronage increased by 32 per cent in the regions where regional councils were responsible for rail services and only 16 per cent in the regions where they were not. The patronage gains were achieved through a large increase in the supply of train services; it appears that elasticity of demand in response to supply was only 2/3. And many regions complained that SNCF drove hard bargains, forcing the regions to pay more than they thought necessary for added train services. When regional responsibility was first extended to the entire country, the regions collectively received 1.3 billion euros per year in compensation from the national government and added roughly 160 million euros per year of their own funds.[8]

Traffic on non-TGV long-distance trains declined, but only enough to offset about one-third of the gains on the TGV and regional services. The non-TGV decline is partly a statistical artefact as some non-TGV lines were converted to TGV service as the new high-speed lines opened. But the decline also reflects a long-term trend of falling patronage on the more lightly travelled corridors. Many of these lines are not profitable, and some are maintained because of public service obligations or political pressure.

In freight, the French railways seem to have done slightly worse than their other European colleagues, which is to say not well at all. As Figure 4.4 shows, freight traffic declined sharply in the 1980s and has hovered around 50 billion ton-kilometres per year since. With rail traffic stagnating, rail's share of the growing freight market has been declining steadily. This trend is due partly to the poor and declining quality of freight service, reflected in the growing numbers and intensity of shipper complaints and the sharp increase in average train delays, which almost doubled between 1995 and 2000 (CSSPF 2001).

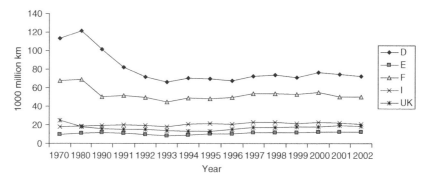

Source: DG TREN statistics.

Figure 4.4   Goods traffic evolution

Productivity

If the recent trends in traffic have been favourable in France, the trends in productivity have not. Friebel, Ivaldi and Vibes (2003) have published one of the few comparative studies of productivity that include data after 1995. They found that the rate of railway productivity growth in France was comparable to or better than the rates in Germany, Sweden, Italy and Spain during the period from 1980 to 1995 but was the lowest of the five countries in the period from 1995 to 2001. Like most of the other productivity studies cited earlier in this chapter, however, Friebel, Ivaldi and Vibes do not adjust for the dramatic changes in the mix of high-speed, normalspeed, and freight traffic in the French railways during the 1980s and 1990s.

Simple productivity analyses that correct for the changing mix of services are shown in Figures 4.5 and 4.6. Three types of output are considered – freight traffic, passenger traffic on ordinary trains, and passenger traffic on high-speed trains – and the different outputs are weighted according to their revenue share in 1995 for SNCF. The inputs considered are rolling stock, infrastructure stock, and labour. Rolling stock and infrastructure inputs are measured according to their investment values and labour by the number of employees. Finally, the rolling stock, infrastructure stock, and employees are weighted according to their share in the total expenses of 1995 for SNCF. The results show that the conclusions of Friebel, Ivaldi and Vibes (2003) are not greatly affected by adjusting for output mix. Total factor productivity (TFP) increased faster on the

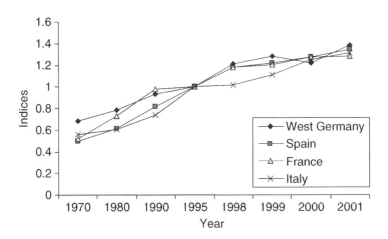

Source: Own calculations from DG-TREN statistics.

Figure 4.5   TFP indices for some large European countries, 1995=100

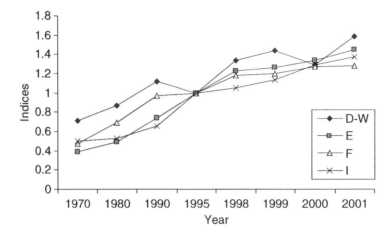

Figure 4.6   Labour productivity evolution, 1995=100

French railways than on other European railways in the 1970s and 1980s but slower in France than elsewhere in the 1990s (Figure 4.5). When only labour productivity is considered the pattern is the same but the gaps between the performance of France and that of its neighbours are larger in both periods (Figure 4.6).

Two factors may have contributed to the recent slowdown in productivity growth. One is the large expansion of regional services without a commensurate increase in passengers and the second is the recent decrease in the maximum working week in France from 39 to 35 hours a week. The railways also continue to suffer from rigid work rules and employment rights, although they may soon gain some relief in this regard. Approximately 40 per cent of the staff is scheduled to retire between 2004 and 2012, which provides an opportunity for an acceleration of cost reductions.

Financial results
Financial trends are difficult to measure, in part because the 1997 restructuring makes it hard to compare financial records before and after. The accounts are also confused by the various and changing subsidies and compensations which are provided by the government. Nevertheless, it is clear that the railway sector continues to lose large sums of money, although whether the losses are higher or lower than before and what effects the reforms have had is hard to say.

The combined current account deficit for the RFF and the SNCF is about 1.5 to 1.7 billion euros per year in recent years. Almost all of the current losses have been concentrated in the RFF, which has been losing about 1.5 billion euros per year, of which about 200 million euros are net operating deficit and the rest is net financial expenses. SNCF experienced a net loss of operating activities of about 150 million euros for 2003 and expects a slight profit in 2004. SNCF's results reflect a combination of the highly profitable TGV services and the unprofitable freight traffic and small passenger lines.

The current account losses come despite many billions of euros in annual subsidies from various levels of government, summarized in the flow of funds diagram shown earlier in Figure 4.2. These include over 2 billion euros that the regions and the Ile de France pay SNCF for regional services, another 2.4 billion that the national government gives SNCF for extra-ordinary pension costs, approximately 1.5 billion the government gives RFF and SAAD to cover old SNCF debts, 675 million it gives RFF for renewals, and 1.3 billion it gives RFF to cover the difference between infrastructure maintenance costs and infrastructure access charges. These various subsidies and grants are partly arbitrary. For instance, the infra-structure maintenance subsidy was initially determined according to eco-nomic calculations (the welfare maximising subsidy to cover the fixed part of maintenance costs taking into account the cost of public funds and the imperfect pricing of competing modes); but it is now determined on an incremental basis, year by year, through negotiations between RFF and the government.

Total debt of the railway system rose from 35 to 41 billion euros between 1997 and 2003 (of which 25 billion euros were obligations of RFF, 7 billion were of SNCF and 8 billion of SAAD). Calculations suggest that about half of the increase is due to new infrastructure investments and half to the current account deficits of RFF and SNCF. Financial simulations show that even if current deficits are eliminated, the debt of the railway sector will increase by about 10 billion euros by 2030 due to future programmed infrastructure investments (see Figure 4.5).

The Effects of the Reforms that don't Involve Restructuring

The trends in traffic, productivity, and finances suggest that TGV has been a clear success, at least so far. The TGV network has induced such a large increase in traffic that half of the railways passenger traffic is now carried on TGV services. The TGV has also generated substantial profits for the sector, covering both capital and operating costs, at least on the initial lines. The danger is that the most profitable TGV lines have already been built and that the future ones will be less profitable; for these reasons, it is both desirable and probable that the building rhythm should slow down. This service has reached its maturity.

Regionalization appears to be a mixed success. On the positive side it has encouraged improved services, well suited to local needs as discerned by the regional councils and presumably profitable to SNCF as well. On the negative side the service expansion has been achieved at a rather high cost. In addition, frequency has increased more than the traffic and has contributed to increased congestion on the tracks around large urban areas, resulting in delays for other services (especially freight).

Freight has been a long-standing disappointment, which has not yielded to the many small reforms tried in the past. The programme adopted in 2003 is more radical than anything tried before, and it is too early to assess its effects. But even if the reform is a success, it will decrease the railway's share of freight traffic even as it cuts the railway's freight costs.

Arguably the most worrisome finding is that these reforms seem to have done little to reduce the slowdown in productivity growth in the railways. The one bright spot is that the coming round of retirements may be enough to cover the decrease in activity in freight and to allow for a reasonable productivity increase for the whole firm.

The Likely Effects of Restructuring

Competition
The main purpose of restructuring, at least from the perspective of the European Commission, is to improve service by introducing competition, or the threat of competition, among train operators. It is clear that many French railway officials do not share this goal, particularly, but not only, at SNCF. Apart from more fundamental or ideological objections, they may believe, with some justification, that the TGV already faces enough competition from the airlines and the automobile while the freight trains are locked in a similar battle with the trucks.

In some respects the prospects for competition appear dim. As of 2005, no independent train operator had challenged the SNCF, and in France, perhaps more than in other countries, a potential competitor faces many obstacles: licences, path allocation procedures, technical capability requirements for staff, technical standards. The small size and limited expertise of the RFF also implies that SNCF will retain some power over the timetables of its future competitors. If competition occurs, moreover, SNCF may be shielded from its full effects through the complex and untransparent system of subsidies RFF and SNCF now enjoy or some other form of government intervention.

Nevertheless, there are some market segments where entry seems likely. Ironically the TGV is probably the service least likely to see entry, even though it is the SNCF's most profitable service. A new entrant to the TGV market would have to make huge and partly sunk investments; it would be hard to improve the quality of service, which is already good; the entrant's costs are unlikely to be lower (since the main costs are for capital, and a private investor would have a higher cost of capital than the interest rate paid on bonds issued by SNCF, and suffer entry and exit costs as well); and, at least at the beginning, the entrant would probably get bad paths. In short, entry to the TGV market is improbable, except perhaps on some fringe or niche service.

Entry is also unlikely in the services which SNCF now finds very unprofitable, such as conventional long-distance passenger trains on lightly travelled routes or freight that does not move in unit trains. A new entrant may be able to provide such services for less cost than SNCF, perhaps sufficiently less to make them profitable. But these services don't represent a large part of SCNF's present market and don't contribute to its profits.

SNCF seems most vulnerable to entry in two services: unit freight trains and regional passenger trains. In the unit freight trains, an entrant certainly could provide better quality service at a lower cost than SNCF, especially if the current programme of freight reforms underway at SNCF fails. It is quite possible that big shippers (steel industry, cement and chemistry companies) will enter the market, at least for their own needs. Such an entry would put pressure on SNCF profits in this lucrative market.

Regional passenger trains are arguably an even greater source of SNCF vulnerability. European regulations do not require competition in local or regional passenger services yet, but competition for subsidized services is likely to become compulsory within a few years, probably in the form of competitively bid service contracts. Furthermore, the regions will almost certainly advocate for competition given their frustrations with SNCF. New entrants probably could offer similar quality service at lower cost and capture some of the regions from SNCF. The effects on SNCF profits might be disastrous given the company's high fixed costs and limited flexibility.

Management improvement

In France there is both a strong fear that vertical restructuring will complicate railway management by making it harder to coordinate infrastructure and train operations and a great hope that restructuring will improve management by developing, in RFF, an independent source of railway expertise that could question or check the decisions of SNCF.

Whether restructuring is proving good or bad for the quality of management decisions is very hard to tell so far. The heads of RFF and SNCF have engaged in some very public disputes which suggests that there is contestation, although whether it is productive or not is another matter.[9] Nevertheless, the disputes take place mainly at the higher level, while at the operational level the coordination between services and infrastructure remains good as both are still provided by the same firm, SNCF. The establishment of RFF as a planning and oversight rather than an operating agency may avoid some of the disadvantages of fragmentation.

The relationship between RFF and SNCF is still marked by asymmetric information, although RFF seems to be gradually developing expertise. The maintenance contract is still uncomfortably vague, although RFF is beginning to insert more few specific targets and incentives to try to hold SNCF accountable and improve performance.

Two points exemplify both the change and its difficulty. The first is related to the timetable policy. The SNCF has traditionally been opposed to timetables which repeat regularly. In most of the rest of Europe, by contrast, the train schedules repeat every hour or two so that, for example, there is a train departing from A to B at 7:10 am, at 8:10 am, again at 9:10 am and so on through the day. Under pressure from RFF, SNCF is revising its policy. Whether regular timetables are good or not, the issue probably would not have been addressed in the previous organization.

Another concern is the declining quality of the infrastructure as reflected in the recent reduction in the maximum speeds on many segments of track because of safety concerns. Many experts think that renewal investments, which are not included in the maintenance contract but financed separately through a special subsidy from the national government to RFF, are too low and that track possession for maintenance is badly managed. To its credit, RFF has helped to put these problems on the industry's agenda and a government investigation is underway.

Nevertheless the separate treatment of maintenance and renewals probably does lead to sub-optimization which might be avoided if RFF had more freedom to switch funds from one use to the other. In this respect the fault is not with fragmentation *per se*, but rather with the peculiar constraints that the national government imposes on RFF management. But it is also clear that the senior government officials who decide on budgetary matters are less well informed than the railway operators, and thus may not allocate government subsidies wisely between RFF (infrastructure) and SNCF (operations). In the effort to recapture freight traffic, for example, would it be better to invest in new rolling stock or in improved marshalling yards or other infrastructure? Senior officials in the Ministry of Finance or the Ministry of Transport are not in the best position to decide such issues.

Challenges of restructuring

Although it is hard to evaluate the restructuring at this early date, two challenges or complications seem fundamental. The first of these is the continuing and intense involvement of national government officials in railway matters. Many of the subsidies that the national government provides are still largely discretionary, which introduces uncertainties and complications in management planning and decision-making. The government subsidies are also typically dedicated to specific purposes, which limits management flexibility. This limitation is a more serious problem for RFF than for SNCF, since SNCF has more opportunities to cross-subsidize activities through accounting games. The dependence of RFF and SNCF on national government decisions makes the two firms sensitive to political pressures. SNCF feels compelled to maintain unprofitable services while the RFF feels obliged to build unprofitable lines and facilities[10].

The second challenge involves the constraints imposed by railway labour. Work-rules and other conditions of employment are extremely restrictive, as mentioned earlier, and these conditions are defended fiercely by trade unions that have strong vested interests and a long history of opposing any changes that reduce their members' advantages. It seems unlikely that restructuring will provide a means of relaxing the labour constraints on the industry, which is a key issue.

CONCLUSION

Perhaps more than other European countries, France has historically organized its railways on the model of an integrated government monopoly dedicated to the broad goals of public service. It is therefore not surprising that many of the reforms initiated by France in the 1980s and 1990s were measures designed to improve the performance of the railways without altering their fundamental institutional character. The most famous reform was the building of the TGV network which opened in 1981 and has expanded steadily since. But other changes took place: regionalization, cooperation with neighbouring railway companies in running international trains, and several successive reforms of freight services.

Given its legacy, France was understandably reluctant to yield to the European directives to restructure its railways and open them to competition. The main response was to establish RFF in 1997 as a small public infrastructure firm independent from SNCF but required to outsource infrastructure maintenance to SNCF. The aim of this unusual reorganization was to conform to the European directives and create some kind of external counterweight to SNCF while avoiding the radical fragmentation of infrastructure and services which the unions opposed and many French railway specialists feared would lead to technical problems. The result is a complex system of financial and contractual relationships between the main actors in the railway system: the national government, regions, SNCF and RFF.

What were the results of these many changes? At the end of the 1990s passenger traffic picked up, probably as the result of the TGV and regionalization strategies. Freight traffic continued to stagnate and productivity growth slowed, however, both troubling developments. Also, partly as a consequence of the productivity slowdown, the railway system as a whole was still running sizable deficits, receiving substantial public subsidies from public authorities and accumulating large debts.

The restructuring of the railways is so recent that one can only speculate as to the likely effects. So far, RFF has not provided an effective counterweight to SNCF. The conflicts between RFF and SNCF have led to high transaction costs without any clear improvement of infrastructure management. Nevertheless, there are some optimistic developments, particularly in improved management of the timetable and a more thoughtful renewals policy. So far, no competitor to SNCF has emerged, although it will happen sooner or later. The SNCF is most vulnerable in unit freight trains and regional passenger services, and the European Commission is likely to require competition in regional passenger services soon. Even if new entrants do not capture a large market share, the effects may be devastating for SNCF because the firm is so inflexible in the short and medium run that a sharp decrease in activity could not be matched by a decrease in costs.

These threats mean that the French railways, and particularly SNCF, will be engaged in a race to improve productivity for the next decade. Will SNCF be able to improve its efficiency fast enough so that it does not suffer greatly from the forthcoming competition? In this race, the system has one advantage – the expertise provided by RFF will be increasing – and the chance that the favourable age structure will lead to the retirement of a significant part of the SNCF staff. But it will have to face two drawbacks: intrusive government involvement and the power and rigidity of the labour force.

NOTES

1. Most studies make comparisons between the western European countries for periods of about 20 years from the 1970s to the 1990s. For instance, Pestieau and Tulkens (1990) use both deterministic parametric methods (with translog form) and non-parametric methods; Cantos, Pastor and Serrano (1999) use a non-parametric approach to build Malmquist indexes; Oum and Yu (1994) use a DEA (Data Envelopment Analysis) procedure; Chane Kune, Mulder and Poudevigne (2000) estimate TFP indices for Germany, France, the UK and the USA; Coelli and Perelman (1999) use both DEA and parametric methods.
2. The subsidies came from the State, the French regions (France is divided in 22 regions), the European Union and the European Investment Bank.
3. According to the text, the CSSPF '*veille au développement et à l'évolution équilibrée du secteur ferroviaire, à l'unicité du service public ferroviaire, à la cohérence dans la mise en œuvre de ces orientations par les deux établissements publics RFF et SNCF ainsi qu'au respect des missions de service public de ces deux établissements*'.

4. The figure includes SNCF and SAAD debt; see note 6.
5. SAAD (*Service Annexe d'Amortissement de la Dette*) is a special account created in 1991 to support 38 billion Francs (5.8 billion Euro) of loans of SNCF, which corresponded to the cumulated deficits of the firm to date. A total of €10.7 billion has been transferred to the SAAD: €5.8 billion on creation on 1 January 1991, plus about €5 billion on 1 January 1997. SAAD resources consist of an annual contribution from the French State of €677 million, paid in equal quarterly instalments and an annual payment by the parent company of €18 million, paid mid-year. The excess of the French State contribution over net annual expenses is capitalised in the SAAD. The role of this account is to isolate that part of SNCF debt in respect of which interest and capital payments are essentially made by the French State. The goal was to wipe off the deficit and to restore the accounting situation of the firm. This procedure can be justified by the 91/440 directive which stipulates (Art. 9) that a specific account can be created for debt amortizing, the liability of which is composed of loans covering the deficits of the firm. The SAAD is run by SNCF, but has no staff nor any decision-making power.
6. Let us note that, as the subsidies given by the State to the *Régions* are lump-sum funds (indexed by the price index), the increases in infrastructure charges do not induce increases in transfers from the State to the *Régions*.
7. They were equal to the expenditure of the State on these services (compensation of public service obligations).
8. These figures exclude the Ile de France. To cover the deficit of these services, they are considered as public service obligation and are priced at about one-third of their cost.
9. The Ministry of Transport has recently summoned the two firms to make their disputes less visible, for instance not to dispute through interviews in papers or through the media. Let us note that the dispute lies at the upper level. Strangely, at the operational level, the coordination between infrastructure and services is good, as both kinds of services are in the same structure.
10. RFF should be constrained by budget balance but both uncertainty of project appraisal and political pressure make the constraint 'soft'.

REFERENCES

Assemblée Nationale (2004), *Rapport d'information sur la clarification des relations financières entre le système ferroviaire et ses partenaires publics*, 8 July 2004, H. Mariton, Journaux Officiel, Paris.

Briard, K., Rémy, A., and Sauvant, A., (2001), 'Analyse des rendements d'échelle et de l'évolution de la productivité de la SNCF par une approche désagrégée', *Notes de synthèse du SES*, ministère de l'équipement, Paris, April–May.

Cantos, P., Pastor, J., and Serrano, L., (1999), 'Productivity, Efficiency and Technical Change in the European Railways: A Non-parametric Approach', *Transportation*, **26**(4), 337–57.

Chane Kune, B., Mulder, N., and Poudevigne, P., (2000), 'Une approche de la productivité du transport ferroviaire à travers notamment l'analyse des services du capital', *Notes de synthèse du SES*, ministère de l'équipement, Paris, May–June.

Coelli, T., and Perelman, S., (1999), 'Theory and Methodology: A Comparison of Parametric and Non-parametric Distance Functions: With Application to European Railways', *European Journal of Operational Research*, **117**, 326–339.

Commission des Comptes de Transport De La Nation (2004), *Rapport Annuel pour 2003*, Ministère des transports, Paris.

Conseil Economique et Social (2004), *Premier bilan de la régionalisation ferroviaire*, 14–15 April 2004.

Conseil Supérieur du Service Public Ferroviaire (2001), *Évaluation de la réforme ferroviaire*, Paris.

European Conference of Ministers of Transport (1998), *Rail Restructuring in Europe*, OECD publications, Paris.

Friebel, G., Ivaldi, M., and Vibes, C., (2003), *Railway (De) regulation: A European Efficiency Comparison*, IDEI Report no. 3 on Passenger Rail Transport, University of Toulouse.

Henry, C., and Quinet, E., (1998), 'Which Railways Policy and Organisation for France?' *Journal of Transport Economics and Policy*, **33**(I), 119–26.

Oum, T., and Yu, C., (1994), 'Economic Efficiency of Railways and Implications for Public Policy. A Comparative Study of the OECD Countries' Railways', *Journal of Transport Economics and Policy*, **28**, 121–38.

Pestieau, P., and Tulkens, H., (1990), *Assessing the Performance of Public Sector Activities:Some Recent Evidence from the Productivity Efficiency Viewpoint*, Nov 1990, Programme d'actions de recherches concertées No. 87–92/106 with CORE and No. 90–94/141 with Université de Liège, University of Liège.

Quinet, E., (2002), *Détermination des coûts marginaux sociaux du rail*, Report for SNCF.

APPENDIX

Annex 1 Infrastructure Charges in France

Infrastructure charges are fixed by an *arrêté* dated 29/12/2003 and signed by the Ministry of Transport. They are composed of several terms:

- An access term.
- A reservation term:
  - for circulation
  - for stops in stations.
- A circulation term.

These terms are differentiated according to the links and according to the hour. The categories of links are as follows:

Category	A+	A−	C	C+	D	D+	E
Type of link	Suburban links		Interurban trunk lines				Other interurban lines
Level of traffic	High	Low	High	High	Medium	Medium	
Speed			<220 km/h	>220 km/h	<200 km/h	>200 km/h	
Total length in km	286.6	984.5	6804.1	404.5	5704.6	95.2	12 699.6

Category	N1	N2	N3	N2*	N3*	Total
Type of link	High-speed tracks					
Level of traffic	High	Medium	Med. Medium	Low	Med. Low	
Speed						
Total length in km	718.2	332.2	194.7	124.3	126.6	28 475.1

Time differentiation is made according to the following definitions:

- Peak hours: from 6 h 30 to 9 h and from 17 h to 20 h:
- Normal hours: from 4 h 30 to 6 h 30, and from 9 h to 17 h and from 20 h to 0 h 30:
- Off-peak hours: from 0 h 30 to 4 h 30.

The unitary prices corresponding to each category are as follows for year 2004:

Price in euro per train × km

		Category										
	A	B	C	C*	D	D*	E	N1	N2	N2*	N3	N3*
Access term	365.9	365.9	3.05	3.05	0.00	0.00	0.00	5295	5295	3384	5295	3384
Reservation term off peak hours	1.52	0.61	0.00	0.00	0.00	0.00	0.00	4.57	1.07	1.07	0.76	0.76
medium hours	4.88	1.22	0.08	0.08	0.00	0.00	0.00	9.30	2.29	2.29	1.60	1.60
peak hours	14.03	2.44	0.08	0.08	0.00	0.00	0.00	10.98	4.57	4.57	3.05	3.05
Coefficient for freight							0.60					
Access to the stations	29.88	0.00	0.00	0.00	0.00	0.00	0.00	0.00	0.00	0.00	0.00	0.00
Ciculation term							0.79					
Circulation term for freight							0.23					

5. Spain: The end of an era

Javier Campos

INTRODUCTION

The inauguration in 1848 of the first railroad service in mainland Spain[1] was widely heralded as a 'clear means of progress, aimed at bringing prosperity to industrialists and peasants alike, by shortening the travel distances among the cities and the regions'. Supporters hoped that the railroad would accelerate Spain's delayed industrialization and become the instrument, some day in the future, for uniting a country with a beautiful but difficult topography.

Once the initial network design was completed and the basic infrastructure deployed (mostly, by foreign private capital), Spain adopted the same 'rail model' as its European neighbors. This model was characterized by the existence of a vertically integrated government-owned monopoly, whose management relied upon social objectives, rather than on commercial ones. RENFE (*Red Nacional de Ferrocarriles*) was born in 1941 to rescue the existing private operators from the ashes of the Spanish Civil War (1936–1939) and remained the uncontested provider of rail services for over 60 years.

As in many other European countries, the model was progressively reformed during the second half of the 20th century. Rail dominated transport in Spain until the 1960s, when competition from other modes started to sharply erode its position. Figure 5.1 shows that about 60 percent of domestic passengers and 35 percent of freight traveled by train in 1950. By 2002, the rail's share had declined to 5.1 percent of passengers and 3.1 percent for freight. Rail passenger traffic continued to grow in absolute terms, but passenger travel by other modes grew even faster. Rail freight traffic failed to grow much even in absolute terms after 1980.

These traffic trends are common to other countries with the same rail model. They can be explained not only by the development of alternative modes of transport, but also by the inability of the railways to adapt to the evolving economic conditions (Campos and Cantos, 2000). For this reason, since the early 1990s, the European Union has pursued an active reform of its rail policy. As in other industries, the change has been aimed at modernizing the sector through the introduction of competition, so as to

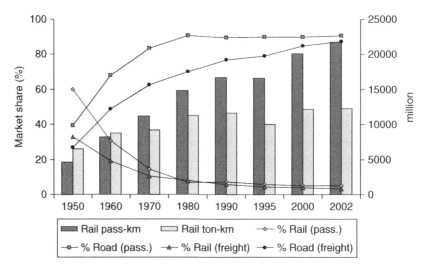

Source: INE (National Institute for Statistics, www.ine.es).

Figure 5.1   The decline of Spanish railways vs. the roads

guarantee the future of the industry by stopping its steady loss of market share and the growing financial deficits of national operators.

As we will see, Spain was at first reluctant to radically change its approach, and chose instead incremental reforms with little, mostly nominal, changes in its rail model. However, RENFE's performance during the 1990s finally convinced the government that a more radical reform – getting rid of the monopoly and opening the tracks to real competition – was needed. This has been finally accepted in the 2003 Rail Sector Law, which went into effect in January 2005. Although it is too early to evaluate the effectiveness of the changes, it is definitely a 'new model', and many observers, economists, 'industrialists and peasants alike', are anxiously awaiting the results.

A BRIEF HISTORY

The early development of the rail industry in Spain was strongly affected by the political turmoil and the uneven economic growth that the country experienced between 1850 and 1940. The benefits of the industrial revolution arrived late and were mostly concentrated in a few areas of the Basque Country, Catalonia and Madrid. The rest of the country remained rural, poor and isolated from the main cities.

In this context, railroads were regarded as an integrating infrastructure, and were soon declared a 'public service of national interest' (1855 General Railroad Law). However, lacking enough public funding and political support to develop the new industry, the law relied on promising financial incentives to foreign investors. As a result, large amounts of capital were attracted into the country, and French-owned private companies, such as MZA (Madrid–Zaragoza–Alicante) and Perèire, dominated the sector initially.

The infrastructure expanded at a very fast pace. By 1860 there were almost 500 kilometers of tracks and more than 25 stations. By 1870 the sector had become an attractive business opportunity for local entrepreneurs as well as foreigners, and government passed a new railways law that encouraged the award of a large number of concessions to build new infrastructure and operate freight and passenger services. In 1877 (after a new government, and yet another new rail law), railway companies extended their networks to other corridors in the north and east of the country and, just before 1900, the figure of 10,000 kilometers of tracks had been reached. By this time, many European railroads had also developed international services that crossed national borders. For political and geographical reasons, however, most of the Spanish network had been built with the so-called Iberian gauge (1.666 meters), instead of the standard European gauge (1.435 meters). This isolated the markets from France (trains had to be switched) and limited further expansion possibilities.

The Birth of RENFE

The financial performance of many rail companies started to deteriorate after World War I. The increase in coal prices and the social and political turbulence that later grew into the civil war reduced traffic. In 1939, just when the companies were on the brink of extinction and the infrastructure was severely damaged, the new government decided to rescue the industry by radically changing its rail model. RENFE was born in 1941 to absorb most of the existing private companies into a centralized and vertically integrated body, directly controlled by the Ministry of Transport. A few companies that operated narrow gauge services, mostly in industrial regions of the north, remained in private hands until 1965 when they were absorbed into another state owned railway company, FEVE.

A new legal framework passed in 1947 explicitly defined the railways as the country's main transport mode, with road being given a secondary role. The monopolistic nature of RENFE, the only long-distance operator, was reinforced by a legal barrier to entry which severely restricted intermodal competition, both in passenger and freight markets, and especially in those corridors already served by the railways. The government also imposed a special tax on truckers (aptly named the *canon de coincidencia*), which increased with truck size and was used to finance the railways.

These policies did not prevent the spectacular growth of road traffic during the 1950s and 1960s (see Figure 5.1), since highway modes were often cheaper, more flexible and more convenient for many users. Until 1971, it was relatively easy to get the permissions needed to establish a small trucking company, and the sector grew exponentially largely through small (driver-owned) companies. Restrictions on trucking were tightened significantly in 1971, with the support of both the trucking associations and the railways, who argued that there was too much 'wasteful competition', because trucking was plagued with low demand and excess capacity. The legislation passed restricted entry in road freight markets, distorting the operators' choice of truck size and the optimal dimension of the industry. It was not enough, though, to reverse the decline of the rail sector, which soon spread to passenger markets with the rapid growth of private car ownership beginning in the 1970s.[2]

The Reforms of the 1980s

It was not until 1984 when a new effort to change the situation of the Spanish railways was made. The government and RENFE signed their first management contract (*Primer Contrato-Programa: 1984–1986*) with the aim of stopping the financial decline of the company by improving its quality, reducing overmanning and closing down some unprofitable lines. The contract was the first attempt ever to deal with the excess capacity and inefficiency problems of the sector and its results were promising: 6.4 percent of the total network was closed down, the workforce was reduced by 28 percent and productivity rose substantially in just two years. Demand remained constant during this period, even though fares were increased with the retail price index (except in 1986, the year which saw the introduction of VAT, when fares rose twice as much as the price index). The company's financial position did not improve as much as hoped, however, so the government decided that new measures had to be implemented.

Another round of reform was introduced in 1987 through the Surface Transport Law (*Ley de Ordenación del Transporte Terrestre*, or LOTT). The LOTT revoked the modal preference for rail transport and promoted instead competition among all modes. For the first time in 40 years, private investors were allowed to build and operate new rail lines (although none did). RENFE was transformed into an autonomous public company, among whose new explicit objectives was the achievement of financial balance.

The LOTT was accompanied by the Rail Transport Plan (*Plan de Transporte Ferroviario*, or PTF), which defined new guidelines for railway transport policy. That same year a second management contract was also signed (*Segundo Contrato-Programa: 1988–1991*), this time including a more specific investment plan, new financing mechanisms, policies for pricing and service levels, and a novel public control system designed to evaluate the results of the PTFs based on an ex-post analysis of performance indicators and a detailed auditing of the investment projects.

Although the policy guidelines of the PTF were not fully implemented at the time, they anticipated many of the principles of the European rail policy in the 1990s. Among others, the guidelines recommended that:

1. Rail infrastructure and services should be responsive to demand, with the introduction of new technologies to improve quality and competitiveness whenever possible.
2. Rail planning and management should be based upon economic targets, introducing financial constraints when necessary, and pursuing, as the ultimate goal, the efficient allocation of resources.
3. Rail services should operate in competition with other transport modes, some of which (such as air transport) were also beginning to be deregulated. In general, prices should cover costs in passenger as well as freight services. If prices were set below costs because of public service obligations (PSO), the company should be compensated.

In 1989, again anticipating some of the changes that other railways would make later, RENFE was reorganized into decentralized management units (*Unidades de Gestión Descentralizada*, or UGD) based upon lines of business rather than geographic territory. The UGDs were grouped into three categories: transport operators (both passenger and freight), service suppliers (such as rolling stock maintenance), and infrastructure (both maintenance and operations). The objective was to induce more commercial behavior since each UGD would operate independently, using transfer prices to charge for services rendered to other UGDs. The hope was that the commercial incentives would encourage efficiency and reduce the need for financial support from the government.

The third management contract (*Tercer Contrato-Programa: 1994–1998*) was designed specifically to support this new strategy by defining detailed financial objectives to be achieved by each UGD. Within the transport operators, the business units for regional services and suburban commuter services were awarded the condition of 'public service', thus deserving sub-sidies to compensate their deficits. Suburban commuter services were granted a subsidy per passenger-kilometer to reflect the reductions in traffic congestion and pollution they achieved. Regional services got a lump sum transfer to compensate for unexpected losses.

The Consequences of the EC Directive 1991/440

In 1991 the European Commission called for fundamental railway reforms based on the experiences of a number of countries (notably Sweden and New Zealand) that had already reformed their industries during the 1980s. The cornerstone of the reform was in EC Directive 1991/440, which set out the objective of unbundling infrastructure from operations by either full separation or, at least, the creation of different organizations and accounts within one holding company in order to increase transparency and make competition easier. Other objectives of the directive were 'to create inde-pendent regulatory institutions for railways', 'to devise a system of infra-structure charges' and 'to open access to national railway markets for competitors'.[3]

Spain responded to the EC directive in 1994, by transforming RENFE's UGDs into proper business units with separate accounts and objectives. Rail services were divided into six major business units: long distance, regional, suburban, AVE (short for *alta velocidad*, or high speed), general freight and intermodal containers. Infrastructure and rolling stock activ-ities were also grouped into several specialized business units, including sta-tions, maintenance, repairs, signaling and computing services. The 1994 statute also increased the internal autonomy of the business units, and the nominal independence of the company from the government. RENFE was allowed commercial freedom in setting fares, for example, although price increases had to be approved by the Ministry of Transport (later, the Ministry of Development).

In 1997, responding again to EC Directive 91/440, the government created the Rail Infrastructure Manager (*Gestor de Infrastructuras Ferroviarias*, GIF), a public body in charge of building and maintaining all new rail infrastructure. The GIF was also responsible for managing the existing infrastructure (tracks, stations, depots and land nearby) and the signaling systems. Its services were financed through track access fees paid by the rail operators, allowing a formal accounting separation of the GIF and RENFE balance sheets in compliance with EC regulations.

A final *contrato-programa* was put in place between 1999 and 2000, designed to consolidate the unbundling model while simultaneously pro-viding RENFE with enough funding to finance the acquisition of the expensive rolling stock for the AVE business unit. The contract was not renewed, however, because company managers and government officials generally agreed that 'regulation by management contract system' had achieved all it could. Additional changes would wait for the passage of a new sector law, a step finally taken in 2003.

EVALUATING THE REFORMS

Over two decades, RENFE had gradually evolved from a centralized and vertically integrated government agency into a firm which, although still state-owned, had been decentralized into business units operating with commercial criteria. Table 5.1 shows that, since 1980, the company has made a considerable effort to reduce capacity by closing unprofitable lines and reducing excess staff. Between 1980 and 2002, RENFE more than halved its staff and closed down above 2,000 kilometers of lines, some of which were transferred to regional governments or to small private companies operating specialized freight services or tourist routes.[4] At the same time, huge amounts of capital were invested in the high-speed passenger services, and the rolling stock was modernized through the acquisition of new locomotives and passenger cars.

RENFE continues to dominate the provision of rail services in Spain despite the possibility, first opened by the LOTT in 1987, of new entry into the rail business. In 2002 it enjoyed a market share of 92 percent of the total passenger-kilometers traveled by train that year with four regional public companies accounting for 7 percent,[5] while the remaining share mostly corresponded to FEVE. In freight, RENFE maintained a share of 95 percent of total ton-kilometers, with FEVE holding a stable 4 percent over the same period. This unchallenged position was reflected in the company's operating and financial performance.

Table 5.1   Evolution of RENFE's infrastructure and fleet

	1980	1985	1990	1995	2000	2002
Network length (km)	15 724	14 804	14 539	14 291	14 251	13 970
Locomotives	1860	2108	2072	2096	1693	1664
Wagons and freight cars	41 007	42 032	37 235	27 863	28 397	26 931
Employees	72 931	74 957	55 551	44 277	32 584	31 422

Source: RENFE (www.renfe.es).

Operating Performance

Between 1990 and 2003, RENFE's passenger traffic increased at an average annual rate of 1.8 percent, while freight grew at an average rate of 1 percent, as shown in Table 5.2. In contrast, Spain's GDP and population grew by 4.6 and 3.4 percent per year during the same period, respectively.

The aggregate traffic trends hide differences among business units. Among passenger services, the AVE and the suburban and regional services experienced notable increases in traffic thanks partly to increases in quality, growing urban highway congestion, and the introduction of specialized services such as the *Talgo* and *Intercity* trains). Traditional (non-high speed) long-distance services, by contrast, have lost much of their appeal among customers, who now prefer air travel for distances above 300 to 400 kilometers. This shift to faster passenger services is common to countries with growing per capita incomes, and is mostly unrelated to the economic competitiveness of the railroad. Among freight service, intermodal containers have grown rapidly since 1965 but general cargo has stagnated in the face of aggressive competition by trucks and the inability of rail services to match the flexibility or, in some cases, the geographic coverage of its highway competitors.[6]

Table 5.3 shows trends in productivity and quality of services in RENFE's business units. The load factor measures the extent to which supply has adapted to demand. Passenger load factors have remained relatively low (around 35 percent) in both suburban and regional services, which

Table 5.2   RENFE's traffic evolution by business units (1990–2003)

	1990	1995	2000	2001	2002	2003	Average change
Long distance	8.455	8.405	7.033	6.986	6.949	6.627	−1.48%
Suburban	4.595	6.132	7.114	7.556	7.775	8.031	3.53%
Regional	2.426	2.074	2.482	2.572	2.575	2.624	2.12%
AVE	–	1.294	1.942	2.077	2.181	2.027	2.69%
Total passenger traffic	15.476	17.905	18.571	19.191	19.480	19.309	1.79%
General cargo	7.745	6.709	7.260	7.397	7.369	7.392	−0.02%
Combined transport	2.473	3.095	4.360	4.352	4.291	4.473	5.05%
Total freight traffic	10.218	9.804	11.620	11.749	11.660	11.865	1.01%

Source: RENFE (www.renfe.es). Data represent billions of passenger-kilometers and ton-kilometers.

Table 5.3   RENFE's performance by business unit (1990–2003)

	1990	1995	2000	2001	2002	2003
Long distance						
Load factor (%)	–	65.5	67.6	68.8	69.6	66.8
Pass-km per employee ('000)	2976.1	3006.7	3060.5	3357.0	3511.4	3458.8
% Punctuality (<10 min)	–	–	95.5	95.7	94.8	90.4
Suburban services						
Load factor (%)	–	35.1	37.4	37.3	37.3	37.8
Pass-km per employee ('000)	1567.3	1773.7	1836.3	1897.5	1983.9	2012.8
% Punctuality (<10 min)	–	–	99.1	98.9	98.8	98.4
Regional services						
Load factor (%)	–	33.7	35.6	35.9	35.5	35.3
Pass-km per employee ('000)	1345.8	1658.7	1733.2	1755.6	1696.3	1649.3
% Punctuality (<10 min)	–	–	96.9	96.8	96.8	94.8
High speed (AVE)						
Load factor (%)	–	–	64.0	64.1	66.2	63.5
Pass-km per employee ('000)	–	7618.5	7139.7	7471.2	6990.4	5774.9
% Punctuality (<10 min)	–	–	98.5	98.2	99.9	99.9
General cargo						
Load factor (%)	–	35.2	35.8	36.3	36.7	37.0
Ton-km per employee ('000)	987.0	1457.9	1915.6	1813.9	1905.6	2018.0
Combined transport						
Load factor (%)	–	46.2	41.4	40.8	40.3	40.9
Ton-km per employee ('000)	1250.7	1550.5	2658.5	2462.9	2531.6	2822.1

Source: RENFE (www.renfe.es) and UIC estimates (www.uic.asso.fr) for 1990.

are affected by public service obligations. For these business units the government sets (and compensates the company for) the minimum level of service to be provided according to social criteria, which yields a generalized excess capacity. But load factors have remained high in long-distance services (where RENFE has reduced capacity in recent years) and in the

AVE high speed business, which is the most profitable and attractive of RENFE's operating units. Neither of these is subject to PSO compensations. The load factors for the two freight business units have remained low, suggesting chronic excess capacity.

RENFE's record on labor productivity is also mixed, as shown in Table 5.3. In the last five years, the number of passenger-kilometers per employee has increased by 15 percent in long-distance service (mostly due to staff reductions) and by 13 percent in suburban services (due to traffic increases). Labor productivity has stagnated in the remaining passenger business units, but has almost tripled in freight largely because of staff reductions rather than output increases.[7]

The primary measure of service quality reported by RENFE is the percentage of trains departing and arriving within ten minutes of the scheduled timetable. By this measure RENFE performs very well, with over 95 percent of passenger services on time. Performance is even better in the case of AVE, due to a highly advertised 'punctuality commitment', used by the company to successfully attract time-conscious customers and steal market share from the airlines.

Overall Financial Performance

One of the primary goals of the three management contracts signed between RENFE and the government during the 1980s and 1990s was to clarify and make more transparent the financing of the different rail activities. Both EC Directive 1991/440 and Spain's 1994 railway law also require a clear reporting of the company's finances, including not only the subsidies received for public service obligations but the operating deficit when commercial revenues are insufficient to cover operating costs.

Table 5.4 shows that RENFE's aggregate financial performance improved substantially from 1980 to 2003. Commercial revenues have never covered costs, but the sum of the PSO subsidies and the operating deficit has fallen from 5.6 billion euros in 1980 to 1.3 billion euros in 2003 (measured in constant 2003 euros). In 1980 commercial revenues represented only 34 percent of total revenues, whereas in 2003 the figure had reached 56 percent.

The improvement is due in large part to considerable efforts to implement cost-reducing strategies such as adjusting capacity to demand whenever possible and reducing staff through incentives for early retirement. Operating costs have been cut substantially in real terms, although the rigid cost structure of the company (where labor's share of costs has remained at 40 percent since 1980) makes it difficult to achieve larger cost savings in the near future.

Although RENFE's performance has improved, the figures in Table 5.4 exaggerate the gains in two respects. First, the company's debt is backed by

Table 5.4   RENFE's aggregate financial results (1980–2003)

	1980	1985	1990	1995	2000	2001	2002	2003
Revenues	5541.3	4100.9	3543.3	3442.4	3024.4	3084.6	3025.8	3019.1
Commercial	1900.2	1851.4	1750.5	1567.8	1730.0	1810.3	1793.2	1700.7
PSO subsidies	3641.1	2249.5	1792.8	1874.6	1294.2	1274.2	1232.6	1318.4
Costs	7537.4	4767.8	3781.4	3937.0	3187.0	3199.2	3121.8	3003.3
Labor	2562.6	2042.9	1643.2	1302.9	1170.5	1178.3	1139.2	1178.6
Energy	376.7	303.8	254.1	191.0	162.7	164.4	157.9	158.8
Other inputs	1582.8	1151.6	845.3	812.7	751.0	787.9	844.7	816.7
Depreciation	1206.1	339.5	413.6	604.6	559.7	541.1	541.2	480.3
Interests	1733.6	930.5	625.3	941.6	475.7	459.6	375.8	289.1
Other costs	75.2	–	–	84.3	67.7	67.9	63.0	79.8
Extra profits	–	–	74.2	−38.0	−34.4	−30.9	−8.7	20.9
Net results	−1996.1	−667.2	−163.9	−532.7	−197.0	−145.4	−104.6	36.7
Financing needs[1]	−5637.2	−2916.7	−1956.7	−2407.3	−1491.2	−1419.7	−1337.3	−1281.7

Note: [1] Total government contribution is the sum of subsidies and net results.

Source: RENFE (www.renfe.es). All figures are expressed in 2003 € millions.

the Spanish government so that the commercial risk of the company is effectively assumed by the Spanish taxpayer rather than by the buyers of RENFE bonds. This artificially reduces RENFE's cost of capital, which in turn may also distort the evaluation of future investments. Second, RENFE's financial statements do not include the costs of some new rail infrastructure projects built by the government. Dogson and Rodríguez (1996), who first identified this problem, argue that the amount of infrastructure provided by and for the company is thus understated in the balance sheets so that larger cost-reducing efforts may be necessary. The problem was partially solved in 1997, when the accounting separation between infrastructure and services demanded by EC Directive 1991/440 was finally implemented. But the financial costs in Table 5.4 are strikingly low, as interest payments have been reduced to just 10 percent of total cost in recent years.[8]

Financial Performance by Business Unit

Financial performance has varied by business unit, as illustrated in Figure 5.2, which shows the trend in cost recovery ratios (percentage of operating cost recovered by commercial revenues and PSO subsidies) by business unit from 1997 to 2003. All the business units except regional passenger services and intermodal containers improved their results within this period, although only the AVE consistently maintained cost recovery ratios above 100 percent. AVE's good performance is misleading, since RENFE's accounts do not include much of AVE's infrastructure costs, which may

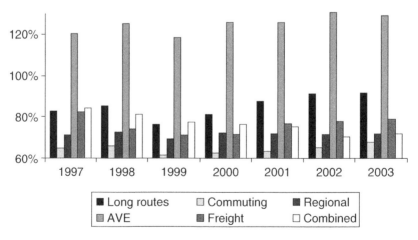

Source: RENFE (www.renfe.es).

Figure 5.2   RENFE's cost recovery ratios by business units (1997–2003)

account for up to 70 percent of total costs. In fact, according to de Rus and Inglada (1997), the first AVE line (between Madrid and Seville) hardly recovers operating costs once the infrastructure costs have been correctly accounted for.

The poor financial performance of some of RENFE's business units is troubling since EC regulations and the likely increase in competition will make it more difficult for one business unit, such as the AVE, to cross-subsidize others in the future. Moreover, it is important to note that the lowest cost recovery ratios are those that already receive the largest PSO subsidies, particularly the suburban and regional business units. Although PSO subsidies are allowed under current European rail policy, it is likely that governments will be pressed to review them periodically. Recent EU policy documents, such as the 2001 White Paper on the future of transport policy, encourage the development of railways because of the external social costs of road transport, but they also call for 'a periodical review of public support mechanisms that could distort the competition within the European market' (European Commission, 2001).

INVESTMENT TRENDS AND THE EXPANSION OF AVE

One of the most important developments in Spanish railway policy has been the decision to invest heavily in rail infrastructure, as shown in Table 5.5. Between 1980 and 2003, the government invested more than 20 billion euros in railways, a sum which allowed the extensive modernization of tracks, stations, signaling systems and rolling stock. Until the late 1990s, RENFE was

Table 5.5   Total public investment in railroads (1980–2003)

	1980	1985	1990	1995	2000	2001	2002	2003
Government	260.1	459.9	783.3	507.3	400.0	438.3	496.1	534.7
GIF	–	–	–	–	1047.2	1535.0	2484.5	2140.8
RENFE	1180.1	630.9	1542.4	575.4	573.6	624.4	632.8	925.2
Rolling stock	279.2	356.2	647.9	307.6	184.6	222.2	189.6	608.9
Infrastructure	900.9	274.7	894.5	267.8	389.0	402.2	443.1	316.3
FEVE	97.1	77.2	75.2	40.0	74.9	74.5	69.2	71.3
Regional railroads	–	121.3	93.2	140.6	119.1	220.3	213.9	272.5
Total	1536.9	1289.1	2494.0	1263.3	2214.8	2892.4	3887.4	4168.6

Source: Ministry of Fomento (www.mfom.es). All figures are in 2003 € millions.

the major investor in infrastructure and particularly in the maintenance and renewal of existing lines, while the government (through the *Dirección General de Ferrocarriles*, DGF, the rail department of the Ministry of Development) was in charge of building a few new lines, junctions and by-passes around the most congested areas. FEVE and the regional operators did not open new lines, but invested in modernizing their fleets, the development of new services and improved technology.

When the Rail Infrastructure Manager (GIF) was established in 1997, it assumed the responsibility of building the largest expansion of the Spanish rail system in the last 50 years. The government, through a combination of the DGF and the GIF, has invested almost 12 billion euros in just four years, and has promised a similar amount for the coming decade. The investment in rail is part of the so-called *Infrastructure Plan* 2000–2007, whose goal is to modernize the country's transport services and infrastructure to achieve the interoperable and open international corridors advocated by European Union transport policy.

As in the old management contracts of the 1980s, the *Infrastructure Plan* includes the broad priority 'to increase rail transport's market share and improve the financial performance of the operators'. Unlike the old contracts, however, the plan also includes a long list of specific targets, such as reducing the travel time by rail between Madrid and Barcelona and all the major provincial cities. The plan attaches particular importance to the development of the high-speed lines, inspired in large part by the example of the French TGV. The government and AVE supporters argue that the environmental damage caused by motor vehicle air pollution and the increasing levels of congestion in both surface and air travel make the railways the preferred transport mode in corridors with enough traffic to justify the substantial investment required by modern railway technology. AVE proponents also hope that shorter time connections between Madrid and the main cities will promote the kind of national integration anticipated from railways as far back as 1848. The European Union has been keen on the creation of a continent-wide high-speed rail network and has committed its financial support for several projects in member countries (European Commission, 2001).

The first AVE service was opened between Madrid and Seville (585 kilometers) in 1992 in conjunction with the international exposition celebrated that year in Seville. The line is widely regarded as a success in terms of passenger acceptance, load factors and quality of service, although ex-post studies show that it drew most of its traffic from modes with already established and costly infrastructure, and that many of its costs were grossly understated. From the point of view of social cost–benefit analysis, it was a doubtful investment (de Rus and Inglada, 1997).[9]

The planned expansion of high-speed corridors in Spain will continue in the near future. The AVE line between Madrid and the northeast city of Lleida (465 kilometers) opened for service in 2003, but with the speed temporarily restricted to 200 kilometers per hour for technical reasons. The line should reach Barcelona in 2007 and the French border by 2009. Other routes in the north and center of the country are either under construction or at the planning stage.

From an economic perspective, Spain's plan for an extensive network of AVE services is risky. The cost of building the required infrastructure is huge and, once built, infrastructure maintenance costs will be high. Demand projections suggest that passenger revenues are unlikely to recover even operating costs. With the EU enlargement towards Central and Eastern Europe and the eligibility of poorer countries for structural and regional funds, Spain is unlikely to enjoy continued generous EU funding for its infrastructure projects. Some observers fear that the displacement of the European center of gravity eastwards will accentuate the peripheral location of Spain, giving increased importance to the necessary passage through French territory with which connections are to be improved. The AVE remains popular as many regional governments have been lobbying for 'their own AVE' in the belief that the original line was an important stimulus to the economy of Seville. Nevertheless, it may be time to reconsider some of the planned investments.

THE 2003 RAILROAD LAW: WILL IT BE ENOUGH?

In 2003 the Spanish government passed a new railroad sector law, the *Ley del Sector Ferroviario* (LSF), 'in order to finally transpose to national legislation the new European directives and establish the basis for the introduction of private competition in the sector'. The law assumes that opening the rail sector to private initiative will improve its economic efficiency and increase its share of passenger and freight, and represents the final step in the reforms begun in 1987 with the LOTT. After years of minor adjustments to RENFE's internal organization and management criteria, the LSF introduced three more fundamental reforms.[10]

The New Industry Structure

The most important change introduced by the LSF is to establish a clean separation between RENFE and the infrastructure manager. The law creates two independent state-owned companies: RENFE-Operator, and the new agency for management of rail infrastructure, ADIF (*Administrador de Infraestructuras Ferroviarias*). RENFE-Operator is to be established from RENFE's current operating and maintenance business units. But while RENFE-Operator will assume the assets, employees and other liabilities of those business units, most of the outstanding debt will be transferred to the government and taken off the company's balance sheets, a decision that has been criticized by some private companies. Like any other rail service provider, RENFE-Operator will be required to obtain a license to operate, and will have to pay the access prices set by the infrastructure manager, ADIF.

In theory, the LSF ends RENFE's 60-year monopoly on rail service. The law does not establish particularly tough requirements for new entrants, requiring only proven financial and technical capability. It is obviously early to predict how competition will evolve, but experience from similar situations (such as railroads in other countries or the telecommunications industry in Spain) suggests that the incumbent will still dominate the market in the initial years. Furthermore, the liberalization of other industries has often included the privatization of the former public monopoly, in order to enhance competition. In the case of the Spanish rail industry, this possibility has been ruled out so far.

ADIF, the new government infrastructure agency, will be responsible for developing and maintaining the traditional network and the high-speed lines, as well as the existing stations and terminals. ADIF will take over GIF's existing infrastructure and personnel and will be also in charge of building new lines, which, for the first time, can be concessioned to private firms in BOT (build-operate-transfer) or other similar regimes. It will report to the Ministry of Development and be financed by a combination of subsidies from the national government, access prices for infrastructure utilization paid by the operators and other surcharges paid by rail customers, such as the so-called 'safety tax' of between 0.02 and 0.30 euros per passenger.

Infrastructure Access Prices

Although GIF had already developed a proposal for infrastructure charging in Spain, the second major change of the 2003 law is to introduce charges for the usage of rail infrastructure, stations and other track elements that conform to EC Directive 2001/14. The new charges, summarized in Table 5.6, intend to recover ADIF's full costs, and include four components: access, capacity reservation, circulation and traffic. The access charge is a general payment to be made by all licensed operators for the right to use the infrastructure. The capacity reservation and circulation fees depend on the kilometers of track used and vary with the type of service or train, the hour of the day and the characteristics of the track. Finally, the traffic charge is

Table 5.6   Charges for infrastructure usage in the new rail law

Concept	Principles	Economic base for calculation
Access	For the right to use of the network	ADIF's administrative costs
Capacity reservation	For the assignment of specific tracks	ADIF's fixed costs of track maintenance and operation
Circulation	For the real use of specific tracks	ADIF's variable costs of track maintenance and operation
Traffic	For the economic value of the services	ADIF's financial and depreciation costs
Stations and yards	For the use of specific stations and yards	Not defined

levied on the operators depending on the economic value of their service as measured by the number of seat-kilometers or ton-kilometers operated.

There are also separate charges for the use of stations and yards, although the law does not explicitly define the procedure for calculating the corresponding prices. It simply states (in article 73.2) that they will be set 'in accordance with general principles of economic viability, effective exploitation of infrastructure, market conditions, and financial balance, providing non-discriminatory treatment to all licensed operators'.[11]

No specific schedule of infrastructure charges has been released so far, so we have yet to see how these principles will be applied in practice. But having a transparent and efficient infrastructure charging regime is a key condition for the successful development of open access in the terms defined by the European rail policy. As Nash suggests in Chapter 2, access rights are of little use if the infrastructure pricing system and other access conditions can still be used to protect the incumbent operator.

Rail Regulation

The final major contribution of the LSF is the creation of a Rail Regulation Committee (*Comité de Regulación Ferroviaria*) to oversee the functioning of the sector and guarantee the equal treatment of all (private and public) operators. The Committee is also charged with resolving disputes that arise between the ADIF and the operators and guaranteeing that access is provided on a non-discriminatory basis.

The Rail Regulation Committee has less independence than similar Spanish regulatory commissions in energy or telecommunications.[12] Unlike the other commissions, the rail committee is an internal department within the Ministry of Development and five of its six members are directly named by the government. These arrangements do not automatically preclude the committee's independence, but they are likely to make suspect any decisions that favor the public incumbent over new private competitors. The EU directives are not very clear about what constitutes an independent rail regulatory agency, and the new law seems to have taken advantage of this ambiguity.

More recently, the government seems to have realized that further efforts may be needed. In the first quarter of 2005, the government announced a new competition policy which includes, among other proposals, a plan to create a truly independent rail regulation agency outside the Ministry of Development. The plan also calls for some specific disinvestments of RENFE to would-be rivals. As a consequence, at least five small firms have formally announced their interest in entering the market for rail services.

CONCLUSIONS

For the last 60 years, Spain, like the other countries of Europe, has had a single, state-owned railway company, responsible for both infrastructure and track services. However, this protective environment, where competition was rare and often discouraged, was not enough to prevent the decline in the railways' market share and profitability. Indeed, the public monopoly model may have hastened the decline by inhibiting the railway's response to the rapid expansion of more flexible transport alternatives and to traveler and shipper demands for higher quality services. Government policy toward other models contributed as well, particularly the lifting of constraints on competition in the trucking industry in 1987, the deregulation of the airline industry since the mid-1980s, and the massive highway construction programs of the 1980s and 1990s.

To face all these challenges RENFE has undergone major reforms in the 1980s and 1990s. The company was gradually transformed into an autonomous commercial body with economic rather than social objectives. It was divided into business units and responsibility for infrastructure management was transferred to a separate government agency. As a result of these changes, RENFE's performance improved greatly in the 1984–2003 period, but the company remained the sole provider of rail services as the development of regulations to allow the effective introduction of competition was put off for more than a decade.

In recent years, the Spanish government, with the support of the most recent strategies defined by the European rail policy, has opted for a long-term strategy of winning back rail customers through the development of high-peed corridors. Following the French model, Spain has devoted considerable resources to an ambitious national high-speed network in order to finally integrate the country regions, reduce congestion and increase personal mobility. Although this risky strategy may prove to be successful, it is also a very expensive one. Besides, high-speed trains sacrifice the rail freight business and its high operating costs will discourage the entry of potential competitors.

In sum, the lack of effective competition has been the most defining characteristic of the traditional rail model in Spain and it is difficult to see that this will change in the near future. The 2003 Rail Sector Law has established a new framework where RENFE becomes only an operator and the infrastructure manager, ADIF, will demand access charges for all operators. However, the unclear definition of the principles for calculating access prices and the low-profile nature of the new rail regulatory body created within the Ministry of Fomento, suggest that we will have to observe the implementation of the new law with caution before endorsing it. Success in the change of the rail model is not guaranteed and the results could be disappointing again.

Therefore, this is a crucial moment for Spain's rail industry. The 2003 law is a big leap forward that could mark the end of an era. But the dream of having the railroad as the 'dorsal spine of the country' will hardly become true without sacrifice. Today, the industry faces the challenge of adapting its structure to competition as other infrastructure sectors have already done, or definitively becoming an expensive public service, with fast and comfortable trains, that would not survive without the caring support of the taxpayers.

NOTES

1. This railroad connected the industrial cities of Barcelona and Mataró (28 kilometers). However, the first Spanish railroad was actually built in Cuba (then, a rich overseas province) in 1837, with more than 90 kilometers of track. For a detailed review of the history of the rail industry in Spain, see Comín et al. (1998).
2. See Carbajo and de Rus (1991) for a detailed analysis of transport policy in Spain during the 1980s.
3. In 2001 a new rail package clarified the principles on which rail infrastructure management should be based and, very recently, through EC Directive 2004/51, the deadlines for implementing 'third party access' have been shortened (to January 2007). However, many of these changes were not implemented in Spain until the 2003 Rail Sector Law (see below).
4. As of 2005, with the completion of some of the new high speed lines, RENFE operated over 13,500 kilometers of track, although less than 10 percent of the network was European gauge and only 16 percent was double-track and electrified.
5. These small companies (*Ferrocarrils de la Generalitat de Catalunya*, *Ferrocarrils de la Generalitat Valenciana*, *Euskotren* and *Serveis Ferroviaris de Mallorca*) are public local monopolies controlled by the autonomous governments. They provide suburban and regional services without competing with RENFE.

6. Due to the coastal nature of the country and the important traffic with the Balearic and Canary Islands, freight maritime transport is also very relevant in Spain. In 2003 it enjoyed a 10 percent market share.
7. These figures represent a major advance in terms of productivity when compared with other European counterparts, as pointed out in Cantos et al. (1999). In general, the company's operating performance improved in comparison to the average of the European railways.
8. In comparable private companies this figure could reach up to 30 percent, according to the International Railways Association, UIC (see detailed statistics at www.uic.asso.fr).
9. It has been widely reckoned that the high-speed expansion in Spain has not been based on purely economic criteria. For example, it is interesting to note that the first *contrato-programa* (1986–1988) ruled out the high-speed alternative because 'its financial viability is uncertain, at least as a general option'. However, when financial support from the European Union was secured this criterion was changed, even though demand and technologies had not.
10. The law was passed in November 2003. However, the new government emerged after the elections of March 2004 decided to postpone it until 1 January 2005 to better prepare its regulations and consequences. At the time of writing this chapter there has not been enough time to fully evaluate its consequences.
11. The principles defined in EC Directive 1991/440 are not much clearer. Article 8 states that (the user fee) 'will be calculated in such a way as to avoid any discrimination between railway undertakings, may in particular take into account the mileage, the composition of the train and any specific requirements in terms of such factors as speed, axle load and the degree or period of utilization of infrastructure'. The 1998 White Paper (European Commission, 1998) did not clarify the concept either. For a recent critical discussion, see Rothengatter (2003) and the reply in Nash (2003).
12. For example, the National Energy Commission (CNE) or the Telecommunication Markets Commission (CMT). For details, the reader could visit their websites (www.cne.es, www.cmt.es).

REFERENCES

Campos, J., and Cantos, P., (2000), 'Railways regulation', in A. Estache and G. de Rus (eds), *Privatization and Regulation of Transport Infrastructure: Guidelines for Policymakers and Regulators*, Washington, DC: The World Bank Institute.

Cantos, P., Pastor, J.M., and Serrano, L., (1999), 'Productivity, Efficiency and Technical Change in the European Railways: A Non-parametric Approach', *Transportation*, November, **26**(4), 337–57.

Carbajo, J., and de Rus, G., (1991), 'Railway Transport Policy in Spain', *Journal of Transport Economics and Policy*, May, 209–215.

Comín, F., Martín, P., Muñoz, M., and Vidal, J., (1998), '*150 Años de Historia de los Ferrocarriles Españoles*', Madrid: Anaya.

de Rus, G., and Inglada, V., (1997), 'Cost–benefit Analysis of the High-speed Train in Spain', *Annals of Regional Science*, **31**, 175–188.

Dogson, J., and Rodríguez, P., (1996), 'La rentabilidad de los diversos servicios de RENFE', in J.A. Herce and G. de Rus (eds), *La Regulación de los Transportes en España*, Madrid: Editorial Civitas.

European Commission (1998), 'Fair Payment for Infrastructure Use: A Phased Approach to a Common Transport Infrastructure Charging Framework in the EU', White Paper, Brussels. Online access at http://europa.eu.int.

European Commission (2001), 'European Transport Policy for 2010: Time to Decide', White Paper, Brussels. Online access at http://europa.eu.int.

Nash, C.A., (2003), 'Marginal Cost and other Pricing Principles for User Charging in Transport: A Comment', *Transport Policy*, **10**(3), 345–348.

Rothengatter, W., (2003), 'How Good is First Best? Marginal Cost and other Pricing Principles for User Charging in Transport', *Transport Policy*, **10**(2), 121–130.

PART II

Competition with vertical integration

6. The United States: Private and deregulated

Clifford Winston

INTRODUCTION

The Rail Passenger Service Act of 1970 and the Staggers Rail Act of 1980 marked a dramatic change in the evolution of the US railroad industry. After several decades of regulatory control over virtually every aspect of their economic operations, the federal government allowed rail carriers to abandon passenger service and created the National Railroad Passenger Corporation, Amtrak, which began operating in 1971. Nearly a decade later, freight operations were substantially deregulated and railroads were given the freedom to set rates (within broad limits) for the cargo they transported, abandon unprofitable routes, and consolidate with other carriers to a much greater degree than they were able to in the past.

Demand for rail passenger transportation had been declining for some time and the railroad industry and policymakers believed that this unprofitable service was contributing to rail's deteriorating financial performance. However, relieving rail of passenger traffic did not significantly improve its bottom line, thus the stakes in the new policy environment for freight operations were huge. Many industry observers feared that if the industry could not substantially increase its rate of return, it faced a real possibility of becoming nationalized. Moreover, if rail freight deregulation failed in the US, it was unlikely that any other country would try this experiment.

Today, countries such as Canada and, to some extent, Australia have deregulated their rail systems and most other countries are considering some form of regulatory reform.[1] Apparently, other nations have interpreted the US railroad deregulation experiment as a success. What aspects of the policy worked and who benefitted? What parts were less successful and who was harmed? What further steps can be taken to enhance industry performance under deregulation? The purpose of this chapter is to address these questions.

THE ECONOMIC MOTIVATION FOR POLICY CHANGE

The Interstate Commerce Act of 1887 is the traditional starting point for rail regulation in the US. Of course, in those days private rail companies carried passengers and freight. As noted, passenger service was transferred to a government corporation instead of being deregulated; thus, I will assess deregulation of freight operations. However, before exploring the motivation for deregulation, it is worth summarizing here the events that led to the change in policy towards passenger service.[2]

The Creation of Amtrak

At the turn of the 20th century, rail transported nearly all intercity passenger traffic in the US. However, rail's dominance in this market changed with the construction of the interstate highway system in the 1950s and the acceleration of air travel in the 1960s. As shown in Figure 6.1, intercity railroad passenger miles fell from roughly 30 million in the early 1950s to some 6 million by the early 1970s.

Because this sharp drop in demand was occurring as the industry's financial performance weakened, rail carriers wanted to abandon passenger service and policymakers did not seem to object. Indeed, the 2003 Congressional Budget Office report quotes a 1961 commission established by the Senate Commerce Committee as concluding: 'Railroad intercity passenger service meets no important needs that cannot be provided for by other carriers and possesses no uniquely necessary service advantages. It serves no locations which cannot be adequately served by air and highway.'[3]

Policymakers gradually took steps that relieved railroads of their common carrier obligation to carry passengers. The Transportation Act of 1958 prohibited state regulators from preventing interstate railroads from exiting unprofitable intrastate passenger services, which forced major metropolitan areas to subsidize commuter rail services to prevent their abandonment. But the burden of remaining interstate passenger services remained. When the Penn Central railroad filed for bankruptcy in 1970, representing for its time the largest corporate bankruptcy in US history, policymakers became alarmed that unprofitable passenger service would spur more bankruptcies, so they decided to relieve freight railroads of that burden and created Amtrak.

The creation of Amtrak was accompanied by two expectations that failed to be realized, although one was addressed by deregulation. First, Amtrak was expected within a few years of its inception to be self-sufficient and operate as a private entity without subsidies. As shown in Figure 6.1,

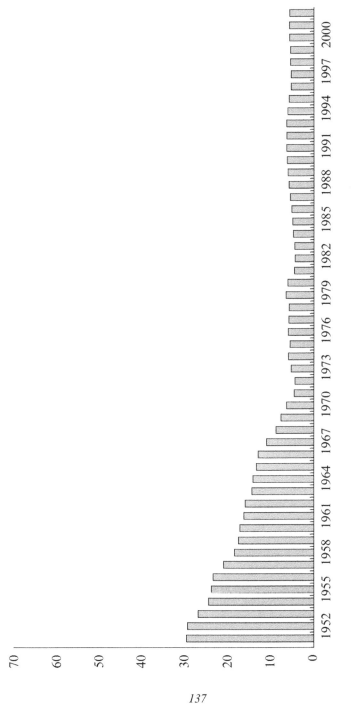

Source: Congressional Budget Office.

Figure 6.1 Intercity railroad passenger-miles, 1951–2002 (billions)

rail passenger demand has hardly increased since the early 1970s and Amtrak has continued to rely on subsidies to continue operations. Recently, those subsidies have accounted for roughly 20–30 percent of its revenues. Among the other private carriers, bus and air, rail's share of US intercity passenger-miles is only 1 percent and may be less if Congress ever acts on its ongoing threat to cut Amtrak's subsidy.[4]

Second, it was expected that freeing private railroads of their passenger obligations would help improve their rate of return. However, as noted, this action did little to return the industry to financial health, especially because its freight operations were still subject to costly regulations.

The Costs of Rail Freight Regulation

Economic regulation of any industry for a long period of time causes that industry to develop a regulatory bequeathed capital structure and a provincial mindset that shapes its relations with labor and the government. Inefficient operating practices and a slow rate of technological progress become deeply engrained in the industry as regulation persists. Deregulation therefore cannot be expected to create an efficient and technologically up-to-date industry overnight. However, it can be expected to jump-start the long-term process of dismantling the most costly aspects of regulation.

In the rail freight industry, the costs include the following:[5]

Distorted prices
Under regulation, railroad rates were in theory determined by value of service pricing, whereby rates for a given commodity were aligned with the value of the commodity rather than the cost of shipping it. Consequently, high-value manufacturing products were charged higher rates than low-value bulk commodities such as coal and grain. The rationale for this pricing scheme was that railroads were characterized by significant scale economies; thus, some form of price discrimination was necessary to enable the industry to cover its fixed costs and earn a normal profit. Indeed, it can be argued that in its inception value of service pricing was tantamount to Ramsey pricing.

Regardless of its theoretical justification, rail's regulated rate structure contributed to the industry's decline when intermodal (truck-rail) competition developed. In this environment it became clear that the demand elasticities for time-sensitive shippers of high-value commodities were higher than the demand elasticities for shippers of low-value commodities. By elevating rail rates for high-value commodities, value of service pricing helped private and for-hire motor carriers capture a large share of rail's high-value manufacturing traffic. Consequently, rail was left with a traffic mix that became increasingly dominated by low-value freight, which generated insufficient revenue to cover rail costs. Rail carriers had little flexibility to respond to competition from trucks or each other by adjusting rates for specific commodities and were prevented from negotiating long-term contracts with shippers that had the potential to benefit both parties.

In addition, rail rates were collectively subject to a rate of return constraint. During the 1970s, this constraint – roughly 2–3 percent of capital invested – was far below market rates of return, thereby preventing the industry from attracting sufficient capital to maintain its plant and equipment.

Barriers to exit

Railroads developed their vast network of track, yards and switching facilities over several decades. During most of the period that the network was built, rail carriers recognized that they would have to compete in some regions of the country with barge transportation for shippers' bulk commodities but they did not envision that they would have to compete with truck transportation for shippers' freight. The construction of the interstate highway system turned motor carriers into formidable competitors and ensured that the nation's rail network would no longer transport the volume of traffic that it was designed to carry.

However, regulation was not reformed to fit the changing times as railroads were prevented from abandoning parts of their network that ceased to be economical. Instead, common carrier obligations forced rail carriers to maintain their network even in situations where it was unprofitable for them to do so.

Labor utilization

In many industries, labor relations evolve through a series of voluntary negotiations. Sometimes an industry must endure a strike but presumably after the strike is resolved, the industry and labor develop a better understanding of how to settle their differences. Because of the importance of rail service to the nation's economy, the federal government has tended to block strikes and forced labor, represented by strong unions, and management to submit to compulsory arbitration.

As pointed out by Keeler, under regulation there was little progress on instituting work rules that would enhance productivity and on setting wages that would reflect productivity. For example, freight train crews were paid for a full day's work for 100 miles of travel, even if that distance entailed less than a day's work. In addition, firemen were still required on locomotives even after locomotives were powered by diesel fuel. Generally, the industry was saddled with excess labor that was paid higher wages than it would be paid in a competitive market.

Technological progress

The railroad industry's poor record of technological advance under regulation was also a source of its financial difficulties. The combination of regulatory constraints on behavior and the lack of economic incentives deterred the industry from improving its operations and offering new services to shippers. For example, shippers frequently voiced dissatisfaction with the unreliability of railroad service. When they asked carriers for information about the location of a shipment and when it might arrive at its destination, carriers could not offer a satisfactory reply. Indeed, during the regulated era, Norfolk Southern tracked its cars and locomotives by the primitive expedient of posting a video camera at the entrance of each rail yard.

The potential for introducing larger, more specialized freight cars represents a classic example of how rail regulation stifled innovation.[6] An innovation in car design would increase the hauling capacity of the equipment, but the car would cost more to purchase. To exploit the innovation, a railroad might want to induce volume by lowering rates for the intended traffic, but the Interstate Commerce Commission could, and in practice often did, oppose the new rate. Presumably, this opposition was motivated by the desire to protect rail carriers that did not invest in larger carrying capacity, thus discouraging other carriers from investing in new types of rail cars. Such episodes were common in the railroad industry, leading the Task Force on Railroad Productivity to conclude during the early 1970s that lapses in railroad technology were a primary explanation of why total productivity in the rail industry had grown at a rate averaging only 1–2 percent per year while other US industries' annual total productivity growth averaged 2–3 percent (Task Force on Railroad Productivity, 1973).

The inefficiencies created by rail regulation put a stranglehold on the industry that prevented it from competing effectively. Rail's share of freight traffic, which stood at nearly 70 percent of intercity ton-miles following World War II, fell to 37 percent by 1975. Moreover, following the bankruptcies of several Northeastern and Midwestern railroads in the 1970s, nearly every remaining railroad was earning a rate of return below that earned in the corporate sector as a whole. Policymakers were increasingly convinced that the industry needed much greater pricing and operating freedom if more bankruptcies were to be avoided; hence, in 1980, Congress passed the Staggers Rail Act to deregulate the railroads in a direct unambiguous fashion. In short, the Act directed the industry to return to profitability by relying on the market.

Policymakers believed that deregulation would help the railroads return to profitability, but they were concerned that railroads might exercise market power and charge some shippers exorbitant rates. Indeed, some academic predictions of the effects of rail deregulation were based on shippers having to pay higher rates (see, for example Levin 1981). Thus, although contract rates were completely deregulated, tariff rates for certain commodities were still subject to maximum rate 'guidelines'.[7] But, as we shall see, one of the major surprises of rail freight deregulation is that railroads *and* shippers benefitted from the policy – with the rate guidelines deserving virtually no credit for this outcome.

THE EFFECTS OF RAIL FREIGHT DEREGULATION

In general, an industry's adjustment to deregulation is shaped by the increased operating freedoms and intensified competition that force it to become more technologically advanced, to adopt more efficient operating and marketing practices, and to respond more effectively to external shocks. As noted, inefficiencies in the railroad industry developed over several decades, so it is going to take considerable time for the full effects of deregulation to be realized. In addition, as rail carriers continue to adjust to deregulation, the full costs of regulation will be better understood because the innovative and entrepreneurial activity that regulation suppressed will become more apparent.

Competition in intercity freight markets occurs at the route level – as defined by a specific origin and destination. In the US, the alternative freight modes include railroads, motor carriers and, in some markets, barge transportation (air freight has a small share of traffic). Thus, from a shipper's perspective, the intensity of intra and intermodal competition at the route level is far more important than the number of railroads at the national level.

Following deregulation, no large railroad entered the industry, while the number of railroads at the national level declined substantially as carriers consolidated through end-to-end (vertical) mergers and parallel (horizontal) mergers. As discussed shortly, these mergers had beneficial effects on shippers and railroads.

The extent of merger activity is exhibited in Table 6.1 by rail carriers that provided service in 1984 but subsequently merged with another carrier. The absorption of Conrail by Norfolk Southern and CSX in 1999 left the US with four large (Class I) railroads – Norfolk Southern and CSX in the East, and Burlington Northern-Santa Fe and Union Pacific-Southern Pacific in the West. But competition among these remaining railroads has become extremely intense (a case study will be presented later). In addition, since deregulation, the number of smaller low-cost (nonunion) railroads, such as

Table 6.1   Major railroad consolidations following deregulation

Carrier Acquired	Ultimate Acquiring Carrier
Atchison, Topeka & Santa Fe	Burlington Northern
Baltimore & Ohio, Chesapeake & Ohio, Seaboard Coast Line	CSX
Chicago & Northwestern, Denver, Rio Grande & Western, Missouri-Kansas-Texas, Missouri Pacific, Southern Pacific, Saint Louis-Southwestern	Union Pacific
Norfolk & Western, Southern Railway System	Norfolk Southern
Grand Trunk & Western, Illinois Central Gulf	Canadian National

Montana Rail Link, has increased substantially; these railroads have formed small systems from track purchased from large railroads. Finally, railroads must compete fiercely with deregulated motor carriers. Deregulation of trucking, effectuated by the 1980 Motor Carrier Act, spurred the development of advanced truckload carriers that are very formidable competitors because of their low costs and superior service.

Effects on Rail Profitability

Railroads had to significantly reduce their costs to improve financial performance. This was accomplished in several ways. First, deregulation gave railroads the freedom to negotiate contract rates. Today, more than half of all rail traffic moves at such rates. Contract rates allowed railroads to tailor their services to shippers' preferences and for both parties to share the resulting gains in productivity. For example, shippers that required service to and from a given destination would receive a reduced rate because they eliminated an empty backhaul (that is, excess capacity) for the railroad. Similarly, shippers that required a unit train to transport large shipments would receive a reduced rate because they helped exhaust economies of traffic density.

Rail improved the efficiency of its network by abandoning thousands of miles of unprofitable low-density lines and eliminating duplicate track in the wake of various parallel mergers. These mergers also enabled rail carriers to choose the most efficient parallel line to keep in the network. Since deregulation, rail's track miles have fallen from 270,000 to 170,000 and its traffic density (measured by millions of ton-miles per mile of track) has increased from 3.4 to 8.9.[8] Railroads also cut costs by eliminating cabooses and related crew members. Bitzan and Keeler (2003) estimate that these actions led to annual industry cost savings of $2 billion to $3.3 billion.

With billions of dollars of sunk, long-lived capital investments, railroads were not immediately able to replace old technology with new technology. Nonetheless, deregulation gave railroads the freedom and incentive to make some important operational and technological improvements that raised service quality and reduced costs. Some of these changes included the greater use of intermodal operations, the introduction of unit trains for coal and grain, the development of double stack rail cars for manufactured commodities, and the further application of computer information systems to track shipments and route cargo. The video cameras that were once placed in rail yards to monitor freight cars were replaced with electronic scanners that automatically recorded each car's arrival.

Gallamore points out that as rail's cash flow improved it was also able to upgrade its technology and replace its worn out capital (Gallamore, 1999). For example, railroads revitalized their plants with stronger and better-maintained track that reduced train derailments and cut the time that track is taken out of service for rebuilding. Rail carriers also acquired newer, larger and more reliable locomotives to handle the growth in traffic.

Collectively, the changes in rail operations and technology spurred by deregulation enabled the industry to substantially cut its costs. As shown in Figure 6.2, real operating costs per ton-mile have fallen steadily, and as of 2002, were 69 percent lower than when deregulation began. Of course, some of the cost decline can be attributed to the long-run trend in rail's traffic mix to include a greater proportion of low-cost bulk traffic. On the other hand, Keeler and Bitzan document that railroads have accrued large cost savings from productivity growth that has continued to accelerate since deregulation, thus deregulation's contribution to observed cost declines is substantial.

In addition to reducing its costs, the rail industry has also increased its traffic. After reaching a postwar low in the mid-1980s, originating rail carloads have grown from 19.5 million in 1985 to 27.9 million in 2002 (Association of American Railroads, 2003). During this period, its share of intercity freight, measured in ton-miles, increased from 37 percent to 40 percent. The combined result of the cost savings and increased output is that rail profitability has significantly improved since deregulation. During 1971–80, the industry's return on equity averaged less than 3 percent; during the 1990s the industry's return on equity has averaged 10.7 percent a year (General Accounting Office, 1999).

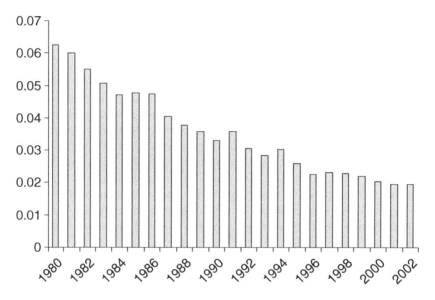

Source: Association of American Railroads (1993, 2000, 2003).

*Figure 6.2   Railroad operating costs per revenue ton-mile, 1980–2002
              (2002 $)*

Effects on Shippers

The evidence that has been presented substantiates that rail deregulation accomplished its primary goal of putting the US rail freight industry on a more secure financial footing. Policymakers were less certain about how shippers would fare under the new policy and, as noted, introduced some safeguards to protect so-called 'captive' shippers from being exploited.

Surprisingly, deregulation has turned out to be a great boon for shippers. Given the intensity of competition in surface freight transportation, rail passed on some of its cost savings to shippers in lower rates. As shown in Figure 6.3, real rail rates have declined since deregulation. Thus far, real rail rates have fallen 65 percent. Some of the decline in rail rates, like the decline in rail costs, can be attributed to the long-run trend in railroads' traffic mix to include a greater proportion of lower-priced bulk traffic but deregulation's contribution has been substantial. For example, Ellig (2002) surveys evidence from various sources and concludes that at least one-third, and possibly much more, of the rate reductions since 1980 can be attributed to the Staggers Rail Act. As a baseline estimate, this implies that deregulation has, on average, lowered shippers' rates more than 20 percent.

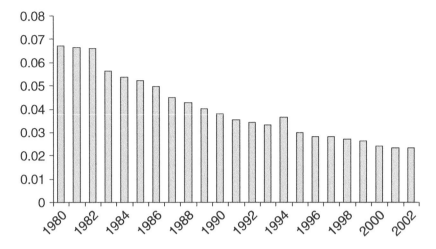

Source: Association of American Railroads (1993, 2000, 2003).

Figure 6.3 Railroad freight revenue per ton-mile, 1980–2002 (2002 $)

To be sure, shippers have not benefitted equally. Large rail shippers in high-density markets have been able to negotiate lower rates than small shippers in low-density markets, but small shippers have been able to increase their rate savings by obtaining lower rates through third-party logistics firms that represent a group of shippers in their negotiations with railroads. As shown in Table 6.2, shippers of all commodity groups have benefitted from declines in their rates, although some shippers have gained more than others. It is striking that coal shippers, who are thought to have more captive traffic than other shippers, have experienced the largest rate declines during the 1990s.

During regulation, rail's slow transit time and its unreliability were a serious problem in an economy that was becoming more service oriented. Indeed, the competitive advantage of trucking largely stemmed from its ability to offer much faster and more reliable service that, for example, facilitated just-in-time inventory practices. Following deregulation, rail greatly improved its service, partly through end-to-end mergers that reduced the frequency with which an originating rail carrier had to switch its cars to another railroad to complete the movement.[9] Based on the first decade of deregulation, Winston et al. (1990) found that the annual benefits to shippers from lower rates and improvements in service time and reliability amounted to at least $12 billion (1999 dollars). In all likelihood, these benefits have grown as rail has continued to improve its operations and lower its costs.

Table 6.2   Average change in real rail rates for selected commodities,
1982–1996

Category	Average annual percentage change in rail rates	
	1982–1989	1990–1996
All commodities	−4.6	−4.1
Farm products	−6.7	−1.1
Metallic ores	−5.2	−5.2
Coal	−3.3	−7.9
Food and kindred products	−6.9	−3.7
Lumber and wood	−6.2	−4.0
Chemicals	−3.9	−2.4
Petroleum and coal products	−5.6	−3.0
Stone, clay, glass and concrete	−5.5	−0.5
Transportation equipment	−2.4	−2.5
Intermodal	−5.8	−2.9

Source: General Accounting Office (1999).

In sum, rail deregulation turned out to surprise policymakers by evolving into a rare 'win–win' outcome for consumers and industry and this outcome has been achieved while rail's overall safety record has continued to improve.[10] Not surprisingly, the gains have come at some expense to labor in the form of reduced employment but not in lower wages.

THE INTENSITY OF RAIL COMPETITION

The benefits to shippers from deregulation may be surprising in light of the substantial industry consolidation that began in the early 1980s, leaving many shippers with at most two rail carriers to compete for their business. Why is that sufficient intramodal rail competition?

Rail competition may arise in several ways. Two railroads can compete directly for a shipper's traffic if their tracks traverse directly into the shipper's plant or if they have access to the shipper through reciprocal or terminal switching.[11] However, shippers captive to one railroad may also benefit from *locational* competition supplied by a nearby carrier. For example, a shipper may be served by Railroad A but threaten to locate a new facility on or build a spur line to Railroad B as a bargaining chip to obtain a lower rate from Railroad A or to get Railroad B to commit to a reduced rate. Shippers could also stimulate railroad competition in some cases through *product* or *geographic* competition. For example, an industrial site served only by Railroad A in a given market may be able to use a substitute product shipped from a different origin by Railroad B, or the site could obtain the same product from an alternative origin served by Railroad B.

Such sources of competition are not simply theoretical possibilities. Grimm and Winston found, for example, that a shipper located 50 miles from another railroad pays roughly 16 percent less in annual freight charges than a shipper located 100 miles from another railroad. They also found that receivers who can be served by two or more railroads from different origins enjoy a 25 percent rate reduction from average charges.

When two rail carriers compete for a shipper's business, economic theory has 'narrowed' the outcomes to marginal cost pricing (Bertrand behavior), monopoly pricing (collusive profit-maximizing behavior), or something between these extremes based on the market demand for the output that is simultaneously offered by the two competitors (Cournot behavior). Winston, Dennis and Maheshri (2005) have performed an empirical test of the duopoly behavior that developed when Union Pacific (UP) entered coal transportation markets in the Powder River Basin in Wyoming and Montana that heretofore had been served only by Burlington Northern-Santa Fe (BN). Their sample was based on the shipping activity of 48 large electric utility plants during 1984 to 1998. Of the 48 plants, 17 experienced entry sometime between 1985 and 1998. Traffic in this market moves under negotiated contract rates. The authors found that the initial entry of a second carrier (UP) into a Powder River Basin market reduced rail rates 16 percent and that this effect became stronger over time, albeit at a diminishing rate. For example, after three or more years of entry, during which time some contracts are likely to have expired, a second entrant reduced rail rates by a third.

The impact of UP's entry on rail rates for coal traffic, *holding other influences constant*, is shown in Figure 6.4 along with an estimate of the long-run marginal cost of rail service. The figure shows that duopoly railroad pricing in Powder River Basin coal markets has evolved slowly, but it can be reasonably characterized by Bertrand competition because rail prices approach marginal cost. From 1985 to 1994, rail prices did not change much from their monopoly level. But since 1994, they have fallen sharply as UP has expanded service to a sufficiently large cohort of plants and as BN has been forced to compete with UP for shippers' traffic because its contracts have expired.

Indeed, the pervasive use of contract rates in rail freight transportation is probably the most important reason why Bertrand's prediction of the outcome of duopoly competition is realized. Each carrier faces the prospect of getting none of an electric utility's business for several years unless it

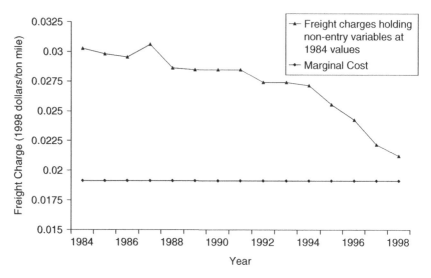

Source: Winston, Dennis and Maheshri (2005).

Figure 6.4 *Rail freight charges and marginal cost in markets experiencing UP entry at some point between 1984 and 1998*

lowers its rate in response to a competitor's bid. Given that a typical contract might call for 5 million tons of coal to be shipped annually for at least five years, a railroad has a lot to lose if it does not compete fiercely for a utility's business and allows the utility to take its traffic elsewhere. Of course, given that some shippers are captive to a single railroad, not every rail shipper in the US pays marginal cost rates. But as discussed in the next section, the extent of this problem is not large.

SOME REMAINING ISSUES

Although the rail freight industry has been largely deregulated, government's oversight has not been completely eliminated. To be sure, the Surface Transportation Board's interventions are limited to a relatively small number of rate cases. But given the legacy of government intervention in this industry, rail carriers' and shippers' instincts are to engage with the Board and Congress to protect and possibly expand their gains from deregulation.

The rail industry is quick to point out that notwithstanding the improvement in its financial performance, it is not revenue adequate. That is, as

Table 6.3   Revenue adequacy of Class I railroads, 1990–1997 (in percent)

Year	Return on investment	Cost of capital	Degree of revenue inadequacy
1990	8.1	11.8	−3.7
1991	1.3	11.6	−10.3
1992	6.3	11.4	−5.1
1993	7.1	11.4	−4.3
1994	9.4	12.2	−2.8
1995	6.9	11.7	−4.8
1996	9.4	11.9	−2.5
1997	7.6	11.8	−4.2

Source: General Accounting Office (1999). Return on investment is based on the Surface Transportation Board's methodology for determining revenue adequacy. These returns may not be the same as returns calculated for non-regulatory purposes.

shown in Table 6.3, railroads' return on investment still falls short of their cost of capital. Thus, the railroads argue that the Surface Transportation Board should refrain from trying to appease captive shippers by either concluding that rail rates are excessive or by supporting a policy of forced access to increase rail competition.[12]

Shippers, and various organizations that represent them, complain that rail rates are not always reasonable and that the Surface Transportation Board's rate complaint process is time-consuming, costly and complex. Hence, few rates are successfully challenged. In addition, shippers have experienced widely publicized service disruptions in the wake of Union Pacific's merger with Southern Pacific and following Norfolk Southern's and CSX's acquisition of Conrail.

The ongoing dispute between captive shippers and railroads should not mar the fact that deregulation has been very good for both parties. Indeed, government intervention at this point of the industry's adjustment to deregulation would be unwise. As noted, coal shippers have experienced declines in their rates. Furthermore, Grimm and Winston (2000) found that the loss to captive shippers of any commodity from elevated rates, as compared with the rates paid by non-captive shippers, is small.[13] Indeed, it can be argued that even with this loss, captive shippers still pay lower rates than they paid under regulation.[14] Thus, in my view government should not pursue policies such as mandatory access to increase competition. Instead, it would be preferable to eliminate the Surface Transportation Board and completely deregulate rail rates while instituting market-based mechanisms to address the captive shipper issue. In the process, the potential for policymakers to adopt measures that effectively re-regulate the industry would be foreclosed.

To achieve this outcome, shippers and railroads should be prodded to negotiate an end to the STB and residual rate regulation. Freed from the Board's oversight, limited as it may be, railroads could focus completely on improving the efficiency of their operations in a less politically charged environment. Shippers would no longer be frustrated by an agency that seems oblivious to their concerns. Moreover, shippers and railroads could extend the benefits they have already achieved through contractual negotiations by achieving additional logistics efficiencies as partners, instead of quibbling over the distribution of an ever-shrinking pie as adversaries.

FINAL COMMENTS

As stressed throughout the chapter, deregulation is a long-term process. US railroads' adjustment to their new economic freedoms, while time-consuming, has raised shippers' welfare and restored financial health to an industry that was on the verge of collapse. Shippers have also played an important role in deregulation's success by negotiating aggressively with railroads to obtain price-service packages that optimize their distribution requirements. Indeed, the extent to which deregulation's success can be replicated abroad depends on how well railroads *and* shippers respond to their new economic freedoms.

It may be surprising to some that railroads have needed more than 25 years to adjust to their new environment – but after 100 years of regulation they clearly need more than 25 years to become fully efficient. In fact, railroads still have a way to go to optimize service times and reliability, to be fully responsive to shippers, and to achieve potential logistical and operational efficiencies. A fully deregulated environment will spur the additional adjustments that the industry must make to accomplish these goals.

The industry's structure has also not fully adjusted to deregulation. It is possible that more rail mergers will be proposed until only two (highly efficient) Class I railroads remain in the industry. This end-to-end restructuring, should it come to pass, would create two transcontinental railroads, but still leave two large railroads in the East and two in the West, and thus have little effect on competition. Indeed, this may be the final equilibrium for the evolution of the US rail freight industry. More importantly, it is likely to result in an industry that contributes mightily to the efficiency of the nation's distribution system for years to come.

NOTES

1. Gómez-Ibáñez in this volume and Pittman (2004) outline various alternatives for rail-road reform and liberalization. These authors point out that vertical integration – single railroads maintain control of both track and trains running over track – generally characterizes operations in North and South America and partial or complete vertical separation – different railroads operate over a single set of track – generally characterizes operations in Europe.
2. A complete overview of passenger rail service in the US is provided in Congressional Budget Office (2003).
3. US Congress, Special Study Group in Transportation Policies (1961).
4. Morrison (1990) estimates that overall Amtrak's social benefits are roughly equal to its federal subsidy. But he also concludes that its social benefits are highly localized – the gains in the well-traveled Northeast corridor offset the losses in the rest of the United States.
5. Two classic sources on the costs of rail freight regulation include Meyer et al. (1959) and Friedlaender (1969). Keeler (1983) provides a detailed discussion of the issues summarized here.
6. This example is discussed in Gellman (1971) and Gallamore (1999).
7. The Surface Transportation Board – the successor to the Interstate Commerce Commission – was given the authority to determine the legality of rates in accordance with maximum rate guidelines. Under these guidelines, shippers can challenge a rate if it exceeds 180 percent of variable costs and if the railroad in question has no effective competition.
8. These figures are from Association of American Railroads (2003).
9. Philips (1999) points out that 'one of the dumbfounding long-term problems with rail-roading is that companies can't seem to hand off a rail car from one railroad to another without delaying it 24 hours or more'.
10. Savage (1999) reports that the rate of derailments and collisions and fatality rates for employees and at crossing facilities have declined since deregulation, although fatality rates for trespassers have slightly increased.
11. Graphical characterizations of these situations are presented in Grimm and Winston (2000).
12. Rail's claim that it is not revenue adequate is not without controversy. Rail's large sunk costs and other capital assets complicate efforts to estimate the industry's financial health, thus the figures in the table should be viewed with caution.
13. They estimate that captive shippers pay rates that are roughly 20 percent higher than rates paid by non-captive shippers, which results in a $1.3 billion (1998 dollars) loss to captive shippers and a deadweight loss associated with this transfer of only about $60 million. The latter is consistent with the view that exchange governed by contracts is generally efficient.
14. As noted, deregulation has reduced rates, on average, more than 20 percent, which exceeds the amount that rates are elevated for captive shippers as compared with the rates paid by non-captive shippers.

REFERENCES

Association of American Railroads (1993), *Railroad Facts*, Washington, DC.
Association of American Railroads (2000), *Railroad Facts*, Washington, DC.
Association of American Railroads (2003), *Railroad Facts*, Washington, DC.
Bitzan, J.D., and Keeler, T.E., (2003), 'Productivity Growth and Some of its Determinants in the Deregulated U.S. Railroad Industry,' *Southern Economic Journal*, **70**, October, 232–253.

Congressional Budget Office (2003), *The Past and Future of U.S. Passenger Rail Service*, September, CBO, Washington, DC provides a complete overview of passenger rail service in the United States.

Ellig, J., (2002), 'Railroad Deregulation and Consumer Welfare', *Journal of Regulatory Economics*, **21**, April, 143–167.

Friedlaender, A.F., (1969), *The Dilemma of Freight Transport Regulation*, Washington, DC: The Brookings Institution.

Gallamore, R.E., (1999), 'Regulation and Innovation: Lessons from the American Railroad Industry,' in Jose A. Gómez-Ibáñez, William B. Tye and Clifford Winston, *Essays in Transportation Economics and Policy: A Handbook in Honor of John R. Meyer*, Washington, DC: Brookings Institution.

Gellman, A., (1971), 'Surface Freight Transportation', in William M. Capron (ed.), *Technological Change in Regulated Industries*, Washington, DC: Brookings Institution.

General Accounting Office (1999), *Railroad Regulation: Changes in Railroad Rates and Service Quality since 1990*, GAO/RCED-99–93, April.

Grimm, C.M., and Winston, C., (2000), 'Competition in the Deregulated Railroad Industry: Sources, Effects, and Policy Issues', in Sam Peltzman and Clifford Winston, (eds), *Deregulation of Network Industries: What's Next?*, Washington, DC: Brookings Institution.

Keeler, T.E., (1983), *Railroads, Freight, and Public Policy*, Washington, DC: Brookings Institution.

Levin, R.C., (1981), 'Railroad Rates, Profitability, and Welfare under Deregulation', *Bell Journal of Economics*, **12**, Spring, 1–26.

Meyer, J.R., Merton, J. P., Stenason, J., and Zwick, C., (1959), *The Economics of Competition in the Transportation Industries*, Cambridge, MA: Harvard University Press.

Morrison, S.A., (1990), 'The Value of Amtrak', *Journal of Law and Economics*, **33**, October, 361–382.

Philips, D., (1999), 'Alliance to Forge U.S.–Canada Rail System', *Washington Post*, 21 December, p. A1.

Pittman, R., (2004), 'Chinese Railway Reform and Competition', *Journal of Transport Economics and Policy*, **38**, May, 309–332.

Savage, I., (1999), 'The Economics of Commercial Transportation Safety', in Jose A. Gómez-Ibáñez, William B. Tye and Clifford Winston, *Essays in Transportation Economics and Policy: A Handbook in Honor of John R. Meyer*, Washington, DC: Brookings Institution.

Task Force on Railroad Productivity (1973), *Improving Railroad Productivity: Final Report of the Task Force on Railroad Productivity*, A Report to the National Commission on Productivity and the Council of Economic Advisors, Washington, DC.

US Congress, Special Study Group in Transportation Policies (1961), *The Doyle Report: National Transportation Policy*, June, p. 322.

Winston, C., Corsi, T.M., Grimm, C.M., and Evans, C.A., (1990), *The Economic Effects of Surface Freight Deregulation*, Washington, DC: Brookings Institution.

Winston, C., Dennis, S.M., and Maheshri, V., (2005), 'Duopoly in the Railroad Industry: Bertrand, Cournot, or Collusive?', Working Paper, July.

7. Latin America: Competition for concessions

Jorge Kogan

INTRODUCTION

During the 1970s and 1980s, the railways in Latin America were all government owned and all in serious difficulty. None of the railways was recovering its costs from tariffs charged to passengers and shippers. Governments were unable to provide enough financial support to cover railway deficits, so that the companies skimped on maintenance and investment and the condition of the infrastructure and rolling stock deteriorated. These factors contributed to slow and unreliable service, which made it harder for the railways to compete with alternative transport modes, principally road transport. Rail's share of passenger and freight traffic was declining steadily.

The situation of the railways was in part a reflection of the economic and political difficulties Latin America faced at the time. Many countries in the region suffered from chronic high inflation rates or episodes of hyperinflation, and many had high foreign debt and had been effectively cut off from further international borrowing. The governments were institutionally weak, and political and social crises were frequent. In this context, governments held down railway tariffs in an often ineffective attempt to preserve their popularity or to control inflation. Railway companies were also pressed to hire more employees than they needed to fulfill the politicians' desires to create jobs. In some cases, railways and other public utilities were the victims of corruption, as public officials siphoned off the companies' resources for private purposes.

By the end of the 1980s, the problems of the railway companies, the economic difficulties of the governments, and the concerns of international development agencies all combined to favor shifting the provision of railway services from public to private hands. Initially, the shift was motivated primarily by fiscal goals. The states could no longer subsidize railway deficits, in part because they could no longer finance budget deficits by issuing debt and any available tax revenues were badly needed to support social services and economic stabilization plans. But the move to private provision was also motivated by a desire to arrest the decline of the railways. Governments hoped to attract private investment and skilled management so as to improve the quality of railway services, and introduce more competition in railway services as a means of both reducing costs and subsidies and increasing transparency.

COMMON FEATURES

The reforms in most Latin American countries had several common elements, although the details often differed. One was that reform was not entrusted to the existing railway companies. Usually the government created or charged a separate agency or bureau with the responsibility for overseeing the privatization of the railways. Buyouts by existing management or labor were rarely allowed, although the government often imposed a requirement to retain some portion of the existing workforce. Instead, the government typically sought to sell all, or a controlling share, of the stock to a consortium of new private investors in the hope that they would inject new capital and fresh management expertise.

Most railways were offered as a concession or lease of limited duration, with the infrastructure reverting to the state at the end. The rolling stock was often sold to the concessionaire with freight concessions, but with passenger concessions the rolling stock usually reverted to the state together with the infrastructure. Freight concessions were usually established for 30 years (20 years for Chile and 50 years for Mexico), and limited extensions for 10 or 20 years were generally authorized with the consent of both parties. Thirty years was the preferred concession term as it was the estimated time required for the full amortization of investments in cars and locomotives; therefore, if concessions were shorter, governments would be required to provide partial funding for rolling stock. Passenger service concessions tended to be shorter, at least for the first concession cycle, since governments wanted to monitor concession performance in detail. The shorter concessions required the governments to participate more in the ownership and financing of passenger rolling stock.

Another common feature was that the railways remained vertically integrated in that the new concessionaires were responsible for both infrastructure and train operations in their service areas. Often the railways were broken up horizontally, so that different concessionaires were given different lines or geographic territories, but within those lines or territories they were vertically integrated. The principal exceptions were in Peru and Uruguay, which will be discussed later, and in the south of Chile, where the government retained control of the infrastructure and passenger transport operations but granted a concessionaire, FEPASA, the right to operate freight trains over its tracks. Vertical separation was never seriously considered by most governments, largely because the railroads were in such a deteriorated condition and already faced such strong intermodal competition that vertical separation seemed a needlessly risky complication.

Some governments allowed competing train companies access to a concessionaire's track, but the grants of access were typically very selective so that the concessionaire had exclusive rights to most of his system. In Mexico, for example, the government attempted to foster competition by requiring that the two northern freight concessionaires grant each other access in the immediate vicinity of the major northern ports. The Mexican government also created a separate company to control the tracks around the City of Mexico; that company was owned by the three main freight concessionaires and tasked with giving all three equal access to shippers in the capital city. Similarly, Brazil and Argentina required that neighboring concessionaires provide access to one another under fair terms, although this provision was hardly ever evoked. The commuter rail and metro concessions were all exclusive, the only exceptions being to provide freight railways limited transit rights to access ports and major facilities in urban areas.

The concessions were almost always offered through some form of open competitive bidding process, either a public auction or, more commonly, the submission of best bids in sealed envelopes. Guatemala was one of the rare exceptions that preferred direct negotiations. In almost every case, the government established some form of pre-qualification process to ensure that those who bid had the technical skills and the financial resources needed.

Most of the freight concessions were awarded to the bidder that promised to pay the state the most for the concession rights. Argentina, one of the first countries to offer freight concessions, used a weighted index of eight different criteria to select the winners, but this scheme was so complex that it proved hard to hold the winners to all of the many promises they had been asked to make. Later countries used a single monetary criterion, although payment terms often varied. Mexico offered its freight concessions to the highest bidder, for example, and winners were required to pay half the amount upon concession award and the remaining half upon actual concession transfer. Bolivia required that the winning bidder deposit the full amount of the bid price in a bank the day of concession transfer. Bolivia wanted to strengthen its railways by 'recapitalizing' them, so the deposit went to the company rather than the government for use in rebuilding railway assets.

Many countries estimated in advance the value of the concessions they were offering, but only a few established minimum acceptable prices or announced those minimums publicly. Brazil was an exception in that Brazilian law requires that the government establish and announce in advance the minimum price for public assets being sold. The Mexican government also calculated a minimum price but did not disclose it until the bids were opened. In one case (the first Mexican railway concession) the bids were below the minimum and the concession was withdrawn to be auctioned again later.

Urban passenger or commuter service concessions usually specified minimum levels of service that had to be offered and maximum fares that could be charged. Since the desired fares were often insufficient to cover costs, negative bids were allowed and the concession could be awarded to the bidder who requested the least subsidy. In Río de Janeiro, for example, bidders for the commuter rail concessions were required to bid for an initial down payment, monthly lease payments, payment for materials inventories, investment commitments, and had to calculate an additional amount for the rolling stock equipment rehabilitation program that was being carried out by the government at the time. In Buenos Aires, bidders had to specify the monthly franchise fee offered or subsidy required to cover operating costs as well as the financial support they needed to complete a capital investment program specified by the government.

Often the role of foreign investors was restricted because of political sensitivities. For example, Mexico required that national investors own a majority interest in any consortium bidding for a railway concession. Similarly, one of the criteria that Argentina used to award its freight concessions was the share of the consortium owned by Argentine investors. At the same time, most countries required that bidders have experience in operating commercial railway services. Since there were few private railways in Latin America at the time, this requirement meant that many consortia included one or more foreign railways, although usually they owned only small shares of the proposed enterprise.

Governments typically established one or several regulatory agencies to monitor the railway concessionaires and determine whether they were living up to their commitments. The performance of these regulatory agencies varied greatly, depending on the discretion given to the agency by the concession contract, the country's economic circumstances and previous regulatory capabilities and experience. Few countries seemed prepared to monitor the concessions, and often the concessionaires' obligations to provide information to the agency were not well worked out in advance. There was also often confusion or disagreement about the principles which the agencies should use in supervising concessions.

One fundamental challenge that virtually every regulatory agency faced was pressure to renegotiate the concession contracts before their terms had expired. The contracts often failed to anticipate events that made them unworkable or undesirable for the government, the concessionaire, or both parties. There were many reasons why this occurred. In some cases the concessionaires found that the assets were in worse condition than they had expected, perhaps because of unexpected delays in the transfer of the concession (Argentina and Brazil). Often national economic crises rendered financial calculations obsolete (Argentina and Brazil). In some cases demand grew more slowly than expected making the fulfillment of highly specific investment programs (Argentina freight) or volume commitments (Brazil freight) irrational. In other cases demand grew more rapidly than expected, making the investment programs inadequate (Argentina commuter and subway lines). Often the governments did not meet all their commitments on such issues as the subsidy payments specified in the contracts (Argentina), track access charges to be paid by the state in its capacity of user (intercity passengers in Argentina), completion of infrastructure construction or rehabilitation programs to be carried out by the government (Brazil), completion of labor adjustment programs (commuter rail lines and Metro in Río de Janeiro), or full access to infrastructure under expected terms and conditions (Chile). Renegotiating these contracts turned out to be highly difficult and controversial. The public was frequently suspicious that the renegotiation was unfair and there were often legal challenges that delayed or limited the scope of renegotiation.

Despite these problems, the reforms appear to have significantly improved railway performance. Demand and labor productivity typically increased after declining or stagnating for many years under state control. Not only did the concessions perform better than their predecessors, but many performed better than had been projected by the architects of reform.

ARGENTINA

Origins of the Reforms

Argentina's experience was typical in many ways. Argentina's first railway was built in the mid-19th century under a concession granted to a private company. At its peak in the early 20th century the rail network consisted of 43,666 kilometers of track operated by 11 companies, many owned by foreign investors, often British. The railways suffered greatly during World War II, and in 1948 the government nationalized them to form a state-owned railway eventually named Ferrocarriles Argentinos (FA).

The railways declined gradually but steadily beginning in the 1960s. Between 1965 and 1990 the number of ton-kilometers of freight carried dropped 50 percent while the number of passenger kilometers fell by 34 percent on commuter services and 26 percent on intercity lines. In Table 7.1,

Table 7.1   Performance of the Argentine railways before reform

	1980	1985	1990
Ton-kilometers (million)	9.459	9.501	7.523
Urban passenger-kilometers (million)	8.458	5.801	5.926
Intercity passenger-kilometers (million)	4.141	4.943	4.716

Source: Kogan (2004, Table 2.1).

the figures from 1980–1990 show an overall reduction of 18 percent. The decline in the railways market share was even more precipitous since the highway modes were growing rapidly at the time. The infrastructure and rolling stock steadily deteriorated for lack of investment and maintenance so that traffic speeds, permitted axle loads and service reliability steadily declined. The company's annual deficit increased to an average of US$1 billion per year for nearly two decades.

Many of these problems arose because the company managers were more sensitive to political than commercial concerns. The labor force far exceeded the levels required to meet actual operating needs and although the network shrank to 34,000 kilometers as the most lightly used lines were abandoned, the railroad continued to operate many unprofitable services for political reasons. Rail tariffs were reduced to 70 percent below road transport tariffs in a failed effort to compensate for the poor service the railway offered and regain market share. The principal result of all these policies was to increase the burden of the railway on the national treasury.

Matters came to a head in 1989, when Argentina suffered a severe economic crisis because of years of high government deficits. As part of a comprehensive package of economic reforms, the Congress passed the State Reform and Public Service Enterprises Law authorizing the transfer of public enterprises to the private sector. This law established that the railways should be offered as concessions of limited duration and it authorized the relevant minister to establish a competitive bidding process to award the concessions. The government subsequently decided to break the railway network up into freight, intercity passenger and urban passenger lines and offer vertically integrated concessions for each type of service.

The Concessions

In the case of freight, the government identified six concessions as potentially profitable, with a combined network of 27,781 kilometers of track. The concessions were offered by international competitive tendering for terms of 30 years with the possibility of ten-year extensions. The bidders

Table 7.2   The Argentine urban passenger concessions

Network	Length (km)	Concessionaire	Takeover date
Mitre	182.1	TBA	05/1995
Sarmiento	186.6	TBA	05/1995
San Martin	55.4	Metropolitano	04/1994
Belgrano Sur	58.4	Metropolitano	05/1994
Roca	252.4	Metropolitano	01/1995
Belgrano Norte	51.9	Ferrovias	04/1994
Urquiza	25.6	Metrovias	04/1994

Source: Kogan (2004, Table 2.6).

proposed the investment programs they would undertake and the payments they would make to the state during the life of the concessions. Prices charged by concessionaires for service provision were not regulated in the case of freight concessions, and the freight concessionaires would not receive any government subsidy. Five of the six concessions were awarded successfully but the sixth, the Belgrano line, attracted no bidders and was eventually given to its employees (through one of the workers' unions) to operate.

A feasibility study of intercity passenger services completed in 1991 concluded that only the Buenos Aires – Mar del Plata corridor was potentially profitable and of interest to a private operator. The Mar del Plata line would be offered as a concession, but the rest of the intercity services were to be transferred to the respective provincial governments who could operate, concession or abandon them as they saw fit. The only provinces that decided to continue to provide rail services were Buenos Aires (they also took the Mar del Plata service and the concession process was interrupted), Córdoba, Tucumán, Salta, Río Negro and Chubut. Although the national government gave the provinces the trains at no charge, the services were never very satisfactory and most were finally discontinued.

For the urban passenger services, the government initiated in 1991 an international competitive bidding process to privatize the seven FA commuter rail lines that served Buenos Aires together with the Buenos Aires Subway. A separate company, Ferrocarriles Metropolitanos (FEMESA), was created to operate the commuter services pending privatization. The services were offered as seven separate concessions, one for each commuter line with the subway included in one of these groups (Table 7.2). The concession that included the subway was for 20 years while the other six were for ten years. The concessions could be extended for an equal term provided concessionaires had met their contractual commitments satisfactorily. The contracts stipulated the maximum fares and the minimum services and investments required, and the concessions were awarded to the bidders requesting the lowest subsidies.

The regulatory agencies that supervised the concessions evolved over the course of the 1990s. The initial plan was for the freight concessions to be supervised by a national rail regulatory agency, the intercity passenger concessions to be supervised by the relevant provinces, and the commuter and subway concessions by a new Buenos Aires Metropolitan Area Transportation Authority (Autoridad de Transporte del Área Metropolitana de Buenos Aires), or ATAM. ATAM was to have been composed of representatives of federal, provincial and municipal governments but it was never established due to disputes with the Province of Buenos Aires about its make-up. As a result, the effective scheme was for intercity passenger concessions to be regulated by the provinces and all other concessions to be regulated by the national government.

The identity and functions of the national regulatory agency changed several times during the 1990s, reflecting some confusion and disagreement about its role. The early agencies had powers to mediate in disputes between the government and the concessionaires and to recommend revisions in the concession contracts if needed. But the final version, the National Commission for Transport Regulation (CNRT), was created in 1996 and its role is limited largely to monitoring the contract compliance by the concessionaires. More significant policy matters, such as renegotiation of contracts, are effectively handled by the Ministries of Transport and Economy.

Initial Performance

The reforms dramatically reduced the amount of financial support the government provided the railways. The government still paid the seven commuter rail concessions subsidies to provide services and to finance their capital modernization projects, but in much lower amounts than those previously required by FA and the Buenos Aires Subway. Moreover, the government was scheduled to receive annual lease payments from the five freight concessions. It is difficult to get a firm accounting of the savings because of the complex schemes of subsidies both before and after the reforms, but the fiscal savings to the treasury ranged from US$500 million to US$1.5 billion per year in the years immediately after concessioning. Another remarkable aspect is that staffing levels dropped from 82,000 employees before reform to less than 13,000 after (the severance program was afforded by the Federal Government with partial finance from the World Bank).

Table 7.3   Traffic carried by the freight concessions in Argentina (millions of ton-kilometers)

Concession	1996	1997	1998	1999	2000
FEPSA	1198.90	1295.00	1195.00	897.00	877.50
FSR	1330.00	1490.00	1656.00	1510.00	1263.30
MGU	524.00	455.00	447.00	441.00	394.50
NCA	1383.00	1903.00	2382.20	2443.70	2490.60
BAP	1582.00	3007.00	2711.00	2510.00	2268.30
Total	6017.90	8150.00	8391.20	7801.70	7294.20

Source: Kogan (2004, Table 2.7).

On the freight services, the number of ton-kilometers carried doubled between 1991 and 1997, reversing the long-term decline in rail traffic. Part of the increase in freight traffic (see Table 7.3) was undoubtedly due to the recovery of the economy, which grew at average annual rates of 6 or 7 percent per year for much of the first half of the 1990s. But most observers credit much of the increase to dramatic improvements in service quality and reliability introduced by the concessionaires and to tariff reductions induced by the outbreak of intense competition between truck and rail.

The freight concessions were not terribly profitable, however, despite the growth in traffic. The concessionaires had thought that traffic would grow even more than it did, and they had not expected that the truckers would drop tariffs and force them to follow suit. With revenues lower than expected, most of the concessionaires responded by ceasing to pay the agreed-upon franchise fees to the government and by reducing the levels of investments they had promised to make.

Traffic also increased substantially on the commuter and subway ser-vices, again reversing a long-term decline (see Table 7.4). As with freight, part of the increase was attributable to the growth in the economy but much was thought to be due to improvements in reliability and service punctual-ity. Unlike freight, however, the increase in commuter and subway ridership was larger than the concessionaires or the government had expected. The service and investment programs required by the government would be inadequate if the growth in ridership were sustained. Also, because the ser-vices were unprofitable at the maximum fares specified in the contracts, the concessionaires would be unable to expand service or increase investment to accommodate the traffic growth unless they received more subsidies from government or got permission to raise fares.

*Table 7.4   Traffic carried by the urban passenger concessions in Argentina
(millions of passenger-kilometers)*

Line and (concessionaire)	1993	1995	1997	1999	2000
Mitre (TBA)	559.5	926.9	1434.0	1496.3	1455.9
Sarmiento (TBA)	N.D	1209.3	2498.8	2503.3	2494.8
Urquiza (Metrovias)	282.0	450.5	432.6	447.4	434.4
Roca (Metropolitano)	1298.1	2419.7	2918.8	2526.0	2472.0
San Martín (Metropolitano)	537.6	831.1	1152.5	1205.0	1151.9
Belgrano Norte (Ferrovias)	242.3	490.3	604.1	632.0	617.0
Belgrano Sur (Metropolitano)	41.5	174.5	283.2	632.0	612.5
All concessions	2961.0	6502.3	9324.0	9442.0	9238.5

Note: 1993 is before the concessions, 1995 onwards is after concessions.

Source: Kogan (2004, Table 2.8).

Contract Renegotiation

By the mid-1990s, it had become apparent that the rail concession contracts as written were no longer realistic and conflicted with the interests of both users and investors. Some observers suspected that the freight contracts had failed not just because of unexpected competition from trucks but also because the overly complex criteria for awarding the concessions had encouraged bidders to inflate their investment proposals and, consequently, traffic and revenue forecasts. There were fewer suspicions of insincere bidding in the case of the commuter rail and subway contracts, but even in the first years of the concessions it was apparent that the investments established in the contracts would soon prove insufficient to accommodate the likely traffic.

The government could have terminated the contracts and put them out to tender again, but renegotiation seemed preferable both to avoid the delays of another competitive bidding and award processes and because the concessionaires had performed in a relatively acceptable manner. The pressures to renegotiate were more acute for the commuter than the freight concessions because the government feared that the commuter and subway services would deteriorate quickly under the pressure of the unexpectedly high traffic.

In 1997, the government authorized the Secretary of Transport to renegotiate freight and commuter concession contracts. The process proved time consuming, and only a few of the concession contracts had been rene-gotiated before the national elections of 1999. The presidential candidate of the opposition coalition made the lack of transparency in the renegoti-ation process an issue in the campaign and, when he won the election, he reopened some of the renegotiated commuter concessions.

The new government was faced with the same economic choices as its predecessor, and eventually renegotiated the commuter concessions on much the same terms. While the previous government had extended the ten-year concession by 20 years, for example, the new government extended it by 14 years. Investments in the commuter system would be increased, but this time they would be mostly financed by the concessionaires instead of the government. The concessionaires would recover their investments through increases in the maximum tariffs allowed and in the duration of the concessions.

These renegotiated commuter contracts were highly unpopular with the public, who never understood why commuter and subway fares had to be increased at all. The economy started to deteriorate in early 1999 and 2000, and the government reneged on subsidy payments due to the commuter concessionaires because of mounting budget problems. These defaults effectively forced the contracts into renegotiation again, but this was sus-pended in early 2002 when a freeze on bank deposits imposed to prevent a banking collapse forced the resignation of the president of the country and the subsequent devaluation of the Argentine currency. The government's attention was understandably diverted by the macro-economic crisis, and as of 2005 the concessionaires were continuing to operate the concessions essentially without a working contract pending a resolution and the quality of service was declining due to growing uncertainties.

BRAZIL

Before the Reforms

As in most of Latin America, the first railroads in Brazil were built by private investors and later taken over by the federal or state governments. Over the years, four major government-owned railways emerged with a combined network of 28,250 kilometers. One, FEPASA (Ferrovia Paulista S.A.), belonged to the State of São Paulo and provided both passenger and freight services to Brazil's most important industrial state. A second, RFFSA (Rede Ferroviária Federal S.A.), belonged to the federal government and provided passenger and freight services to much of the rest of the country. The remaining two railways, EFVM

(Estrada de Ferro Vitória a Minas) and EFC (Estrada de Ferro Carajás), both belonged to CVRD (Companhia Vale do Rio Doce), a giant mining and steelmaking company owned by the federal government. EFVM and EFC primarily served to carry iron ore from CVRD's mines to its mills and to ports for export.

Brazil's railways suffered greatly during the country's economic crisis of 1982 to 1992. Rail freight traffic growth slowed from an annual increase of 7.9 percent between 1975 and 1980 to an average of 2.5 percent between 1982 and 1992. The slowdown in traffic growth was probably just as well since the budgetary problems of the federal and state governments prevented them from assisting the railways as they had in the past. The level of investment in the rail industry in 1989 was just 19 percent of the investment recorded in 1980. During this period, moreover, roughly 40 percent of the rail investment was absorbed by the construction of the AÇO Railroad, a specialized line serving a steel company and the remaining 60 percent was barely sufficient to prevent the collapse of the rest of the system. By 1996, the combination of inadequate investment and poor maintenance had reached the point where only 64 percent of the locomotives were available for service. For the locomotives used in urban passenger service the availability was even lower: 59 percent for diesel and 42 percent for electric. The two non-mining railroads, FEPASA and RFFSA, accounted for 91 percent of Brazil's rail network and suffered from the worst investment, overstaffing and budgetary problems. By the end of 1995, the railways debt had reached US$3 billion and the companies required a subsidy of over US$250 million per year.

The Concessions

The federal government took charge of reforming both RFFSA and FEPASA. The two railroads were divided into seven separate concessions, as shown in Table 7.5, each for 30 years with the possibility of extension for another 30 years. RFFSA was retained as a legal entity to assume responsibility for the old RFFSA and FEPASA debts and to hold title to the railway infrastructure, rolling stock and other assets. RFFSA no longer operated the railways, however, but leased its assets to the seven concessionaires. The EFVM and EFC lines were part of the privatization of CVRD in 1997 and they remain under the company's control although they have to provide access to other operators to their networks if required.

The concession contracts established the maximum tariffs the concessionaires could charge. These maximums varied according to network, product and region and were indexed to inflation. In the case of disputes,

Table 7.5   Freight concession in Brazil

Network	Concessionaire	Bidding date	Takeover date
West	Ferrovia Novoeste	01/03/1996	Jun 96
East Center	F. Centro Atlantica	01/06/1996	Sep 96
Southeast	MRS Logistica	01/09/1996	Dec 96
Tereza Cristina	F. Tereza Cristina	01/11/1996	Feb 97
Sul	F. Sul Atlantico	01/12/1996	Mar 97
Northeastern	Cia. Ferr. Nordeste	01/07/1997	Jan 98
Paulista	Ferro Bandeirante	01/11/1998	Jan 99

Source: Kogan (2004, Table 2.23).

the contracts called for tariffs to be set to cover long-run variable costs and to provide an adequate return for the company. The concessionaires did not have to make specific investment commitments, but they were obliged to file annually investment plans for the coming three years so that the government could review them to see that the safety and integrity of the system was being maintained. The contracts also specified the minimum number of RFFSA or FEPASA employees that the concessionaire had to hire, roughly half of those employed previously.

The concessions were awarded between 1996 and 1997 to the highest bidder through a public auction and without any pre-qualification. In accordance with Brazilian law, the government established a minimum price and announced it in advance. Investors were allowed to participate in more than one concession, but an investor or investor group could own no more than 20 percent of the shares in any one concession.

The performance of the railways improved greatly under the concessions. Between 1997 and 2000 the concessionaires invested nearly US$1.6 billion in rehabilitating or extending tracks, bridges, rolling stock and fixed facilities. Partly as a result, by 2000, locomotive availability had increased to 88.5 percent and freight car availability reached 90.5 percent. The number of ton-kilometers of freight carried increased by 20.1 percent, as shown in Table 7.6, and the concessionaires were earning an operating margin of 12.8 percent (as percentage of total revenue).

One disappointment was that the number of intercity passengers declined from 4.3 million in 1996 to 1.6 million in 2000 as the concessionaires cut money-losing services. This decline was not completely unexpected as the relatively low population densities in Latin America make for relatively low traffic volumes in most intercity corridors, and low volumes are often more economically carried by bus or air than rail.

Table 7.6   Traffic carried by the freight concessions in Brazil (millions of ton-kilometers)

Line	1996	2000	2000/1996
ex-RFFSA	33 500	47 310	41.2%
ex-FEPASA (Ferrovias Bandeirantes)	5270	5060	−3.9%
Estrada de Ferro Vitoria a Minas	51 330	5667	10.4%
Estrada de Ferro da Mineração Rio do Norte	3020	34 000	12.6%
Estrada de Ferro Carajás	38 250	43 880	14.7%
Other lines	324	1610	396.9%
All lines	128 980	154 870	20.1%

Source: Kogan (2004, Table 2.27).

Regulatory Problems

Although the performance of the industry improved significantly, the experience revealed some significant weaknesses in the system for overseeing or regulating the concessionaires. One problem is the relationships among the regulatory commission (COFER), the Secretary of Transport and RFFSA. COFER is composed of seven commissioners and is charged with solving conflicts among concessionaires, customers and the government. COFER has only a small staff with limited technical capabilities, however, and is frequently forced to depend on consultants hired by the Secretary of Transport, who, in turn, often rely on the residual staff at RFFSA for expertise and historical records. The result is that the information and analytic capability necessary for resolving regulatory disputes is diffused across several agencies with potentially conflicting interests. This in turn leads to confusion about who is in charge and unpredictability in regulatory decisions.

The controls over tariffs and access have also been controversial. Most observers believe that the maximum tariffs set in the concession contracts are relatively generous. Moreover, the provision that tariffs should not exceed long-run variable costs is not terribly helpful since there is no specified or widely agreed upon formula for calculating long-run variable costs. There is similar ambiguity in how the regulatory system is to resolve disputes about how much railways can charge for allowing another company access to its tracks and customers. The diffusion of expertise and authority among COFER, the Secretary of Transport and RFFSA makes such technical issues harder to resolve. These problems are mainly of concern to shippers who are 'captive' to a particular railroad because they have no alternative means of transportation and do not face locational or product competition. Just how serious the captive shipper problem is in Brazil is hard to say, but some shippers feel captive and complain that the regulatory system provides them inadequate protection.

Finally, there is some unhappiness about the restrictions on concession ownership. Some argue that the 20 percent limit on the shares of a concession that any one investor group can own has served to reduce competition. The requirement means that each concession is owned by at least five different groups, which restricts competition in the concession award process and which may, through overlapping ownership, discourage competition among railroads after the awards have been made. Despite the 20 percent limit, moreover, some observers believe that several of the concessions are effectively controlled by investors who are the major customers of the concessions. These railways (particularly FCA, MRS and CFN) are alleged to give their investor-customers preferential prices and service.

MEXICO

The Reforms

Mexico's principal railway was nationalized in 1937 and was consolidated with several other railways into Ferrocarriles Nacionales de México S.A. (FNM) in the early 1980s. By 1994, on the eve of reforms, FNM was suffering from many of the same low investment, low productivity and high deficit problems that affected other state-owned railways in Latin America. Only 40 percent of FNM's 26,000-kilometer network was considered in good condition and no new lines had been built for more than 16 years. Staffing was excessive and thefts and accidents were common. Passenger and freight revenues were inadequate to cover costs, forcing the federal government to subsidize rail operations. In the period from 1990 to 1996, government subsidies to FNM rose to an average of US$ 400 million per year. The government had other budgetary priorities and problems and could not afford to finance rail deficits of this magnitude indefinitely.

In 1995, Mexico began to divide up FNM into nearly a dozen different concessions. The most important are three large or trunk railways: the Northeast Railroad and the Northern Pacific Railroad, both connecting Mexico City with the US border to the north, and the Southeast Railroad, which goes south from Mexico City. The networks of the trunk railways were designed so that the major Caribbean and Pacific ports are served by two of the trunk concessions and the two northern railways connect with different US railways at the border.

A fourth important railway, the Mexico Valley Terminal Railroad (Ferrocarril de la Terminal del Valle de México), is responsible for the tracks in the Mexico City area. This terminal railway is designed to give the three trunk railways access to Mexico City on a non-discriminatory basis. Toward that end, each trunk concessionaire owns 25 percent of the terminal railroad while the national government owns the remaining 25 percent.

In addition to the trunk railways, a number of short-line and specialized railways were offered as concessions as well. Some rail passenger lines were also separated from trunk lines and offered as concessions awarded on the basis of the lowest requested subsidy.

Under the concession scheme, the government continues to own the infrastructure and leases it to the concessionaire for a 50-year term, renewable for an equal term in the case of trunk lines and for 25 to 30 years for short lines. Concessions were awarded by competitive bidding and there were restrictions on the extent of foreign ownership allowed in the bidding consortia. Under certain circumstances, concessions could be 'assigned' to state or local authorities rather than bid competitively; this process was used primarily for passenger lines or services that were unprofitable but which state governments were prepared to support.

A Rail and Multimodal Transport Tariff Board, the DGTTFM (Dirección General de Tarifas, Transporte Ferroviario y Multimodal), was created within the Secretariat of Communications and Transport (SCT) to serve as the regulatory agency. Its main responsibility is to supervise the concessions although it also advises on general policy towards the industry. It monitors the concessionaires' compliance with technical and quality regulations and acts as arbitrator in the case of conflicts between concessionaires. Concessionaires are required to submit information on safety and security, quality and performance to the board on an annual basis.

The DGTTFM's authority to regulate railway tariffs is sharply limited. The concessionaires can set their own tariffs, subject to the provision that the tariffs are filed with the SCT and applied on a non-discriminatory basis. The DGTTFM can intervene only if it determines that a shipper has no effective alternative to the railroad that serves it, including other railways, other modes of transport and other routes. Even then, the Federal Competition Commission must review and approve the DGTTFM's analysis of alternatives before the regulatory agency can adjust the tariff.

The architects of the reform hoped that competition among railways or with other modes would be sufficient to prevent monopoly abuse in most cases. As noted earlier, the networks of the three trunk railways were carefully designed so that they would overlap or compete in the Mexico City Valley and at key ports and border crossings. The trunk concessionaires are required to provide each other access to those key points. Access charges are required to cover fixed and variable rail costs, but the participating concessionaires are authorized to negotiate these charges directly, with the government intervening only in an impasse.

By 2001, the government had awarded a dozen concessions totaling nearly 17,400 kilometers of track (84 percent of FNM's network), as listed in Table 7.7. The companies that won the three trunk lines and the Mexico Valley Terminal Railroad are Transportación Ferroviaria Mexicana, S.A. de C.V. (TFM); Ferrocarril Mexicano, S.A. de C.V. (Ferromex); and Ferrocarril del Sureste, S.A. de C.V. (Ferrosur). Four short lines were awarded, two to the trunk line operator Ferromex and the others to Línea Corta Coahuila-Durango, S.A. de C.V. (LCCD); and Compañía de Ferrocarriles Chiapas-Mayab, S.A. de C.V. (CFCM). Four concessions were 'assigned', including three to state governments.

Performance

The concession system has provided important budgetary relief for the Mexican government. Annual railway subsidies have declined from US$400 million before the reforms to roughly 10 or 20 percent as much. Moreover, the government has begun to collect the franchise fees provided under the concession contracts, which amount to 0.5 percent of gross income during the first 15 years of the concession and 1.25 percent in later years. These savings and revenues are offset in part by the US$1.5 billion that the government paid in severance to laid-off FNM employees.

Traffic growth has been mixed, with freight increasing by an astonishing 48 percent between 1994 and 2000 while passenger traffic fell almost to zero (Table 7.8). The increase in freight traffic is due in part to the growth of the Mexican economy and exports under NAFTA, but most believe that the greatly improved quality of rail service also played an important role. Two new tourist or scenic passenger railways were established since the reforms, but much of the prior FNM passenger service was abandoned. The government has continued to support passenger services to isolated communities either through competitive bidding for subsidized concessions or by assigning the line to a state government that was willing to take responsibility. Such rail services are likely to be replaced eventually by road transport since several studies estimate that building a road would be less expensive than maintaining rail service. Freight tariffs have declined by 20 percent, as shown in Table 7.9.

Finally, the system of promoting competition through the design of the trunk networks and the requirements for access seems to have worked reasonably well. Government authorities note with pride that in the first five years of the reforms only one shipper has filed a formal complaint about the

Table 7.7   Mexico: rail system concessionaires and 'Asignatarios' after reform

Concessionaire	Concessioned network	Type of service	Date	Price Mx $ (millions)	Term (years)
TFM, SA de CV	Northeast Railroad	Freight	12/02/1996	11072[1]	50
Ferrocarril y Terminal del Valle de México, SA de CV	Valle de México Terminal Railroad	Freight	12/02/1996	–	50
Ferrocarril Mexicano, SA de CV	Pacific-North Railroad	Freight	06/22/1997	3941	50
Ferrocarril Mexicano, SA de CV	Ojinaga-Topolobampo Line	Freight and Passenger	06/22/1997	256	50
Línea Coahuila-Durango, SA de CV	Coahuila-Durango Line	Freight	06/14/1997	180	30
Ferrosur, SA de CV	Southeast Railroad	Freight	06/29/1998	2898	50
Compañía de Ferrocarril Chiapas-Mayab, SA de CV	Chiapas-Mayab Rail Unit	Freight	08/26/1999	141	30
Ferrocarril Mexicano, SA de CV	Nacozari Short Line	Freight	08/27/1999	20.5	30
'Asignatarios' Ferrocarril del Itsmo de Tehuantepec, SA de CV	Itsmo de Tehuantepec Railroad[2]	Build, Operate, and Develop	12/23/1999	–	50

Baja California State Government	Tijuana-Tecate Short Line	Freight	71	04/01/2000	–	50
Baja California State Government	Tijuana-Tecate Short Line	Passenger	71	10/31/2001	–	30
Aguascalientes State Government	Adames-Peñuelas Segment of the Northern Pacific Railroad	Passenger	78	12/20/2001	–	30

Notes:
[1] This represents 80% of shares. In all the other cases, 100% of shares is involved.
[2] For the Medias Aguas-Salina Cruz segment.

Source: Mexico Communications and Transport Secretariat. All prices are stated in million of Mexican pesos as of award dates. The total is equivalent to US$2.3 billion.

Table 7.8   Trends in traffic in Mexico

	1990 (before concessions)	1994	2000 (after concessions)
Ton-kilometers	36 417	37 315	48 333
Passenger-kilometers	5336	1855	82

Source: Kogan (2004, Table 3.12).

Table 7.9   Changes in freight tariffs between the first concession year and 1999

	First year	Tariff in first year (US$PPP/ ton-km)	Tariff in year 1999 (US$PPP/ ton-km)	Tariff change (%)
Argentina:				
Broad Gauge	1993	0.039	0.036	−7.7
Standard Gauge	1994	0.032	0.043	+34.4
Brazil:				
FCA	1996	0.051	0.032	−37.3
Novoeste	1996	0.043	0.027	−37.2
Nordeste	1996	0.056	0.026	−53.6
MRS	1996	0.027	0.022	−18.5
ALL	1996	0.044	0.033	−25.0
Tereza Cristina	1996	0.12	0.101	−15.8
Bandeirantes	1998	0.038	0.023	−39.5
Mexico:				
TFM	1997	0.054	0.043	−20.4
Ferromex	1997	0.041	0.036	−12.2

Source: Kogan (2004, Table 4.6).

absence of competition, and that was for a single segment and type of product. This could be because shippers view the appeal process as very cumbersome to use, but it also suggests that the extent of monopoly abuse is limited.

OTHER COUNTRIES

Most of the other Latin American countries have followed the practice of Argentina, Brazil and Mexico in dividing their national railway into several regional concessions but keeping each concession vertically integrated and requiring only limited grants of access to other railways. Colombia in 1998, for example, divided its national railway, Ferrovías, into two concessions: one serving the Atlantic and the other the Pacific regions. The concessions were for 30 years, with the concessionaires obligated to conduct a major rehabilitation during the first four years. The contracts provided for government subsidies to support this rehabilitation, but no state support afterwards. The reforms significantly improved the quality and safety of rail service, but rail's share of the freight market remained disappointingly low. Bolivia and Chile also divided their railways into several vertically integrated concessions (although Chile allowed extensive access on one southern railway).

Only two Latin American countries – Peru and Uruguay – have attempted to vertically unbundle their railways. Peru's reforms are the farthest along, although not so far as to provide many useful conclusions. Before the reform, Peru had one national railway, ENAFER (Empresa Nacional de Ferrocarriles), and two specialized mining railways (CENTROMIN, owned by a government mining company; and Southern Peru Cooper, owned by a private mining company). ENAFER operated three separate networks: the Central, South, and South-east lines. The latter included the rail line from Cuzco to Machu Picchu, which provides the only access to the world-famous ruins other than by hiking or helicopter. The company reported to the Ministry of Transport and although it did not receive government subsidies (in part because of profits on the Machu Picchu line), it was deeply in debt, its infrastructure was in terrible shape, and the quality of service was poor. Rail freight had suffered particularly from competition with Peru's Autopista Central (Central Highway).

ENAFER was divided into three infrastructure concessions corresponding to its three lines. Concessions started in June 1998, state operations ceased and ENAFER entered into liquidation. The concessions are for 30 years with the possibility of five-year extensions to a total of 60 years. The concessionaire is responsible for maintaining the infrastructure and rolling stock, granting train operators access but it cannot operate trains on its own concession. The concessionaire can set its own track access and rolling stock lease fees, subject to review by a regulator, and pays the government a franchise fee calculated as a percentage of the gross receipts from track access and rolling stock revenues. A regulatory agency, OSITRAN, was established to monitor the performance of the concessionaires, promote competition in the industry, and act as an arbitrator in the event of conflicts between the concessionaires and train operating companies.

In the first two years after the reforms, the quality of service has improved but this has not necessarily translated into increased freight traffic. The South concession saw traffic decline slightly in the first year of the concession but then grow by 21 percent in the second. The Central and

South-east concessions have not seen an appreciable increase in freight traffic. Tourist traffic to Machu Picchu is providing good returns to operators given the growing demand and high fares.

Uruguay had unsuccessfully experimented with a number of different approaches to revitalizing its national railway, AFE, during the 1990s. By 2000, AFE had declined to the point where it carried only 1.3 million tons of freight and 369,000 passengers but required an annual subsidy of about US$20 million. That year the government decided to separate the infrastructure from train operations, leave the infrastructure in state hands, and introduce competition among train operators.

In late 2002, AFE's infrastructure and the employees that maintained it were transferred to the Ministry of Transport and Public Works (MOPT). MOPT was allocated a portion of AFE's annual subsidy intended for network rehabilitation and maintenance, amounting to US$5 million for 2003 and US$10 million for 2004. MOPT will charge train operators, including AFE, for the use of the network. AFE will continue to receive subsidies for the unprofitable train services that it operates, but these are to be gradually phased out so that AFE competes on an even footing with private operators. As of 2004, no private company had approached MOPT for permission to operate trains and AFE remained the sole rail operator. In the last few months a new government came to office, and is now putting back the infrastructure under AFE, and at the same time is calling for private interests to form a private–public partnership with AFE.

THE REVIVAL OF LATIN AMERICA'S RAILWAYS

Accomplishments

During the 1980s there was a real possibility that some of Latin America's railways would simply collapse. The quality of service was so poor that traffic was fleeing to the highway and air modes, even for many shipments of bulk agricultural products where rail normally has a great advantage over other modes. The railways were recovering only a portion of their costs from the tariffs they charged passengers and shippers, and the financial burden the companies imposed on governments was becoming unbearable.

By the turn of the century, the fear of railway collapse had abated significantly, although not disappeared completely. Most observers credit rail concessions with improving the prospects of the industry. The concession system seems to have benefitted both governments, by reducing the level of subsidy required, and many customers, by increasing the quality of services and in some cases reducing prices as well. Management became more market and productivity oriented. Tariffs went down, as shown in Table 7.9, which meant that a large portion of the benefits was transferred to shippers and users. Perhaps the most convincing sign that customers were better off was that freight and urban passenger traffic grew in all concessions, reversing decades of decline under government management.

The performance improvement is important since railways have potentially a key role to play in the region's future. Rail freight is particularly critical because some of Latin America's most important exports, such as agricultural products and minerals, are very suitable for carriage by rail. The projected increases in exports of these products are large, and the recent improvements in railway performance open the possibility that the railways will attract the lion's share of this growth. Efficient, high quality rail transport will help ensure that Latin American products and minerals are competitive on world markets. The railways are better positioned to take advantage of this opportunity than they have been for decades, although they will have to continue to improve and invest in modern rolling stock and heavier weight track if they are to reach their full potential.

The railways also have an important role to play in passenger traffic, although more for urban than intercity services. Commuter rail ridership is thought to be important to keep down levels of congestion and pollution in Latin America's largest cities. Concessions have been relatively successful in increasing commuter rail ridership while also reducing the subsidies such services normally require. The concession system has seen the appearance or great improvement in tourist railways, particularly in Mexico and Peru. But in contrast, the concession system has led to the abandonment of most intercity passenger services, although this may be a blessing in disguise. Most of these services were highly unprofitable, largely because they faced very effective competition from buses and cars. In the end, most governments decided that the social benefits from preserving these services were not worth the subsidies required. This judgment was probably correct, and helped lift a considerable burden for providing obsolete services from the railway system.

Challenges

Despite the overall satisfactory results of reforms in terms of quality of service, efficiency, safety and security, a number of challenges remain. The most important of these revolve around the regulatory system and public expectations.

While the concession system has worked well, we still have much to learn about drafting concession contracts that are less vulnerable to renegotiation. It is essential that objectives, terms and conditions in the contract be carefully thought out and clearly defined to reduce the chances that unanticipated problems or ambiguous language become sources of controversy or make the contract unworkable. In addition, contracts should spell out the conditions and procedures governing subsequent renegotiations (if any) and the role of the regulatory agencies and others in those renegotiations.

As part of this effort, governments should be careful to avoid contractual commitments that they are likely to find difficult to honor. This problem has arisen frequently with concessions where negative bids (that is, requests for subsidies) are allowed; such contracts have often failed when budget or economic crises force the government to renege on its monetary commitments.

Regulatory agencies have, for the most part, been relatively poorly equipped to handle the controversies that have arisen. Many Latin American regulatory agencies were established late in the privatization process (in some cases even after the concessions had already been granted) and provided with relatively few resources. In some cases, as in Peru and Mexico, concessionaires are not even required to furnish the information necessary to assess their performance. In other cases, the regulatory office was staffed with former rail employees who had opposed the reforms and, consequently, had unconstructive attitudes. A poorly equipped and informed regulatory agency is likely to make it harder to resolve disputes fairly.

Finally, it is worth noting that the potential benefits of many privatization programs were exaggerated, sometimes because of the need to 'sell' the reforms to the public, the natural optimism of most reform advocates, or simple ignorance. Whatever the reasons, the result was often unrealistic public expectations about the likely results of the reforms. Citizens sometimes perceived some concessions as 'failures' largely because their expectations were too high. Opponents took advantage of this problem, and the recent economic and social crises in the region only served to reinforce the problem. As of 2005 the atmosphere in the region is largely suspicious of reform, arguably unfairly so. But the debate continues.

ACKNOWLEDGEMENT

Ricardo Sánchez (ECLA/UN) contributed to some sections of this chapter.

REFERENCE

Kogan, J.H., (ed.) (2004), *Rieles con Futuro. Desafíos para los Ferrocarriles de América del Sur* (Rails with a Future. Challenges for South American Railroads), Caracas, Venezuela: Corporación Andina de Fomento.

8. The prospects for competition

Ginés de Rus

INTRODUCTION

Public regulation, public ownership and vertical integration have characterized the world's railways during the last half of the 20th century. The railways began as private and unregulated companies in the mid-19th century, but by the end of the 19th and the beginning of the 20th centuries governments had moved to regulate railway tariffs and safety. During the middle of the 20th century most countries, with the exception of the United States and Canada, had nationalized their railways and reorganized them as publicly-owned monopolies. The establishment of competing private railways was often prohibited and competition from alternative transportation modes was sometimes discouraged by various measures as well. The idea was that a single company could establish an integrated and efficient national network and that public ownership would ensure that the railway was run in the best interests of consumers.

Within a few decades it was clear that the public monopoly model was not performing well. The railways had long been under intense pressure to meet the competition from other transport modes and to adapt to the changing composition of freight and passenger demand. Public ownership seemed to inhibit rather than encourage the railways to meet these challenges even though it was often accompanied by public subsidies, which softened the blows delivered by the changing environment. But the availability of subsidies and the strong influence of public sector managers and unions seemed to discourage effective adaptation in railway efficiency or service offerings and the railway's share of traffic and financial performance declined steadily in most countries, with no apparent end in sight.

The disappointment with the public monopoly model has set off a search, chronicled in this book, for an alternative approach that would reduce the level of public involvement in the industry and substitute more the forces of competition. But while there is agreement on the need for more competition and less government, there is disagreement as to how this is best achieved. The principal debate is whether it is better to promote competition through vertical unbundling or among vertically integrated companies. In addition there is some debate as to whether the railways ought to be privately owned or not.

This chapter synthesizes and assesses the evidence offered in the previous chapters from the experiences of rail reform in Europe, Latin America and the United States. In short, neither unbundling nor integration has proven to be the best approach in a wide variety of circumstances. Unbundling, although attractive in theory, has so far proved complex to implement and has delivered only some of the promised benefits. Competition among vertically integrated railways has had more demonstrable success in the freight systems of North and South America, but it is still untested in the more complex railway networks of Europe or for passenger services. The evidence is arguably slightly stronger for integration than for unbundling, but the jury is still out.

RAILWAYS AS INTEGRATED PUBLIC MONOPOLIES

Railway technology is characterized by large economies of traffic density and sunk costs which give the railways both advantages and disadvantages over other modes. Economies of traffic density occur when the average cost of transport declines as the volume of traffic carried on a corridor increases. The main sources of economies of traffic density and sunk costs are in the railway infrastructure (right of way, track, signals, power distribution and stations) rather than in operations (rolling stock, crew and energy). Infrastructure costs increase with traffic volumes because additional traffic requires or makes it economical to use heavier track and ballast, more sophisticated signals, more passing sidings, a straighter and more level route, and so on. But infrastructure costs usually do not increase proportionately with traffic since the basic costs for right-of-way acquisition and grading often change little as traffic increases. Also, infrastructure investments are generally long-lived and immobile, which means they are sunk in the sense that it is difficult to redeploy them to other corridors or uses if they are no longer needed.

Economies of traffic density mean that railways can offer the cheapest (although not necessarily the fastest) means of transporting passengers and freight in corridors where traffic volumes are very high. It is difficult, for example, to find a more efficient alternative to transport high volumes of coal from a mine to a power plant or high volumes of grain from an agricultural region to an export port.[1] High sunk costs mean that the short-run marginal cost of carrying additional units of traffic may be very low as long as the railway has excess capacity. But economies of traffic density have disadvantages as well, in that railway average costs rise as traffic declines, making the mode uneconomical at low volumes. Also, sunk costs are seldom sunk forever: eventually there is a day of reckoning when the durable and immobile assets reach the end of their service lives or capacity and must be replaced or expanded.

One of the basic reasons why government became so deeply involved in railways is because the economies of traffic density and large sunk costs give rise to fears that railways are what economists call natural monopolies.[2] Large economies of scale mean that it is more efficient for a single railway to serve a corridor rather than several, and large sunk costs mean the incumbent railway need not fear 'hit and run' competition from other railways. If railways are to be disciplined by competition it must come from other modes of transport or, indirectly, from the fact that businesses located on one railroad must compete with businesses located on other railroads. During the 19th century and the first decades of the 20th century there was little effective competition from other modes of transport, except on routes where river or coastal shipping was an option, and for much of that period the potential of locational or product competition was not well understood.[3]

Government involvement was also encouraged because railways have always been seen as central to national economic development. In the 19th century the railways' dramatic savings in transport costs made the rail service essential for commerce and as a tool for integrating remote or lagging regions into the national economy, essentially heightening the fears of monopoly thus encouraging governments to regulate tariffs and services. When the railways began to decline in the face of competition from highway and air modes in the mid-20th century, many communities and industries still seemed so dependent on the railways that their fears of intolerable service cutbacks often helped provoke nationalization.

Another source of pressure for government involvement was railway management and trade unions. They too feared cutbacks in service, which made them natural allies of the communities and industries that felt dependent on railways. Once the railways were in public hands, well organized unions often became very effective lobbyists for policies to protect the railways from competition or change.

Whatever the causes, the government's deep involvement in the railways led to pricing, investment and other decisions that often contributed to the railways' decline. The tariff structure typically included substantial cross-subsidies in that the prices for some services were set above their avoidable costs in order to generate surpluses that could be used to support politically sensitive but unprofitable services. This cross-subsidization was ultimately unsustainable in that it encouraged competing modes, such as trucks and buses, to go after the traffic with high markups. Similarly, railways were often prevented from closing freight and passenger lines with little traffic, or required to construct new high-speed passenger lines that had few prospects of profitability (Vickerman, 1997; Steer Davies Gleave, 2004). Government subsidies were usually provided in recognition of the railways' 'public service obligation' to maintain socially worthwhile but unprofitable services. But these subsidies were seldom sufficient and, worse, the prospect of subsidy seemed to reduce the pressure on management and labour to increase productivity or reduce costs.

The negative effects of these decisions were exacerbated because the railways faced such strong adverse external trends. In the case of freight, economic growth and technical change were reducing the importance of the high-volume, low-value, high-weight traffic that rail was best adapted to carry. As Gallamore (1999) eloquently explains:

> Plastics were replacing metals, making products lighter and less 'rail intensive'. Aluminium substituted for steel, paper and plastic for glass, composites for lumber, individually packaged products for bulk, and fresh and frozen foods for canned fruits and vegetables. Stock-keeping units of all kinds of finished consumer goods proliferated and became smaller, lighter, more valuable per pound – and more suitable to trucking than to rail. Even heavy bulk commodities were affected, for example, oil or natural gas (efficiently moved by pipeline) replaced coal for home heating.

In the case of passengers, rising incomes were encouraging similar demands for speedier and more convenient services that were often more readily supplied by the auto and airplane than by the train. Research has shown consistently that the value that travellers place on travel time savings is closely related to their earnings (Mackie et al., 2001), so that rising per capita incomes result in an increase in the willingness to pay for speed. The auto offers advantages in this regard in that it provides a door-to-door service, on demand and is not restricted to railway timetables, and the plane is usually faster (door-to-door journey time) than rail for intercity trips beyond 400 kilometres unless the rail line is high speed.[4]

Public policy often attempted to insulate the public railways from competition, but with little apparent effect. In some countries, such as Mexico, railways were deemed the exclusive responsibility of government and private railways prohibited. In other countries, such as Britain, there was no ban on building new private railways but there was also no requirement for the public railways to provide a competitor access to its tracks. Potentially more significant were restraints on other modes. As Campos explains (in Chapter 5), for example, Spain attempted to restrain trucks and favour trains by taxing trucks heavily and limiting truck permits. Similarly, France restricted intercity bus services to encourage rail ridership. These restraints on other modes were seldom (if ever) enough to prevent the railways from losing market share, however, because the advantages of the competing modes were so strong that only unacceptably draconian restraints would have been effective. Nevertheless, the history of the railways in the 20th century is intriguing in that extensive regulation, restraints on competition and heavy subsidies were not enough to prevent road and air transport from replacing the railways as the dominant mode of transportation.

Many countries attempted to introduce more commercial behaviour to their public railways in the 1980s, principally by reorganizing them as publicly owned corporations rather than government departments or by introducing explicit performance contracts with management. These measures often brought some labour and cost savings, as Quinet and Campos recount in the cases of France and Spain (Chapters 4 and 5). But the reforms were not enough to gain the commercial edge that these organizations, often burdened with a bureaucratic culture, needed to fight with truck operators and private cars for freight and passengers. The chronic fiscal crises associated with low traffic, relatively high average costs, substantial public service obligations and barriers to exit, forced governments to pursue more fundamental reforms.

INTRODUCING COMPETITION

At the heart of the current reforms are efforts to introduce competition in at least one of three ways: vertical unbundling, so that train operators can compete with one another; privatization, so that investors can compete for control of the railway company; or deregulation, so that railways are allowed to compete directly or indirectly with other railways and other modes.

These three options are not mutually exclusive as both vertical unbundling and deregulation are often combined with privatization. Deregulation typically includes some degree of vertical unbundling in as much as the various vertically integrated railways established are often required to provide competitors with access to their tracks at certain key places. But as Gómez-Ibáñez points out (Chapter 1), the more extensive or complete forms of vertical unbundling are incompatible with deregulation in that the independent infrastructure company is usually presumed to be a natural monopoly, and thus requires regulation.

In practice, the most hotly debated choice is whether to introduce competition through vertical unbundling or while maintaining vertical integration. Correctly or not, many analysts take it for granted that the railways will be privatized, with the possible exception of the infrastructure company under full vertical unbundling.

COMPETITION THROUGH VERTICAL UNBUNDLING

The theoretical advantages and disadvantages of vertical unbundling are clear, as set out by Gómez-Ibáñez and Nash in Chapters 1 and 2. The main advantage cited by proponents is to introduce competition in train operations and to restrict regulation to infrastructure. Entry will be encouraged because new rail operators do not have to incur the sunk costs associated with the construction of rail infrastructure. Other advantages claimed are the promotion of international through services and the facilitation of fairer intermodal competition. The European Commission argues that separation of infrastructure and operations will make it easier to develop international services. The Swedes and others contend that separating infrastructure from train operations will put the railways on the same basis as the roads, ports and airports, thereby making it easier to compare the subsidies that the different modes receive and the environmental damage that they cause and to eventually move to full social cost pricing of all transport. In France, Quinet reports that government officials also hope that the creation of a separate infrastructure company will provide an alternative source of railway expertise to counteract the near monopoly on information enjoyed by the incumbent national railway.

  The main disadvantage cited by sceptics is that unbundling will make the coordination of infrastructure and train operations more difficult. The coordination of infrastructure and train operation strongly affects the quality and cost of railway service. Coordination that was internal to the vertically integrated firm now must be achieved by contracts between separate firms with conflicting interests. Moreover, those contracts must be supervised by a regulator since the infrastructure company is still a monopoly. The regulator must guarantee fair or equal treatment to competing operators in track access and charges, and provide the right incentives to the infrastructure company to maintain the network and to invest in new capacity. Sceptics also argue that the parallels with other transport modes are misleading because the infrastructure of roads, airports and seaports is fundamentally simpler than that of railways, which makes coordination easier. Even so, airlines and shipping lines are often vertically integrated in that they invest in and operate their own terminals within an airport or seaport.

Whether the advantages of unbundling outweigh the disadvantages in practice is, unfortunately, not terribly clear. Part of the problem is that relatively few countries have been unbundling for very long, the principal ones being Sweden, Britain, Australia and Germany. France, Spain and others have reacted more slowly and with less enthusiasm to the European Commission's directives.

Moreover, the European Commission's directives allow some latitude in implementation so that differences in strategy may be confused with differences in performance. The Commission does not require that the infrastructure company be completely independent from the former integrated public monopoly, for example, but only that the accounts be separate. France and Spain have taken advantage of this to design arrangements which seem to leave the infrastructure company oddly dependent on the old public company, as explained in Chapters 4 and 5. The Commission also does not require that the infrastructure company be privately owned, so that while Britain privatized its infrastructure company and Germany announced its intention to do so, Sweden left the company in public ownership. One effect of the British railway crisis of 2001, in which the private infrastructure company (Railtrack) went bankrupt and was converted by government into a non-profit organization (Network Rail), may be to discourage other countries engaged in vertical unbundling from privatizing their infrastructure operator.

Finally, the record is confused by allegations of half-hearted or incompetent implementation. For example, there is some concern that qualitative requirements could be unduly used as a barrier to entry, so the independence of the rail regulator from the government may be especially important when the main rail operator is the former state-owned monopoly. No doubt, competition is the best force to avoid market power in rail markets, but the independence of the regulatory agency could help to make competition effective.

The most widespread allegation of poor implementation is in Britain. The bankruptcy of Railtrack and the renegotiation of most of the train operating contracts before they had expired are taken by many as evidence of the difficulties of vertical unbundling. But Nash (in Chapter 2) argues that the problems were due to hasty implementation while Glaister (in Chapter 3) contends that the governments under both the Conservative and Labour Parties were too risk averse to let competition take its course. Glaister argues that:

> No evidence or experience has demonstrated that one cannot separate rail infrastructure from operations if that is what is desired . . . Unfortunately, the British experience on railways may also illustrate the possibility of ending up with the worst of all worlds: to incur the costs of privatisation in order to

harness the forces of competition but then to intervene to prevent that competition from delivering its benefits. And to end up paying private risk-bearing rates of interest on large debts without achieving any real risk transfer from the public sector.

The relatively brief experiences and the differences in policies and enthusiasm among countries help explain why the econometric or statistical studies of the effects of vertical unbundling are inconclusive. As Nash explains in Chapter 2, some studies show that unbundling improves railway productivity while others show that it does not.[5] The difficulty, one suspects, is that there is so much variation in the types and intensity of implementation that the variable 'reform' in the econometric analysis is unable to account for the real content (effort, commitment, credibility) of the policies.

A reading of the various national experiences recounted in this book suggests a similarly mixed result: while there is evidence that unbundling can bring benefits in certain circumstances there is also evidence to suggest that unbundling risks substantial costs. There are two ways of providing competition in train operations with vertical unbundling. The first is to competitively tender franchises to provide specific train services – this approach is often used where the train services desired are unprofitable, and the franchise is usually awarded to the bidder requesting the least subsidy. The second approach is to open access to the tracks to all comers, letting the market determine what services will be provided. This approach typically assumes that train services should not or need not be subsidized, although an open access regime can be designed with subsidies as well. In Sweden, for example, the government-owned infrastructure company charges track access fees that are thought to be below cost, so that all train operators enjoy some subsidy.

The benefits of unbundling are clearer in the case of competitively tendered franchises than in the case of open access. Nash regards Sweden as one of the most successful examples of vertical unbundling largely because tendering for passenger services has gradually brought down subsidy costs. Germany is beginning to realize similar savings in the services tendered by regional governments. In Britain the evidence is more ambiguous: competitive tendering of passenger services brought dramatic promises of reduced subsidy, but the bids proved unrealistic and had to be renegotiated before the terms of the franchises expired. Glaister implies that the government could have been tougher in holding the operators to their promises and the results were confused by the collapse of Railtrack, but in the end it seems the savings were small, if any.

Open access has been more of a disappointment in that it has failed to stimulate much new service. Even Nash, who is a supporter of unbundling, concedes that 'virtually no' open access operations have emerged in Europe despite the fact that the European Commission requires open access for international services. In a number of cases, most notably Britain, governments unbundled the railways but then restricted access for domestic services. Britain allowed open access for domestic freight services only and essentially prohibited access for domestic passenger services out of concern (which Glaister suggests was exaggerated) that the prospect of open competition would discourage bidders for its passenger franchises. Elsewhere in Europe, a few countries allow open access for domestic services and all are required to allow access for international services, but these options are seldom exercised. Nash implies that half-hearted implementation is to blame 'because the existing legislation only provided for minimal rights of access for international rail freight operators, and left the administration of those rights, and the charges to be levied, in the hands of the existing rail operators, who had a vested interest in preventing them from being exercised'. But this argument seems less convincing in the cases of countries, like Sweden and Germany, which have been leaders in unbundling and allow access for domestic services. It may be that there are simply not that many profitable opportunities for new private train services in Europe.

Given that competitive tendering seems more effective than open access it is unfortunate that the European Commission abandoned a proposal to require competitive tendering for all subsidized train services. The Commission backed down because of resistance from the European Parliament and the Council of Ministers, who were concerned about the effects on the incumbent public railway companies. Quinet argues convincingly that competitive tendering is likely to spread regardless, however, particularly in countries like France and Germany which have decentralized some of the responsibility for train services to regional or metropolitan authorities. These regional governments are likely to have more interest in competitive tendering than the national government if only because they are more concerned with getting value for money in their train services and have fewer ties to the national train operator.

While there have been some gains from competition for tendered train services, there are also signs that the costs in lost coordination could be high. So far the problems of coordination between infrastructure and train operations have not been severe outside of Britain. But virtually every observer agrees that the implementation of vertical unbundling has proven devilishly complex. For example, it is a major (and some would argue still unresolved) challenge to design a regime of infrastructure access charges that simultaneously (1) provides incentives for train operators to use existing capacity wisely, (2) establishes incentives for infrastructure providers to adequately maintain existing capacity and invest in new capacity when needed, (3) treats both incumbent and new train operators fairly, and (4) generates an adequate revenue stream for the infrastructure company.

The difficulties of coordination may be masked, as Gómez-Ibáñez suggests in Chapter 1, by the fact that there has been relatively little entry or new service in most countries, so that the operators have not put the infrastructure system under stress. Indeed, in Sweden, often cited as the most successful model of unbundling, Nash reports that the government-owned infrastructure company may be overinvesting in capacity. Meanwhile in Britain, where unbundling experienced its most notorious problems, the franchise train operators greatly expanded service without any investment in new capacity by the infrastructure company. Glaister is undoubtedly correct in arguing that political concerns undermined the implementation of unbundling in Britain, but it is hard not to also conclude that the difficulties in implementation helped give the politicians the excuses they were looking for.

COMPETITION WITH VERTICAL INTEGRATION

There are two principal methods of introducing competition while maintaining vertical integration: concessions or deregulation. The first approach, used mainly in developing countries, is to competitively tender concessions of limited duration to operate vertically integrated railways. The basic idea is to rely on competition for the concession to get performance improvements, and then to regulate the concessionaire to ensure promises are honoured over the life of the contract. In essence, this approach is no different than the competitive tendering of franchises that is often used with vertical unbundling, except that the concession operator is responsible for the infrastructure as well as the train operations. The term concession is often used instead of franchise because concession implies some responsibility for investment, and often the terms of the vertically integrated concession require the concessionaire to make certain investments.

The second approach, seen in its simplest form in the freight railroads of the United States and Canada, is to allow vertically integrated railways to compete with other modes and one another with relatively minimal government regulation. The idea is to allow competition from other modes and both direct and indirect (locational and product) competition among railroads to generate the desired performance gains. This approach is seldom pure in that some residual regulatory authority is usually maintained to protect customers who have no effective alternative. Similarly, an element of vertical unbundling is often introduced in as much as railways are often required to grant competitors access to their tracks at certain key locations where authorities feel it is important to enhance competition. But the powers of regulators to set tariffs and force access are tightly circumscribed, so that the emphasis is on competition with minimal government interference.

In practice, the approach of deregulation or limited regulation has been applied in freight but not passenger services. In fact, many of the freight concessions in Latin America are so lightly regulated that they are essentially similar to the American and Canadian system of deregulation. In Brazil and Mexico, for example, the freight concessions are for many decades, tariffs are not regulated for most intents and purposes, and access is required on certain tracks but the railroads are left to negotiate terms with the regulator intervening only in the case of an impasse. The passenger systems in Latin America adhere more closely to the traditional concession model. Urban passenger fares are usually strictly regulated, for example, because the government wants to keep fares low to reduce traffic congestion and pollution.

As Kogan reports in Chapter 7, the concession system has worked fairly well in improving performance. Ridership on the urban rail concessions of Buenos Aires tripled in only seven years, for example, reversing decades of stagnation and decline. Similar, if less dramatic, turnarounds were seen elsewhere. The fact that the performance of these railways improved so dramatically is testimony both to the inefficiency of the old public railways in the region and to the effectiveness of competition for concessions in motivating improvement.

The main limitation of the concession approach is in devising a scheme to regulate the concessions that is fair to both consumers and investors. The original idea was that the concession contract would completely define the commitments of the concessionaire to the government (in terms of tariffs, services, and so on) and of the government to the concessionaire (in terms of subsidy, and so on). The fact that the concession was competitively tendered provided reassurance to the concessionaire and the government that the terms were fair. But, as Kogan recounts, the trends in traffic or other key variables have often been so different than those anticipated as to make the contracts unworkable for the government, the concessionaire or both parties. The regulatory agencies have been poorly equipped to cope with the challenge of renegotiating the contracts, and the process has often raised public suspicions of unfairness or corruption.

Deregulation has also led to dramatic turnarounds in both North and South America. Winston's account of the US experience is striking: rail freight tariffs declined by 65 per cent in real terms (at least one-third of the rate reductions can be attributed to deregulation) and rail traffic increased by 40 per cent in the two decades since deregulation. Kogan reports similar reductions in real tariffs and increases in freight traffic in the Argentine, Brazilian and Mexican freight concessions, which are so lightly regulated that they are similar to the North America model.

The turnarounds in North America have been confirmed by more elaborate econometric studies that attempt to control for the other factors that may influence performance. In their comprehensive review of rail productivity and efficiency studies, for example, Oum and Yu (1994) concluded that the Canadian railways achieved higher productivity growth than their US counterparts during the 1960s and the 1970s because Canada deregulated rail tariffs in the 1960s while the United States did not do so until 1980. They also found that rail productivity growth accelerated significantly in the United States after 1980.

It is important to note that the US freight railways and one of the two major Canadian railways had always been privately owned, so that the reform was to introduce competition through deregulation rather than through privatization. In that respect, the turnaround in the North American railways suggests how inimical government regulation can be if it is done badly and over a long period of time. Given the relative sophistication of the countries involved, it also suggests how difficult it is for governments to regulate well.

The North America freight experience also provides a striking demonstration of how important indirect competition among freight railways can be. Canada has only two major railways (both transcontinental) and the United States has only four (two east and two west of the Mississippi River). In practice this means that many rail shippers are 'captive' in the sense that their plants are served by only one railway, are not located on a waterway and rely on shipments of a commodity, such as coal, that are unsuitable for trucks or pipelines. Winston shows (in Chapter 6) that rail tariffs are lower in the United States when shippers have a choice of rail carrier. But the fact that most shippers don't have a choice and that average tariffs have declined so dramatically suggests that threat of indirect competition from plants at other locations or from similar products can protect the captive shipper, especially if they are locked in with private long-term contracts. The captive shipper may not enjoy the same rates as the non-captive shipper and both the United States and Canada feel compelled to retain residual powers to set tariffs in cases where the abuse is significant, but that regulatory power is apparently invoked only infrequently.

One of the unresolved questions is whether the deregulation approach could be applied successfully to passenger railways or to mixed passenger and freight systems, such as those in Europe. Gómez-Ibáñez is the most optimistic of our authors, arguing that the railways face so much competition from road and air that they have little monopoly power in intercity passenger service. He is less confident about the effectiveness of intermodal competition in urban passenger services, however, and, in any event, we have yet to see a practical demonstration of deregulation in either intercity or urban passenger services.

CONCLUSIONS

It is still far too early to draw a definitive conclusion about what method of reform is best, and we may well find that the best policy depends on the type of country or railway service involved. Nevertheless, the experience to date with railway reform seems to favour the introduction of competition with vertical integration rather than through vertical unbundling.

Vertical unbundling has worked best in driving down the subsidy costs for competitively tendered passenger service franchises. Unbundling has been less successful in promoting competition through open access, however, and the issue of whether we can avoid serious problems of coordination between infrastructure and train operations is still unresolved. Some of the problems experienced are undoubtedly due to half-hearted or incompetent implementation, but it is also striking how complex the implementation seems to be – and complexity invites problems.

Competition while maintaining vertical integration has been very successful in improving railway performance, although not without problems. In the case of concessions, the big question is whether we can devise a regulatory system that can cope fairly with the prospect that the concession contract may need to be renegotiated. In the case of deregulation, the issue is whether the successes achieved in freight can be translated to more complex passenger or freight and passenger services.

If forced to take a position, competition with vertical integration seems more promising than competition through unbundling if only because unbundling has not yet delivered the kinds of striking turnarounds seen with integration. The reforms of the North and South American railways are striking in that they reversed decades of decline. The only similar turnaround achieved with unbundling was in Britain, where passenger services and ridership increased and subsidies declined dramatically during the first years of the reforms. The British record is hard to interpret, however, in light of the subsequent problems, and it could well be that the situation in Europe or elsewhere is so much more complex or different that the successes in the North and South American systems will prove hard to replicate. One can only hope that these efforts to reform continue so that we can learn and benefit more from them.

NOTES

1. Water transport can be even more economical if a water route is available.
2. The classification of an industry as a natural monopoly is not independent of the level of demand and product mix to be served. A natural monopoly exists when the cost curve shows *subadditivity*, which means that the demanded level of outputs can be produced at a lower cost by a single firm. A cost function can be *subadditive* within a particular range of one or more outputs, but outside that range more firms can produce more cheaply. The theoretical definition of natural monopoly has to be applied to actual markets: the proof for the existence of natural monopoly is a market test.
3. This is not entirely true. In the United States, for example, railway tariffs were regulated in the 19th century in part because of complaints by small businesses that very large businesses (the 'trusts') were receiving secret rebates from the railways which left them at a competitive disadvantage. The railways presumably gave these rebates because they recognized that the very large businesses had more possibilities to shift production to plants served by railways that treated them well.
4. It is interesting to see the rise of high-speed services over medium distances. Rail services substitute private transport thanks to the new technology running trains at 300 km per hour, and the increasing congestion experienced by land and air transport.
5. More efficiency is associated with financial and managerial autonomy (Oum and Yu, 1994; Gathon and Pestieau, 1995; Cantos, Pastor and Serrano, 1999; Cantos and Maudos, 2000), with competition (Rivera-Trujillo, 2004), and the gradual introduction of reforms (Friebel, Ivaldi and Vibes, 2003); on the contrary, subsidies contribute to inefficiency (Oum and Yu, 1994; Cantos and Maudos, 2000). Regarding vertical unbundling, the empirical evidence is inconclusive: Cantos, Pastor and Serrano (1999) find that the separation of infrastructure and operations increases efficiency. The opposite result is reported in Rivera-Trujillo (2004) and in Friebel, Ivaldi and Vibes (2003) no significant effect is found, though they exclude the UK due to lack of data availability.

REFERENCES

Cantos, P. and Maudos, J. (2000), 'Efficiency, Technical Change and Productivity in the European Rail Sector: A Stochastic Frontier Approach', *International Journal of Transport Economics*, **27**.

Cantos, P., Pastor, J. and Serrano, L. (1999), 'Productivity, Efficiency and Technical Change in the European Railways: A Non-parametric Approach', *Transportation*, **26**, 337–357.

Friebel, G, Ivaldi, M. and Vibes, C. (2003), *Railway (De) regulation: A European Efficiency Comparison*. IDEI Report n. 3 on Passenger Rail Transport, University of Toulouse.

Gallamore, R.E. (1999), 'Regulation and Innovation: Lessons from the Americam Railroad Industry' in J.A. Gómez-Ibáñez, W.B. Tye and C. Winston, *Essays in Transportation Economics and Policy: A Handbook in Honor of John R. Meyer*, Washington: Brookings Institution Press.

Gathon, H.J. and Pestieau, P. (1995), 'Decomposing Efficiency into its Managerial and its Regulatory Components: The Case of European Railways', *European Journal of Operational Research*, **80**, 500–507.

Mackie, P.J., Jara-Díaz, S. and Fowkes, A.S. (2001), 'The Value of Travel Time Savings in Evaluation', *Transportation Research*, E 37, 91–106.

Oum T.H. and Yu, C. (1994), 'Economic Efficiency of Railways and Implications for Public Policy: A Comparative Study of The OECD Countries' Railways', *Journal of Transport Economics and Policy*, 28–2, 121–138.

Rivera-Trujillo, C. (2004), *Measuring the Productivity and Efficiency of Railways (An International Comparison)*, University of Leeds, forthcoming.

Steer Davies Gleave (2004), *High Speed Rail: International Comparisons*, London: Commission for Integrated Transport.

Vickerman, R. (1997), 'High-Speed Rail in Europe: Experience and Issues for Future Development', *The Annals of Regional Science*, **31**, 21–38.

Index

Printed and bound by CPI Group (UK) Ltd, Croydon, CR0 4YY

23/04/2025

14660963-0002